CODEBREAKER

Marc Mc Menamin is an author, documentary maker and teacher originally from Ballyshannon, Co. Donegal. He holds an MA in History and a PGDE in Education from the National University of Ireland, Galway, and works as a teacher in Oaklands Community College, Edenderry, Co. Offaly, where he teaches English, History and Politics and Society.

He has produced a number of award winning radio documentaries for RTÉ Radio 1's The Documentary on One including *Richard Hayes, Nazi Codebreaker*, which was a finalist in the Best Radio Documentary Category at the 2018 New York Festivals. His 2013 radio documentary *Peter Daly Good Cop/Bad Cop* was shortlisted for numerous prizes including the 2014 Prix Europa and Prix Italia awards while his 2015 radio documentary *Seamus Darby and the Goal that Made Champions* was shortlisted for Sports Documentary of the Year at the 2016 Celtic Media Awards. He also occasionally works as a reporter for RTÉ Radio 1's *The History Show*.

Marc has worked as a researcher and assistant producer on a number of documentaries, most notably TV3's *Sinn Féin: Who Are They?* As well as a stint on *Tonight with Vincent Browne*, he also worked as an intern to Stephen Donnelly TD in Dáil Éireann.

Based in Dublin, he is an avid fan of cycling, Donegal GAA and the Republic of Ireland soccer team and tries to get home to Ballyshannon as often as possible.

Codebreaker is Marc's first book.

CODEBREAKER

The untold story of Richard Hayes,
the Dublin librarian who helped turn
the tide of World War II

MARC MC MENAMIN

Gill Books

Gill Books
Hume Avenue
Park West
Dublin 12
www.gillbooks.ie

Gill Books is an imprint of M.H. Gill and Co.

978 07171 8161 2

Print origination by O'K Graphic Design, Dublin
Edited by Neil Burkey
Proofread by Esther Ní Dhonnacha
Map adapted from Stock/Getty Premium
Printed by TJ International, Cornwall
This book is typeset in 11/16 pt Minion.

The paper used in this book comes from the wood pulp of
managed forests. For every tree felled, at least one tree is
planted, thereby renewing natural resources.

A CIP catalogue record for this book is available from the British
Library.

5 4 3

ACKNOWLEDGEMENTS

This book would not have come to fruition without the help of many people. To all of them I owe a huge debt of gratitude. Firstly I'd like to thank Conor Nagle and the team at Gill Books for believing in this project from the outset and for sharing my enthusiasm to tell the story of the quiet patriotism of Dr Richard Hayes. Indeed, not a word of this book would have been written if it weren't for the help and support of the Hayes family. In particular I'd like to thank Faery Hayes for access to family documents and photographs and her unwavering patience and assistance in answering my many queries. Jim Hayes gave me a great insight into his grandfather and his friendship and numerous cups of tea were very much appreciated. Similarly Jim's mother Yvonne Dixon was a fountain of information in relation to her father-in-law.

During the course of the research for this book I was fortunate enough to meet Sheila O'Sullivan of Kenmare, Co. Kerry, daughter-in-law of Captain John Patrick O'Sullivan. Sheila is a fantastic local historian in her own right and I am very grateful to her and her daughter Christine for all their help and for allowing me access to family papers and for answering my many questions in relation to Capt. O'Sullivan.

I wish to thank the staff of the National Library of Ireland, who were most diligent in helping me gain access to the Hayes papers. In particular I would like to acknowledge Gerry Long, Dónall Ó Luanaigh and my neighbour Orla Sweeny. I'd also like to thank fellow south Donegal historians Brian Drummond, Joe O'Loughlin and Marc Geagan for their encouragement when undertaking this project.

This book had its genesis as the radio documentary *Richard Hayes, Nazi Codebreaker* on RTÉ Radio One's *Documentary on One* programme. I wish to sincerely thank the *Doc on One* team for helping bring this story into the public domain and for their support of me as a documentary maker over the years. In particular I want to acknowledge Donal O'Herlihy, whose help, guidance and expertise made the Hayes radio doc such a special project. Similarly, Series Producer Liam O'Brien has been the most wonderful mentor, teacher and friend over the last few years and for that I am eternally grateful.

Many people gave up their time to answer questions for the radio documentary and their insights have found their way into this book. Among those who deserve my thanks are Prof. Eunan O'Halpin TCD, Dr Mark Hull Kansas, Dr Gary McGuire UCD and Dr Chris Smith Coventry. In addition to this I wish to thank Marcel Krüger, Dundalk, Capt. Daniel Ayotis of the Irish Military Archives and Keith Farrell, producer of RTÉ's *Ireland's Nazis*.

My thanks to Principal Gerry Connolly, Deputy Principals Richard Murphy and Mairead O Shea and all the staff and students of Oaklands Community College, Edenderry, Co. Offaly. In particular I wish to thank Ken Crann, Tina O'Toole, Michael Dore, Michael and Tricia Cummins and Evelyn Lynch for their support and friendship at Oaklands over the past number of years.

I wish to pay special tribute to a number of people who have been a great support and loyal friends to me over the years. In particular I'd like to thank Triona O'Neill, my oldest and dearest friend. Without Triona a lot of the things I do wouldn't happen and her belief in me and unwavering friendship mean everything. I'd also like to thank Johnny Keenaghan, Daire O'Neill, Paul Gerard Duncan, Terry O'Doherty, Simon McGarrigle, Aaron Ó'Maonaigh, Aaron Vaughan, Paul Cleary, Patrick McGahern, Brian Mullaney, James Mc Intyre and Chris and Joe McGurrin.

Also my many friends and colleagues in Dublin who have assisted me in one way or another over the years deserve special mention. In particular, Colin Murphy, Mary Elaine Tynan, Richard Stearn, Mick Burns, Conor Tiernan and Conor Sweetman.

My family deserve special thanks, especially Catherine, Ellie, Louis and Mark McIvor as well as Johnny, Harry and Molly Golden. In particular I'd like to thank my aunt Margaret Golden, someone who is very dear to me. The cups of tea and chats beside the range in Churchill on the drive back home from Dublin are something I look forward to and cherish.

Over the years I've had the great fortune to know many wonderful people who sadly have since passed on. My grandmothers Elizabeth Leslie and Mary McMenamin, uncles George Leslie and Harry Golden and dear friend Ronan McGee are never far from my thoughts and I hope that this book has done them proud.

Finally this book is dedicated to my parents Patrick and Florence McMenamin and to my brother Jason. Their love and support of me made the writing of this book possible and to them I'm forever grateful.

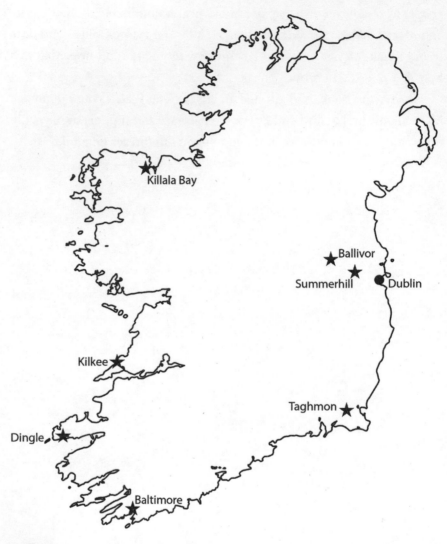

Dublin, home of librarian Richard Hayes, and the known landing zones of Nazi spies during World War II.

CONTENTS

'*History is punctuated with codes. They have decided the outcomes of battles and led to the deaths of Kings and Queens.*'

SIMON SINGH, Historian

'*In the written history of the world there is not so much as a glimpse behind the heavy curtains that enshroud the background of secret diplomacy.*'

MAJOR HERBERT O. YARDLEY, Cryptographer

FOREWORD

I first came across the story of Dr Richard Hayes in an article in the *Irish Times* property section in early 2016. The piece dealt with the sale of a house at 245 Templeogue Road and had been shown to me by a teaching colleague who quipped, 'There's a story there', as I read through it. The house had been known colloquially as the 'Nazi house' and its story was local lore in Dublin 6. It was erroneously said that the Art Deco house looked like a swastika in aerial photographs.

Truth, however, is always stranger than fiction. In 1940, it was used as an IRA safe house and a man named Hermann Görtz had stayed there on an ill-fated mission to Ireland to spy for the Third Reich. Given my interest in history I decided to investigate the matter further.

After much research, I came across the name of Dr Richard Hayes. He had interrogated Görtz during his incarceration in Arbour Hill prison and subsequently broke the communication code he was using. A similar cipher had baffled staff in Bletchley Park, and such was its importance, MI5 had an entire hut with 16 staff working on breaking it. In addition to this, Hayes's code-cracking expertise was to have a direct impact on various Allied engagements such as the Battle of the Bulge. He was also the first person in the world to break the German microdot encryption method.

Astonishingly, Hayes wasn't a military man at all. He had been seconded to Irish Military Intelligence for his obvious intellect. He spoke several languages, including fluent German, and was also a highly skilled mathematician. He uniquely possessed all the talents needed for the job that was at hand.

I was fascinated that a man such as Hayes was virtually unheard of in Ireland, given his achievements in the field of cryptanalysis and his contribution to the Allied war effort. The striking thing was that the more I read about Hayes, the more it became apparent how unassuming he was. He cycled to work every day in the library and after work he cycled to

McKee Barracks near Phoenix Park to work on the German codes that had been intercepted during the day.

Often he would take messages home to work on while simultaneously raising his young family. In his spare time, he compiled a bibliography of Irish manuscripts that is still being used today. Despite Hayes's obvious achievements, finding written material on him was a difficult task. He was merely a footnote in the more 'interesting' stories of others from that period. A good starting point was the pioneering research into this period of Irish history by Prof. Eunan O'Halpin, Dr Mark Hull and authors James Scannell and Enno Stefan. It is on the shoulders of that work that this book stands.

Despite Richard Hayes's name being not widely known, his contribution to Irish history is immeasurable. He masterminded the Irish counter-intelligence programme during World War II and helped ensure that Germany felt it could not directly invade Ireland.

It is my hope that now, 42 years after the death of Richard Hayes, the story of his life reignites public debate on how we commemorate World War II in Ireland and that he and other Irishmen who played such a crucial role in the Allied victory are suitably commemorated.

Marc Mc Menamin
Ballyshannon
June 2018

MAIN CHARACTERS

Dr Richard J. Hayes – Director of the National Library of Ireland during World War II. He was seconded to the Irish Defence Forces, where he headed the cryptography unit. He became Ireland's most prolific and brilliant codebreaker as well as a formidable interrogator of captured German spies.

Hermann Görtz – The most formidable German spy sent to Ireland during World War II, he remained at large for over a year. Görtz was a German spy in Britain and Ireland before and during the war.

Politicians and Civil Servants:
Frederick Boland – Assistant Secretary of the Department of External Affairs from 1939 to 1946 prior becoming the Secretary, a post he held until 1950.

Admiral Wilhelm Franz Canaris – a German admiral and chief of the Abwehr, the German military intelligence service, from 1935 to 1944.

Winston Churchill – British politician, army officer and writer, Prime Minister of the United Kingdom from 1940 to 1945 and again from 1951 to 1955.

Éamon de Valera – Irish political leader in 20th-century Ireland. His political career spanned over half a century from 1917 to 1973; he served several terms as head of government and head of state. Served as Taoiseach and Minster for External Affairs during World War II.

Herman Göring – a German political and military leader as well as one of the most powerful figures in the Nazi Party that ruled Germany from 1933 to 1945. A veteran World War I fighter pilot, he was a recipient of the Pour le Mérite and leader of the German Air Force, the Luftwaffe.

Adolf Hitler – German politician who was the leader of the Nazi Party, Chancellor of Germany from 1933 to 1945 and Führer of Nazi Germany from 1934 to 1945.

Franklin D. Roosevelt – American statesman and political leader who served as the 32nd President of the United States from 1933 until his death in 1945.

Joseph (Joe) Walshe – Secretary of the Department of External Affairs of the Irish Free State from 1923 to 1946.

Joachim von Ribbentrop – Foreign Minister of Nazi Germany from 1938 until 1945.

The Irish Defence Forces:

Col Liam Archer – The Director of Irish Military Intelligence (G2) from the outbreak of the war until his promotion to Deputy Chief of Staff in 1941.

Col Dan Bryan – Director of Irish Military Intelligence from 1941 until 1952. Bryan was responsible for recruiting Dr Hayes as a codebreaker and formulating Irish defence policy in the late 1930s.

Commandant Éamon De Buitléar – worked for G2 alongside Dr Hayes as an interrogator and cryptographer.

Capt. Joseph Healy – Professor of Spanish at University College Cork, seconded into G2 during World War II where he worked as a codebreaker and interrogator.

Lt. General Dan McKenna – Chief of Staff of the Irish Defence Forces during World War II.

General Hugo MacNeill – Irish general who became involved in political intrigue with German spy Hermann Görtz.

General Eoin O'Duffy – an Irish nationalist, political activist, soldier and police commissioner. He was leader of the quasi-fascist Army Comrades Association, commonly known as the Blueshirts.

Captain John Patrick O'Sullivan – Irish Army Signals Officer who monitored the German Legation from listening stations in Collins Barracks and his home in Chapelizod.

The Irish Republican Army:

Stephen Hayes – a member and leader of the Irish Republican Army from April 1939 to June 1941. Served as Acting Chief of Staff while Séan Russell was abroad.

Stephen Carroll Held – an IRA member who visited Germany in 1940 as an emissary of the IRA to discuss Plan Kathleen, the projected German takeover of Ireland.

Pearse Paul Kelly – IRA man who was arrested along with Hermann Görtz at 1 Blackheath Park, Clontarf, in 1943.

Patrick Mc Neela – IRA man who picked up Hermann Görtz from Jim O'Donovan's house Florenceville in Shankill, Co. Dublin.

James 'Jim' O'Donovan – a leading volunteer in the Irish Republican Army where he acted as Head of Munitions and Chemicals. Travelled to Germany to set up the link with the Nazi Party.

Séan Russell – an Irish republican who held senior positions in the IRA until the end of the Irish War of Independence. From 1922 until his death on board a Kriegsmarine U-Boat in 1940 he remained a senior member and chief of staff of the IRA, while it divided and was outlawed by the Irish state.

Frank Ryan – an Irish politician, journalist, intelligence agent and paramilitary activist. A prominent figure on the left in the IRA.

Maurice 'Moss' Twomey – an Irish republican and former chief of staff of the Irish Republican Army. Used mainly as a hard man in his later years.

German Spies:

Dieter Gärtner and Herbert Tributh – South African nationals who were sent by the Abwehr to Ireland carrying explosives.

Walter Simon – trained at the Abwehr branch in Hamburg, which was responsible for subversive activities against the United Kingdom.

Henry Obéd – An Indian native who accompanied Gärtner and Tributh.

Wilhelm Preetz – the first German agent to be captured in Ireland. Married to an Irish woman from Tuam, Co. Galway.

Günther Schütz – a German citizen who performed a mission for German intelligence to Ireland. Arrived in Wexford using a state-of-the-art system of microdots for encrypting messages.

Werner Unland – A German sleeper agent who had arrived in Dublin with his wife prior to the war. Used his home on Merrion Square as a base for spying.

Jan van Loon – A Dutch sailor and opportunist who volunteered his services as a spy to the German Legation.

Ernst Weber-Drohl – a professional wrestler, strongman performer and German Abwehr agent during World War II.

German/IRA Intermediaries:

Helmut Clissman – the best-informed German about Ireland and the I RA during World War II. The Nazis twice failed to smuggle him into Ireland to act as an intelligence agent and link with the outlawed IRA. Mr Clissmann first came to Ireland as a young Trinity College student in the 1930s.

Oscar C. Pfaus – German intelligence agent with the Abwehr. In 1939 the Abwehr sent Pfaus to Ireland to set up a link with the IRA for the forthcoming war with Britain.

Native Irish German Spies:

John Codd – an Irish national who, after being captured as a British Army corporal during World War II, went on to serve in the German intelligence service and SS intelligence.

John Kenny – Amateur radio operator who accompanied John Francis O'Reilly on his mission to Ireland.

Joseph Lenihan – Member of the Lenihan political family, recruited by the Abwehr in the Channel Islands and later selected for the Double-Cross system by MI5.

John Francis O'Reilly – An opportunist who was recruited by the Abwehr and sent to Ireland on a spy mission.

James O'Neill – Trained by the Abwehr as an agent and unsuccessfully sent to Ireland via Spain.

Irish German Conspirators:

Joseph Gerard Andrews – An opportunist who became involved with Görtz and continued using his code after Görtz's arrest.

Caitlín Brugha – an Irish Sinn Féin politician. Sheltered Hermann Görtz and Günther Schütz while they were on the run.

Anthony Deery – IRA member and Hermann Görtz's radio operator.

Christopher Eastwood – A chef on board the SS *Edenvale* who passed messages to Portugal for Andrews using Görtz's code.

Mary and Bridie Farrell – Sisters who sheltered Görtz at their home in 7 Spencer Villas, Glenageary. The sisters campaigned for Görtz's deportation to be reversed.

Liam Gaynor – Author of Plan Kathleen, the blueprint for the German invasion of Northern Ireland.

Maud Gonne MacBride – Widow of 1916 leader Major John MacBride and mother of Iseult Stuart.

Charles 'Nomad' Mc Guinness – An Irish adventurer, author and sailor supposed to have been involved in a myriad of acts of patriotism and nomadic adventures. A friend and confidant of Hermann Görtz.

Helena Moloney – A prominent Irish republican, feminist and labour activist. She fought in the 1916 Easter Rising and later became the second female president of the Irish Trade Union Congress. She harboured and aided Hermann Görtz while he was on the run.

Francis Stuart – Irish writer and Nazi sympathiser. Travelled to Germany to liaise with the Abwehr. Offered his home at Laragh Castle, Co. Wicklow, as refuge to Hermann Görtz.

Iseult Stuart – the daughter of Maud Gonne and Lucien Millevoye, and the wife of the novelist Francis Stuart. Had a romantic relationship with Hermann Görtz during his stay at her home in Laragh, Co. Wicklow.

Foreign Diplomats posted to Ireland during World War Two:

David Gray, United States – an American playwright and novelist who served as the United States minister to Ireland from 1940 to 1947.

Dr Eduard Hempel, Germany – the Nazi German Minister to Ireland between 1937 and 1945 in the build-up to and during the Emergency.

John Maffey, 1st Baron Rugby, United Kingdom – At Churchill's request he became the first United Kingdom representative to Ireland in 1939 and served in the role until the end of the war.

MI5:

Cecil Liddell – Older brother of Guy and head of MI5's Irish section which worked in conjunction with Col Dan Bryan in the Dublin Link. Visited Ireland to be shown the Görtz coding system by Dr Hayes.

Guy Liddell – MI5's Director of Counter-Espionage during World War II.

United States Army:

General Lucius D. Clay – a senior officer of the United States Army who was known for his administration of occupied Germany after World War II.

I

SHAKING HANDS WITH THE DEVIL

'Ireland is important to the Commander in Chief of the Luftwaffe [Hermann Göring] as his base for attacks on the north-west ports of Britain, although weather conditions must be investigated. The occupation of Ireland might lead to the end of the war.'

ADOLF HITLER, Wehrmacht situation conference,
3 December 1940

This is a story of many characters, but chief among them is a humble librarian from west Limerick, whose efforts alongside his colleagues in Irish Military Intelligence helped turn the tide of the Second World War. During that destructive conflict that swept through Europe from 1939 to 1945, Nazi Germany attempted, through espionage, to penetrate the Irish Free State at every level. They did this for a variety of reasons; primarily they did it to assess the IRA's suitability as an asset to the Nazi regime, but they were also interested in weather reports from Ireland due to the similar climate the country shared with the United Kingdom. Such information could have been used to great effect in the planning of military operations by the German forces against the Allied Powers. Ireland had never before faced such a threat to her sovereignty.

Spying missions into Ireland posed myriad problems for the Irish authorities. Foremost was the very real threat of a German invasion but there was also the possibility of a pre-emptive invasion by the Allies in order to counter the German threat. In the latter years of the war, information leakage through German agents active in the Irish Free State also posed a serious threat not only to Ireland, but to the very course of the war itself. Ireland needed the right people in the right place, to do the right thing at the right time.

Two such gentlemen were Dr Richard J. Hayes, the Director of the National Library of Ireland, and Colonel Dan Bryan, the Director of Irish Military Intelligence from 1941 to 1952. Hayes's brilliance as a codebreaker and interrogator, and the foresight of Bryan to utilise him in this role, ensured that Germany felt they could not directly invade Ireland, while also playing a significant role in crucial Allied operations such as the Battle of the Bulge. Much of this story has been hidden in plain sight for several decades, but the story of Hayes, Ireland's enigmatic and unassuming Nazi codebreaker, is an exceptional one. When Ireland faced her darkest hour, alone and vulnerable on the periphery of Europe, Richard Hayes was all that stood between Ireland and Nazi Germany.

Germany had long fixed her gaze on the British Isles. As early as the mid-1930s Ireland was identified as being of strategic importance to the Reich. While Ireland possessed very little in the way of natural resources, its proximity to England ensured that it would always be of interest to the German authorities. Ireland was in many ways a gateway to the Atlantic, and control of her meant control of the supply routes from the United States, on which the British relied. While the German Luftwaffe and the Kriegsmarine were ill-equipped to totally disrupt convoys that passed close by neutral Éire and directly into British-controlled Northern Ireland, a line of thinking soon developed that if Ireland were to be turned into a German ally it would help create a new front from which to attack the British – right on its own doorstep.

German contacts with Ireland predated the outbreak of the war in 1939. As early as the mid-1930s Germany maintained political and cultural links with Ireland, liaisons that were to draw considerable suspicions from the Irish authorities, particularly G2, the Irish Directorate of Military Intelligence. G2, which is still in existence today, is the military intelligence branch of the Defence Forces, the Irish armed forces, and the national intelligence service of Ireland. It is essentially Ireland's version of

MI5 or the CIA. G2 has responsibility for the safety and security of Irish Defence Forces personnel, and supports the national security of Ireland.

During the war years the Directorate operated domestic and foreign intelligence sections, providing intelligence to the Government of Ireland concerning threats to the security of the state and the national interest from internal and external sources. It was during this period that Military Intelligence first became known as G2, which was an American designation. It had had many different titles over the years from its genesis as the intelligence section of the IRA, led by the IRA's Director of Intelligence, Michael Collins. But the rise of fascism was to give G2 its toughest challenge yet.

Initially Military Intelligence was concerned with assessing external threats to Ireland. This resulted in a devotion to the study of foreign armies, something which wasn't an onerous task, as there was no foreign army posing a threat to the Irish state at that period. There was of course the United Kingdom, with which from 1921 Ireland had a very complex defence and security relationship. However there were limited resources available to intelligence, and it was pointless devoting them to the study of the British Armed Forces. But during the 'Emergency' G2 did build up its resources for assessing the strength of the British and American forces in Northern Ireland.

In the 1920s and 1930s G2's main role was to deal with the internal threat of the IRA, and to assess the threat of republicans being manipulated by foreign powers. This eventually evolved into counter-intelligence, subversion and the prevention of other countries using Ireland as a base for spying, and as such Irish Military Intelligence was structured into various sections during the war. Assuming overall command was the Army Chief of Staff Lt Gen. Dan McKenna. His Assistant Chief of Staff was Liam Archer, who assumed this role in 1941, and the rest of Intelligence was subdivided into the following sections: G1, which dealt primarily with personnel; G2, which dealt with Intelligence, and which from 1941 was headed by Dan Bryan, who was headquartered in Dublin with four regional commands; G3, which dealt with operations; and G4, which handled logistics. Bryan was able to liaise through G2 with the Garda Síochána Special Branch as well as with the Garda Aliens Section, Naval Service, Coastal Service, Immigration and the Departments of Justice, Posts and Telegraphs and External Affairs. With all these powers at his disposal Dan Bryan was well placed to take on the looming Nazi threat.

Daniel Bryan, known as Dan to his friends and colleagues, was born in Dunbell, Gowran, Co. Kilkenny in 1900. From 1916 he studied medicine for two years at University College Dublin. In November 1917 he joined the Irish Volunteers to fight against British rule in Ireland, serving in C and G companies of the 4th Dublin Brigade. He entered the National Army in 1922 and was formally commissioned to the rank of Captain in the Defence Forces on 4 September 1923. Bryan was to serve most of his career at army headquarters, with the majority of it in the Intelligence section. In 1941 he was appointed as Chief Staff Officer of G2, and he held this post throughout the Emergency. He was a man of huge intellectual ability, known for his shrewdness, analytical thinking and considerable memory for facts, figures and faces – skills that were to be tested to the extreme as the darks clouds of fascism began to gather over Europe.

From the early 1930s, prior to his elevation to Director of Intelligence, Dan Bryan had been writing internal memoranda arguing that if Ireland didn't deal with foreign powers developing relationships with the IRA, such powers that threatened countries such as Britain and France would start operating secretly in Ireland. Bryan argued that if Ireland wished to be truly neutral, a policy which had been at the heart of Irish foreign policy since independence, it could only be so by practising a very shrewd realpolitik, ensuring Ireland couldn't be used as a base to attack British interests. Bryan's views were quite unpopular in the army at the time, because there prevailed an attitude that if Germany went to war against Britain, Germany might help Ireland regain the lost territory of Northern Ireland.

This naïve theory was endorsed by some senior officers and prompted Bryan to courageously put his thoughts in writing. Mindful of the growing threats of National Socialism in Germany and Mussolini's Fascist Brigades in Italy, Bryan penned a long essay entitled 'Fundamental Factors affecting Irish Defence' as part of his application for promotion to commandant.

The 60-page document would eventually make its way to the government, where ministers were suddenly spurred into action by his writings. Bryan argued that 'we are not relatively but totally disarmed; the big danger is not from the United Kingdom but from Britain's enemies. The danger is Britain's enemies will establish a link here with the IRA and that may provoke them into action against us.' While many around him took the view that the war wasn't Ireland's concern, Bryan continued warning the authorities about the imminent threat, as his concern at Ireland's vulnerability grew with each passing day.

In the course of the document Bryan anticipated what would be necessary in terms of resources and personnel if Ireland should get involved in the war. Staffing and money were problems for G2, but they had done the heavy lifting in terms of intelligence and counter-intelligence functions, mostly in terms of preventing England or Germany or the US from interfering with Ireland. Essentially Bryan wanted G2 to be able to detect foreign spies entering the country and to deal with them as quickly and quietly as possible.

While Bryan had written this paper in 1936, it wasn't fully implemented until 1939, at the outbreak of the war. His paper had been written at the correct time, however, and politicians became slowly but surely aware of the threat posed to Ireland by the developing political situation in Europe. The British government was desperately trying to appease Hitler; however, slowly but surely, Europe was headed towards war. While Neville Chamberlain preached 'peace in our time', in Ireland a cabinet committee on press censorship was re-established, and groundwork was laid down for press and communication censorship based on the British experience of World War I.

Bryan and Col Liam Archer, the Director of Intelligence until 1941,were given a significant input in the formation of the government's security policy, and debates were held in the Dáil with regard to aligning Irish neutrality with British security interests. A committee composed of the Departments of Justice, Defence and Local Government was also formed. The committee was to be chaired by the Taoiseach, and its sole brief was to coordinate all government departments in relation to national defence while a new Defence Forces bill was being drafted. Crucially, Dan Bryan had reawakened Irish defence policy as a major political interest in the nick of time.

Under the stewardship of Archer and Bryan, G2 was to concern itself with coordinating all aspects of state security. This included maintaining files on all suspects and persons of interest, as well as suspect organisations, both domestic and foreign, operating in Ireland. Part of this role was to include monitoring of the German presence in Ireland. While Ireland had quite a small German population at the outbreak of the war in 1939 (estimated at 200 known aliens), it was highly organised and respected, and posed an intelligence and security threat to the state. In order to counter this, a joint security operation between G2 and An Garda Síochána was set up to monitor potential threats.

As early as 1931 the National Socialist German Workers' Party (NSDAP), commonly known as the Nazi Party, had an overseas affiliate group known as the Auslands-Organisation operating in Dublin. While on the surface it posed as an organisation dedicated to promoting trade and cultural links with Ireland, it was in fact engaged in intelligence gathering and the recruitment of informants who would endeavour to monitor goings-on in Ireland and report them back to the German High Command in Berlin.

The Dublin branch of the Nazi Party had a very small but influential membership largely made up of aesthetes and members of the intelligentsia. While the party only had 30 members, its influence in Dublin society was extensive, particularly in the arts. The most prominent member of the group was Dr Adolf Mahr, an Austrian archaeologist who later became leader of the Dublin branch of the Nazi Party. Mahr arrived in Ireland in 1927 to work as keeper of antiquities in the National Museum of Ireland in Dublin, and in 1934 Éamon de Valera appointed Mahr Director of the museum. Mahr joined the Nazi Party in 1933, and during his spell as Nazi leader in Dublin he recruited roughly 23 Germans to his organisation. G2 monitored Mahr closely, but he was also kept under close surveillance by George Furlong, Director of the National Gallery from 1935 to 1950, who was clandestinely working as a spy for MI5 himself.

In 1939 Mahr was recalled to Germany due to a general order calling all German citizens to return home at the outbreak of the war. He had hoped to return to Ireland by late September 1939, believing that the war with Britain would be brief and would result in a decisive German victory. Events were to take a different turn, however. After the war Mahr was arrested and accused of being a Nazi spy, and for using his position as Director to plan a Nazi invasion of Ireland. It was alleged that he had escaped with maps and plans that would be of use to a potential invading army. After his release Mahr tried to return to Ireland, but he was ultimately prevented from doing so on the advice of Dan Bryan to Taoiseach Éamon de Valera.

Other high-ranking Germans and Austrians prominent in the Nazi Party in Ireland included Col Fritz Brase, who became head of the Irish Army's School of Music; Otto Reinhard, who was Forestry Director with the Department of Lands; and Heinz Mecking, chief advisor with the Turf Development Board. This group of intelligentsia were vociferous in their sense of national pride, and proudly espoused their beliefs publicly. They were regulars in the most high-end restaurants and bars of the era. Mahr had a particular fondness for the Red Bank Restaurant on D'Olier Street and the Gresham Hotel on O'Connell Street.

In 1937, the Auslands-Organisation organised an ostentatious Christmas party in the Gresham where the party faithful wined and dined in a main hall that was festooned with swastika flags, tricolours and a large portrait of Herr Hitler. A toast was raised to salute the Führer, and Nazi salutes were given during raucous renditions of *Deutschlandlied*, the Nazi Party anthem. While giving the impression that he was an aesthete, Mahr was without doubt a very serious doctrinaire Nazi. He would later attend a conference in 1944 organised by the ss and Propaganda Ministry under Joseph Goebbels which sought to deal with the 'Jewish Question'. Mahr and other members of the German community living in Ireland also successfully collected intelligence and relayed this to Berlin to be used in future invasion plans for Ireland.

The presence of this German colony posed the Irish authorities with a unique problem, in that there was a branch of the Nazi Party in Dublin in the lead-up to the outbreak of the war when Ireland was trying to operate a policy of neutrality. Eventually the problem was taken out of the government's hands, when all members of the Auslands-Organisation were recalled to Germany at the outbreak of the war as part of a general recalling of all German citizens resident abroad. De Valera facilitated their passage via a mail boat named the *Cambria*, and breathed a sigh of relief to be rid of a potentially tricky diplomatic problem.

While the Auslands-Organisation was a visible presence in Dublin it had no direct links with the IRA, as had been feared by Dan Bryan. If Germany could in some way link with republicans it would lead to an unholy alliance and create an extra front from which Germany could attack the British. That all changed with the arrival into Ireland of a young language exchange student.

———

Helmut Clissmann first arrived into Ireland in the mid-1930s as a student with the German Academic Exchange Service, and he later studied at Trinity College Dublin. He was also an officer in the Abwehr, the German military intelligence agency during the war. Despite the fact that the Treaty of Versailles prohibited the Germans from establishing an intelligence organisation, they formed an espionage group in 1920 within the Ministry of Defence, calling it the Abwehr. The initial purpose of the Abwehr was defence against foreign espionage, and they essentially gathered domestic and foreign information about individuals who were a threat or of potential use to Germany.

When Hitler came to power he absorbed the Abwehr into the Oberkommando der Wehrmacht (OKW), essentially the German High Command. The OKW was part of the Führer's personal working staff from June 1938, and the Abwehr became its intelligence agency under Vice Admiral Wilhelm Canaris. Its headquarters were located in an ominous-looking building at 76–78 Tirpitzufer, Berlin, where agents were briefed for spying missions. Shortly before the war the Abwehr was subdivided into three broad sections: Foreign Intelligence Collection, Sabotage and Counter-Intelligence.

Clissmann was tasked by the Abwehr to develop his knowledge of English and to assess the capacity of Irish republicanism to be an asset to Germany in the event of a conflict with the United Kingdom. On the surface he was involved in what seemed a cultural mission to promote links with Nazi Germany in Ireland. At one stage Clissmann championed the idea of an academic prize for students who came first in the German exam in the Leaving Certificate. The winner of the prize would get an all-expenses-paid trip to Nazi Germany, where they would stay in a Hitler Youth Camp; the idea was eventually rejected by de Valera.

Clissmann operated under the direction of Adolf Mahr, and was successful in making contact with senior republicans in Dublin – even if he was ultimately unsuccessful in attracting the attentions of the Abwehr to Ireland, as the organisation felt it would be more appropriate to wait for a more opportune time in the future. Clissmann was, however, encouraged to maintain contact with the IRA. In September 1939, he was recalled to Germany along with other German nationals and travelled to mainland Europe on board the *Cambria*. He continued his work with the German Academic Exchange Service before being called up to active service in July 1940. He was posted to the Brandenburg Regiment and assigned military missions related to Ireland. Among these was an aborted attempt to land in Sligo during the war. Despite the various underground German movements in Ireland the main threat to Ireland in the years coming up to the outbreak of the war was actually from Irish republicans, as opposed to German or Italian intelligence agents.

———

By the mid-1930s the IRA was an organisation in disarray, diminished by a decade-long campaign against the Irish Free State. But despite the organisation being subjected to internment and sustained scrutiny by the government, the IRA was still potent enough to provide a threat to both the British and the Irish state. The majority of republicans had sided with Fianna Fáil after the Civil War, leaving behind a rump of extremists who were determined to liberate Northern Ireland from British rule by force of arms. De Valera's government had been particularly severe in dealing with the IRA, to the extent that they were perceived to be of no imminent threat to the security of the state.

In truth they were a faction-ridden group led by various ideologues. The 'conservative' wing of the group was led by Chief of Staff Maurice 'Moss' Twomey, with Seán MacBride serving as Adjutant General and Seán Russell as Head of Munitions. The 'left' wing of the group was led by Frank Ryan, editor of the IRA newspaper *An Phoblacht*. Ryan and others on the left took up arms in the International Brigade in the Spanish Civil War in 1936. By the outbreak of World War II in 1939, it was estimated (depending on sources) that the IRA had between 5,000 and 30,000 active members, which left the organisation well placed to attack at the heart of British society.

In April 1938 an IRA General Army Convention was held and Seán Russell commanded enough support to be installed as the new Chief of Staff. Moss Twomey stood aside from the role and semi-retired to open a confectionery and newsagent's on O'Connell Street, though he maintained links with the IRA. Russell immediately set about reorganising the IRA into a formidable threat to British interests, and appointed an Army Executive. He immediately set his sights on beginning a new bombing campaign in England, ensuring that IRA training classes in explosives were held in various secret locations across the country.

In January 1939, the IRA declared war on England, and began a bombing campaign which targeted London, Manchester, Birmingham and Alnwick. On 19 January the IRA unsuccessfully targeted Prime Minister Neville Chamberlain's only son in a botched attack in Tralee, Co. Kerry, and in early February the campaign was escalated further when bombs exploded at Leicester Square and Tottenham Court Road tube stations in central London. When some young IRA volunteers were arrested in London following an intense security operation by Scotland Yard they had in their possession a document entitled the 's-Plan'.

The 's' stood for Sabotage and it contained a detailed set of instructions for a terrorist campaign in England: acts of destruction to bring about the paralysis of all official activity in England and inflict the greatest possible destruction on British defence installations. It divided the IRA campaign into two main lines: propaganda and offensive military action. The document listed six different types of action, including the destruction of armament factories and the disruption of civil/public utilities such as transport and gasworks. Attacks were also planned against industrial plants, commercial premises and newspapers.

The IRA's attacks were to be strictly concentrated on the island of Britain and in and around centres of population, where IRA volunteers could operate freely without drawing attention. No attacks on targets in Northern Ireland or other areas under British control were planned as part of the s-Plan. On 28 and 29 November 1938, British customs posts along the border were demolished using explosives. The only fatalities were three IRA volunteers, Jimmy Joe Reynolds from Leitrim, John James Kelly from Donegal and Charlie McCafferty from Tyrone, killed by the premature explosion of a mine at a house in Castlefin, Co. Donegal on 28 November. IRA units were expected to raise any money needed for the campaign themselves, and the men who acted within IRA teams were unpaid and expected to support themselves while on missions. Despite being not very well equipped in some respects, the IRA posed a considerable security threat, and was determined to stoke fear within the British establishment.

In an attempt to escalate the campaign, the IRA unequivocally delivered a written ultimatum to British Foreign Secretary Lord Halifax:

I have the honour to inform you that the Government of the Irish Republic, having as its first duty towards its people the establishment and maintenance of peace and order here, demand the withdrawal of all British armed forces stationed in Ireland. The occupation of our territory by troops of another nation and the persistent subvention here of activities directly against the expressed national will and in the interests of a foreign power, prevent the expansion and development of our institution in consonance with our social needs and purposes, and must cease. The Government of the Irish Republic believe that a period of four days is sufficient notice for your Government to signify its intentions in the matter of the military evacuation and for the issue of your Declaration of Abdication in respect of our country. Our Government reserves the right of appropriate action without further notice if upon the expiration of this period of grace, these conditions remain unfulfilled. –Óglaigh na h-Éireann (Irish Republican Army)

De Valera was outraged by the declaration, and in a debate in Dáil Éireann he excoriated the IRA for claiming they had any right to assume the title 'Government of the Irish Republic'. He assured the Dáil he would bring forth strong measures to deal with the IRA and to give the government the necessary powers to uphold its authority. While Ireland and England tried desperately to deal with the ongoing crisis, a man of average build wearing a grey coat and carrying a small suitcase boarded a train for the Hook of Holland in Hamburg Central Station. His destination: Ireland.

———

The German passport carried by the man as he boarded the train identified him as the author Oskar Karl Pfaus, born on 30 January 1901 in Württemberg, southern Germany. He had obtained an entry visa for England, granted to him in the weeks prior by the British Consul in Hamburg. Pfaus, 38 years old, had an oval face and brown eyes and hair, and spoke with an American accent. He also insisted on using the American version of his name: Oscar C. Pfaus. He had spent a considerable amount of time in the United States, living what many would consider a colourful life. He had at various stages been a volunteer to the United States Army, a hobo and a mineral prospector in California. Pfaus had returned to Germany on a passenger liner in 1938, having been placed on a list of people of potential use to the Reich. He was soon recruited by the Abwehr in Hamburg to take on a mission that was to be kept secret at all costs.

Pfaus presented himself at the Abwehr headquarters on Knochenhauerstrasse in Hamburg. This was a sub-office of the Berlin Abwehr, whose interest in Ireland had been piqued by the IRA bombings in London and elsewhere. Pfaus was asked by the Abwehr if he would be interested in travelling to Dublin to try and establish contacts with IRA headquarters, and to try to find out whether there was an appetite for collaboration with Nazi Germany. Such was the clandestine nature of the mission entrusted to Pfaus that even the Foreign Office in Berlin was unaware of it. They had imposed a strict veto on contact with subversive elements in Ireland in order to preserve the integrity of the German diplomatic mission in Dublin and, most importantly, to avoid attracting any unnecessary attention to its headquarters on Northumberland Road.

Eager to make his mark as an elite agent and trustworthy son of the Fatherland, Pfaus arrived in Ireland via Holyhead on the morning of 2 February 1939, carrying with him his English visa and, concealed in his jacket, a .45-calibre Smith and Wesson automatic pistol which he had taken back from America. Pfaus stayed overnight in O'Neill's boarding house on Lower Gardiner Street in Dublin's city centre before making contact with General Eoin O'Duffy, the leader of the quasi-fascist Army Comrades Association, more commonly known in Ireland as the Blueshirts. O'Duffy had been in correspondence with Pfaus via letter, and he and some of his supporters were the only contacts the German had in Ireland.

Such was the level of trust between O'Duffy and Pfaus that he didn't need to use his cover story that he was a journalist working for the *Deutsche Allgemeine Zeitung* newspaper. Pfaus broached the subject of collaboration between the IRA and Germany with O'Duffy, to which the Blueshirt leader expressed his revulsion. While O'Duffy had fought in the IRA in Ulster during the War of Independence, politics had of course moved on in Ireland, meaning that Pfaus's knowledge of what was happening on the ground was outdated.

O'Duffy was now a vehement opponent of the IRA, a group which he considered to be illegal and criminal. He had originally set up the Blueshirt movement to protect the ruling government party Cumann na nGaedheal's meetings from attack by the IRA, and he was revolted by the thought of any sort of reconciliation with them. This posed a dilemma for Pfaus, who would have to look elsewhere in order to make contact with the IRA. The opportunity came when he was introduced to a young philology student named Joy Payne. Pfaus stayed for a time with Payne's parents, who were O'Duffy supporters in Glenageary, and the young Joy fell head over heels in love with Pfaus. Within a few days, through contacts in the Irish Hospitals Trust, an organisation which had liaisons with the IRA, Pfaus received a message to meet a contact outside a newspaper shop on O'Connell Street on 13 February 1939, almost ten days after his arrival in Ireland.

The shopkeepers had closed up their premises by the time Pfaus arrived on O'Connell Street. After waiting some time he began to question whether anyone would come to meet him. Pfaus soon began to feel uncomfortable, and he had just decided to head home when he was greeted by a large man with a Cork accent and the build of a rugby player, who suddenly bundled him into a car. The two zigzagged across Dublin, eventually arriving, unbeknownst to Pfaus, in Clontarf. Little did the shaken German know that his chauffeur was actually Moss Twomey, the former IRA Chief of Staff. While Twomey had stood down from the position in favour of Seán Russell, he was still aiding the IRA with logistical help and target selection for the bombing campaign in England. Pfaus didn't need to ask where he was; he knew as Twomey motioned him into the house that he would be meeting the IRA very soon.

The car pulled up to a house and Pfaus was led inside to a large, dimly lit room, where half a dozen men sat around a table. The door closed behind him as he entered, and without warning one of the men barked, 'Who are you?' With trepidation Pfaus asked for proof that he was standing in front of the IRA Army Council, assuring the men assembled that he could not state his mission until he was sure who they were. As Pfaus scanned the room he noticed that a number of the men were blocking the windows, doors and any other means of escape, standing menacingly with their hands in their coat pockets.

Pfaus was beginning to question the wisdom of his visit when one of the men standing at the door insisted that he disclose his identity first. Pfaus hesitantly stated his name, and one of the men demanded to know what his business with them was. Somewhat evasively, he stated that he wished to establish propaganda contacts. One of the men asked, 'Contacts with whom?' Pfaus explained that he simply wished to know who the men were. Two of the men present were Seán Russell and Jim O'Donovan. Unbeknownst to Pfaus, Russell was IRA Chief of Staff and O'Donovan was

Head of Munitions and Chemicals, and the author of the s-Plan.

Ignoring their guest's request for their identities, Russell began to interrogate Pfaus at length about German intentions for Ireland. Pfaus explained the idea of possible collaboration between the IRA and Nazi Germany. And any fears he may have had were proved unnecessary, as the proceedings were called to an abrupt halt. The IRA men shook Pfaus's hand warmly as they indicated interest in his plan. All parties agreed that an IRA member would travel to Germany to further discuss the idea of cooperation between republicans and the Germans. O'Donovan took a £1 note from his pocket and tore it in half, giving half to Pfaus and keeping the other himself. The note was to act as a recognition signal for the as yet undetermined IRA contact and the Abwehr once the IRA operative reached Germany.

Pfaus left Ireland on 14 February 1939, feeling his mission had been a success given that the link between the IRA and Nazi Germany had been made. But while Pfaus was in Ireland he had disseminated propaganda materials, and his visit to Ireland didn't go unnoticed; his movements were recorded by G2 operatives who had been secretly monitoring him since he arrived from Holyhead. They noted that he departed Ireland in a nervous and erratic state.

——

Following Pfaus's return to Germany, IRA Chief Seán Russell decided that Jim O'Donovan would be sent to Berlin as the IRA's representative. O'Donovan was a natural choice, given his role as Head of Munitions and the fact that out of all the IRA's leadership he spoke enough German to carry out the task. Russell instructed O'Donovan to find out what military items the IRA could hope to obtain from Nazi Germany, as by the time of Pfaus's visit munitions were running low. These would have to be replenished if the IRA were to keep its war with Britain going.

Séamus (James) O'Donovan was born in Roscommon town on 3 November 1896. Known to those close to him as Jim, he fought in the Irish War of Independence and then on the Anti-Treaty side during the Irish Civil War. O'Donovan was an explosives expert, and was imprisoned a number of times, having reputedly invented the 'Irish War Flour' explosive (named after the flour sacks in which it was smuggled into Dublin aboard ships). He subsequently became IRA Director of Chemicals in 1921, and in his mid-20s O'Donovan married into republican royalty when he wedded Monty Barry, the sister of IRA martyr Kevin Barry. In 1930, he became manager at ESB headquarters in Dublin, where he perfected his knowledge of electronics. O'Donovan was of slim build, with very striking features, most distinguishing of which was the fact that he was missing three fingers on one hand due to an accident involving transport of explosives while on an IRA operation in his early 20s.

O'Donovan was to visit Germany three times in 1939. On his first visit Pfaus was alarmed to answer the door of his house near Hamburg's Central Station to find O'Donovan standing there holding his torn half of the £1 note. Pfaus ushered him inside the house and a meeting was soon arranged between O'Donovan and Abwehr agent Hauptmann Marwede where the two men discussed the role that the IRA was to play in the forthcoming war against Britain. The Germans impressed upon O'Donovan that they could not provide weapons immediately to the IRA to aid them in their bombing campaign. In reality the Germans secretly thought the S-Plan was foolhardy and provocative. The Germans also expressed scepticism about the IRA's ability to carry out offensive operations against Northern Ireland should the war break out as expected. After three days O'Donovan returned to Ireland, but not before the Germans had given him the codename 'Agent V-Held'.

O'Donovan and the rest of the IRA were hugely encouraged by the meeting, and O'Donovan returned on 26 April 1939 to firm up details regarding radio contact and courier routes for messages and armaments. A safe house in London was also established during the meeting. With the link adequately set up, O'Donovan returned to Ireland on 15 May, testing the route himself on his way back to Dublin. In his absence Seán Russell had decided to leave for the United States on a propaganda tour to try and raise funds from Irish-Americans for the ongoing bombing campaign. Stephen Hayes had been installed as Acting Chief of Staff in his absence; however, his appointment as head of the IRA was to later prove disastrous.

While he was a committed republican, he didn't command the same respect among his peers that Russell had due to what many perceived as his poor judgement.

Stephen Hayes was born in Enniscorthy, Co. Wexford, and during the War of Independence he was Commandant of the Wexford Brigade of the IRA's youth wing. He took the Anti-Treaty side during the Irish Civil War, during which he was interned. As a militarist with a severe hatred of the British, Hayes sought to intensify the war against Britain, and as a result the IRA bombing campaign escalated in Russell's absence. London and Liverpool were again targeted in violent explosions. The British estimated that during this period 'one hundred and twenty-seven terrorist outrages' had been committed: 57 in London and 70 in the provinces. One person had been killed and over 55 injured, while 66 persons had been arrested on terrorism-related charges. The police had seized 55 sticks of gelignite, 1,000 detonators, two tons of potassium chlorate and oxide of iron, seven gallons of sulphuric acid and 400 containers of aluminium powder.

Such was the state of alarm in the United Kingdom over the seizures that when King George VI and Queen Elizabeth visited the United States, Seán Russell was taken into custody at the behest of a Scotland Yard request to US authorities, as an assassination attempt was feared. MI5 were also aware that the IRA had plans to blow up the Houses of Parliament, and the IRA came close to blowing up Hammersmith Bridge and Southwark Power Station. Meanwhile in Ireland the security forces were stretched to their limit when violence erupted during a march for the annual Wolfe Tone republican commemoration in Bodenstown, Co. Kildare. The Nazi regime in Germany looked with disbelief at the British government's inability to deal with the escalating situation.

In the midst of all this chaos, Jim O'Donovan made his last visits to Berlin and Hamburg in August 1939. This time he brought his wife Monty with him, primarily as cover. The two were given a hostile reception upon arrival by German customs officials, who strip-searched Monty for contraband. This incensed O'Donovan, and he vented his displeasure. The couple were eventually met by Oscar Pfaus, who was dismayed at O'Donovan's newfound hostility towards Germany. The IRA man openly mocked the swastika flag and the brown uniforms of the SA, and questioned the fitness for war of the Wehrmacht, whom he considered 'cadaver like in their obedience'.

Once settled, O'Donovan met with Herr Neumeister of the German Foreign Office and the Abwehr to discuss the IRA sabotage campaign in England, as well as the standard of IRA equipment, arms and ammunition. The Germans were also interested in hearing about IRA intentions towards the Irish Free State and Northern Ireland and the likely reaction of the Dublin government to any outbreak of war between Germany and Ireland. It was agreed that a radio link would be established between the IRA and the Germans, and that any transmissions should be coded for the purposes of secrecy. When the meeting concluded O'Donovan and Monty boarded a KLM flight bound for Croydon, and made their way back to Dublin.

As the couple left the meeting one of the Nazi officers had called out to them, 'There is to be war, Mr O'Donovan. Probably in one week.' His words were to prove prophetic, as within a few days of the O'Donovans' arrival back into Ireland the German officer's prediction came to pass. Following several staged incidents that German propaganda used as a pretext to claim that their forces were acting in self-defence, the first regular act of war took place on 1 September 1939, at 4:40 a.m., when the Luftwaffe attacked the Polish town of Wieluń. The German forces destroyed much of the city, killing over 1,000 people, most of them civilians. France and the United Kingdom declared war on Germany on 3 September, but failed to provide any meaningful support to the beleaguered Poles. For the second time in the 20th century the world was at war.

———

As O'Donovan settled back into his routine in Dublin, in Berlin the Abwehr agents he had dealt with were concerned. They had forgotten to agree on a keyword for the coded radio transmissions that would be sent from Germany to the IRA in Dublin. In an effort to rectify the situation the Germans sent a Breton national to meet O'Donovan with the code word 'HOUSE OF PARLIAMENTS'. The key phrase contained an intentional error so as to prove the authenticity of the receiver should the code be inadvertently broken. Once O'Donovan received the keyword transmissions could begin; the first coded message between the IRA and the Abwehr was transmitted on 29 October 1939 in which O'Donovan requested the supply of weapons and other equipment begin as soon as possible.

While the radio was strong enough for transmission to Germany, the IRA had other plans. They began to use the machine to make regular anti-British, anti-de Valera and sometimes anti-Semitic illegal broadcasts from the transmitter's operations base at Ashgrove House off Highfield Road in Rathgar. The transmissions were made on open channels and in December 1939 Gardaí raided Ashgrove House and seized the transmitter. Four IRA members were arrested, though O'Donovan escaped. Despite the fact that the transmitter was seized O'Donovan kept monitoring and transcribing the coded messages from Berlin, though his diligence at recording the messages varied. The link with Germany was temporarily severed, but it was only a matter of time before the IRA and the Germans found a way around what they considered a minor inconvenience.

On 2 September 1939, de Valera convened an emergency session of Dáil Éireann to deal with the threat posed by the British and French declarations of war against Germany. He explained to the various members gathered that in his estimation neutrality was the best policy for the country given the current situation in Europe. In this view he was almost universally supported by the Teachta Dála and the country at large, future Fine Gael leader James Dillon being a notable exception. Dillon, who felt that Ireland should take the Allied side, gave an impassioned speech in the Dáil in favour of entering the war, outlining what he felt were the moral obligations to do so.

His words fell on deaf ears, however, and the 1937 constitution was duly amended to allow for the Emergency Powers Act 1939 to be passed. The act enabled censorship of the press and mail correspondence, and in addition the government was able to take control of the economic life of the country under the new Minister of Supplies, Seán Lemass. Liberal use was made of all of these powers, along with internment of those who had committed or were about to commit a crime, which would be used extensively against the IRA and other subversive elements. Censorship was under the charge of the Minister for the Coordination of Defensive Measures, Frank Aiken.

But as Ireland came to grips with the realities of neutrality, both the government and the Irish people were unaware that the war was about to come to Irish shores whether they liked it or not. In a room in Berlin, the Abwehr were secretly plotting on sending German agents to Ireland to revive the link with the IRA. The outbreak of the war had a disastrous effect on the IRA's ability to carry out attacks in England. The German Navy's blockade of entry points into England reduced the cash and arms flow from the United States that republicans had been relying on. In desperate need of arms and ammunition, the IRA decided to raid the Magazine Fort in Dublin's Phoenix Park. It was an audacious plan, but if the IRA were to be successful it would further bolster their war against the British.

The Magazine Fort was built in 1735 in the west of the city, north of the River Liffey within the Phoenix Park. The building is in the south-eastern end of the park, by a wooded ridge. During the British occupation the fort had been seen as a symbol of the occupation, but by 1939 its purpose was to house the Irish Defence Force's stocks of arms and ammunition. On 23 December 1939 the IRA targeted the arms shelter with the Acting Chief of Staff Stephen Hayes giving the go ahead for the raid. The fort was lightly guarded, and on the evening of the raid the officer responsible for the defence of the fort had little in the way of resources. He had held the post for 24 years preceding the raid, and had at his disposal one non-commissioned officer, six men armed with rifles and one Lewis automatic gun. Also stationed there during the raid were a military policeman and a fire picket.

The Magazine Fort's guard party were briefed for duty on the evening of 22 December and given clear instructions as to their duties for the next morning. Crucially, the fort did not have its own troops; instead these were supplied from infantry units stationed in a command area. On the night of the raid the 7th Dublin Infantry Battalion, stationed at Portobello Barracks (the modern-day Cathal Brugha Barracks), was responsible for supplying the guard, while the fire picket was supplied by a unit stationed in Islandbridge Barracks. At eight o'clock the officer-in-charge left his post to go into the city.

For him to do this the guard manning the gates had to switch on the outer lights illuminating the entrance, open the inner gate, then open the outer gate. This was of course against all normal operating procedure. Once the officer had cleared the gate the guard closed both gates and went back to his post. Shortly afterward the son of the officer-in-charge appeared at the gate and was let in. Around half eight the gate bell rang again, and the guard saw a civilian who said he had a parcel to deliver to the officer-in-charge. The guard said he would take the parcel and bent down to unbolt the gate. When he stood up straight again the barrel of a revolver was pointed at his face.

The gunman shouted at the guard to open the gate fully and put his hands up. Out of the darkness IRA teams appeared from both inside and outside the fort, confiscating the weapons of the sentry and the guard. The two hostages were then forced to act as human shields for the two intruders to the guardroom, where the remaining soldiers were caught by surprise and surrendered without a fight. While this was happening, a second IRA team disarmed the fire picket troops. The troops attached to the fort and the gatekeepers were then held prisoner until around ten o'clock that evening, and with the guards neutralised the IRA began to move ammunition and weapons out in heavy trucks. The guards were locked into one of the ammunition holding areas and warned not to give away details to the authorities that could identify their capturers.

Eventually the alarm was raised at Islandbridge Barracks when one of the lorries failed to stop at a gate on the way out. At 10 minutes to 11 a party of soldiers were dispatched from Portobello Barracks to investigate what was happening at the fort. They managed to capture two of the raiders, who were seen hiding near the fort's entrance. In the meantime the duty officer at Portobello had raised the general alarm. By midnight a new guard was ordered and posted at the Magazine Fort, while the old guard were taken into custody.

The IRA had audaciously escaped with a total of 1,084,000 rounds of ammunition, which they removed in 13 trucks. It was a huge propaganda coup for the organisation, and gave the IRA the shot in the arm it needed. Despite this, however, the arms would not fully fill the deficit that the Emergency Powers Act had on IRA munitions.

Observing all of this from a distance, the Abwehr became convinced that the IRA were a force to be reckoned with, an underground army that could be called upon to rise at the right moment and destroy the British from within. This false perception was solidified in the minds of the Abwehr by the success of the bombing campaign and the meetings in Germany with Jim O'Donovan, who did everything he could to sell the organisation as a formidable force. Having allowed the IRA carry on their campaign indefinitely without major interference, de Valera sought to clamp down on them after the raid on the Magazine Fort.

Sickened by the audacious manner in which the raid was carried out, de Valera began to see the IRA as a genuine threat to the state, and at his behest the Dáil further bolstered existing emergency powers to deal with the republican menace by ordering a round-up of known IRA members. Under the Emergency Powers Act, any offence that was deemed a threat to the security of the state was punishable by death. These included the possession of arms or explosives or being an accessory to these crimes. In reality de Valera was hoping he could crush the IRA in one fell swoop; however his measures were to prove to be too little, too late.

———

De Valera's emergency legislative measures and the seizure of the transmitter had left the IRA in a state of limbo, and temporarily severed the link with the Abwehr. However in January 1940, the Irish writer Francis Stuart arrived in Berlin in an attempt to revive the link. Stuart slipped through the authorities' radar, as he was known mainly as an artist rather than a subversive.

Francis Stuart was born in Townsville in Queensland, Australia on 29 April 1902 to Irish Protestant parents, Henry Irwin Stuart and Elizabeth Barbara Isabel Montgomery. His father was an alcoholic, and killed himself when Stuart was an infant. This prompted his mother to return to Ireland, and Stuart's childhood was divided between his home in Ireland and England.

In 1920, at the age of 17, Stuart converted to Catholicism and married Iseult Gonne, Maud Gonne's daughter. Iseult had lived a privileged but unsettled life. Her stepfather, Maud Gonne's estranged husband John MacBride, had been executed in 1916 for taking part in the Easter Rising. Iseult Gonne's own father was the right-wing French politician Lucien Millevoye, with whom Maud Gonne had had an affair between 1887 and 1899. Because of her complex family situation, Iseult was often passed off as Maud Gonne's niece in upper-class social circles in Ireland.

Iseult grew up in Paris and London, and in her early twenties she had been proposed to by W.B. Yeats. Yeats had previously proposed to Maude Gonne, and at the time of his proposal to Iseult he was 30 years her senior. Iseult also had a brief affair with modernist poet Ezra Pound prior to meeting Stuart. Pound and Stuart both believed in the pre-eminence of the artist over the masses, and both men became interested in fascism. While Pound eventually found common cause with Mussolini's Italian Fascist brigades, Stuart found himself drawn to Hitler's Nazi Germany. It was a fascination which the Abwehr sought to exploit through Helmut Clissmann, who became acquainted with the Stuarts during his visits to Ireland.

Clissmann had married Elizabeth Mulcahy, a native of Co. Sligo and daughter of well-known republican Denis Mulcahy. He was eventually posted to North Africa and then captured at the end of the war and interned in the notorious Bad Nenndorf prisoner of war camp, where he was tortured by the British. The Clissmanns settled in Ireland after the war, and were instrumental in founding St Killian's German School in Clonskeagh and the Irish section of Amnesty International. They had seven children who are today active in many prominent professions throughout Ireland. The family made a considerable living through business that was built on representing various German firms in Ireland, including the giant Schering pharmaceutical company.

In 1939, Helmut Clissmann was facilitating academic exchanges between Ireland and the Third Reich while forming connections which might be of benefit to German Intelligence. Iseult Stuart intervened with him to arrange for Francis to travel to Germany to give a series of academic lectures in conjunction with the academic exchange. Stuart travelled to Germany in April 1939, and his host there was Professor Walter F. Schirmer, the senior member of the English faculty with the Deutsche Akademie and Berlin University. He eventually visited Munich, Hamburg, Bonn and Cologne.

At the completion of his lecture tour he accepted an appointment as lecturer in English and Irish literature at Berlin University to begin in 1940, two years after Jews had been barred from German universities by the Nuremberg Laws. In July 1939, Stuart returned home to Laragh Castle in Co. Wicklow, and confirmed at the outbreak of war in September that he would still take the place in Berlin. When Stuart's plans for travelling to Germany were finalised, he received a visit from his brother-in-law, IRA member John MacBride. This meeting followed the seizure of the IRA radio transmitter on 29 December 1939, which had been used to contact Germany.

Stuart, MacBride, Jim O'Donovan and Acting IRA Chief of Staff Stephen Hayes then met at O'Donovan's house, Florenceville in Shankill, Co. Dublin. Stuart was told to take a message to Abwehr headquarters in Berlin. He travelled alone to Nazi Germany, something that was only possible because of Ireland's neutrality, arriving in Berlin in January 1940. Upon arrival he delivered the IRA message, and had some discussion with the Abwehr on the conditions in Ireland and the fate of the IRA–Abwehr radio link. His travels didn't go unnoticed by G2, who subsequently put the Stuarts' mail under surveillance.

Based on the information supplied by Stuart and the Germans' reading of the situation it was decided that they would send a number of Abwehr agents to Ireland to seek IRA help in the war against the British. The first of these German agents arrived on Irish soil in early 1940, having left Wilhelmshaven naval base in northern Germany on board the German U-boat U-37. His mission was to strengthen the connection with the IRA and to enlist their aid in the ongoing war.

———

The night of 8 February 1940 was cloudless and calm. Out of the silence a German U-boat broke the surface of the water in Killala Bay on the Sligo–Mayo border. Inside the submersible craft Abwehr agent Ernst Weber-Drohl blew up the Luftwaffe-issue rubber dinghy which he would use to reach the shore – an unusual choice for a 60-year-old who suffered from arthritis.

Weber-Drohl had spent the majority of his life working as a circus strongman and weightlifter, performing under the name 'Atlas the Strong'. Born near Edelbach in Austria, he toured extensively in America and Ireland with the circus. His knowledge of Ireland and the English language drew the attention of the Abwehr in Nuremberg, and on this basis he was selected for a mission to Ireland. Weber-Drohl was given money and instructions from the Abwehr to Jim O'Donovan. After making contact with O'Donovan he was then to return to Germany by whatever means possible.

Inexpert in the use of the rubber dinghy, the would-be Abwehr agent capsized his vessel on the way to shore, and was eventually brought to land in a dishevelled state by his comrades before they departed. Weber-Drohl eventually made his way inland alone, and began the long march to meet O'Donovan. Along the way Weber-Drohl was met in Sligo by Stephen Hayes, who briefed him and saw to it that he could travel to meet O'Donovan undetected by the authorities. When Weber-Drohl delivered the cash and instructions to O'Donovan (who must have been shocked to answer his door to the soaked, exhausted German agent, who complained incessantly to him of swollen knees), he informed him that the Germans requested that the IRA send an operative to Berlin to discuss weapons and munitions required by the IRA, as well as financial requirements for the bombing campaign. He gave O'Donovan a total sum of $14,450, keeping $650 for himself to replace the money he had lost in his boating accident. O'Donovan put Weber-Drohl up in his home at Florenceville, and later arranged for him to stay in a room in a boarding house in Westland Row in Dublin.

But despite having been able to travel from Sligo to Dublin undetected, Weber-Drohl's freedom was short-lived; he was arrested on 24 April 1940 for violation of the 'Aliens Act', and was held in Garda custody pending a hearing in the Dublin District Court. In court, Weber-Drohl pleaded his innocence, arguing that he was a victim of poor circumstance, having fallen off a Dutch steamer near Waterford, losing his passport and marriage certificate and beloved pipe in the process. He told a sob story to the court, lamenting that he, a poor arthritic man, was surely deserving of sympathy. A gullible court bought the story, and he was fined £3 and released.

While he may have fooled the court, Weber-Drohl was being closely monitored by Dan Bryan and G2, who had him arrested under the Emergency Powers Act within three days of his release from the District Court. G2 had been investigating Weber-Drohl's cover story, and found that it was radically different from the delicate web of lies he had spun for the court.

Weber-Drohl had concocted a story where he claimed that he had two missing children from a relationship with an Irish woman, and that he had come to Ireland to try and find them. Weber-Drohl had fathered two children with a woman named Pauline Brady, and soon after the birth of the children Weber-Drohl headed for America, promising he would send for Pauline and the two children once he had set himself up there. Eventually Pauline was told by an American friend of Weber-Drohl that he was dead. The friend had pretended that he had seen his obituary in an American newspaper, a revelation that was to send Pauline into a paroxysm of despair. She was eventually placed in Grangegorman Mental Hospital, and died there in 1923, while Weber-Drohl's children were sent to the Sacred Heart Home in Drumcondra.

Based on this evidence, G2 were able to persuade the authorities that Weber-Drohl was certainly not who he said he was, and that his story was an elaborate hoax. Weber-Drohl, furious at having his cover blown, went on hunger strike, and was released after eight days of his protest. He was subsequently rearrested and interned until the end of the war. The authorities were eager to avoid the publicity that would surround a German spy in Ireland, and it was reported in the newspapers that Weber-Drohl was being detained in relation to 'passport difficulties', although deportation proceedings against him were suspended until after the war. Despite G2's best efforts, the Abwehr had struck the first blow, and soon more spies would follow Weber-Drohl to Irish shores.

While Weber-Drohl was certainly incompetent, he was still a dangerous individual. He was successful in paving away for another German spy whom he said would soon follow him to Ireland: a mysterious individual named 'Dr Schmelzer', who would further bolster the link between the IRA and Nazi Germany. Dan Bryan and G2 knew that the situation was becoming quite grave. They were aware the IRA had made a deal with the devil in their pact with Nazi Germany. Bryan recognised this as the threat that it was, and immediately sought to increase surveillance on any foreign subversives who might enter Ireland.

But unbeknownst to Bryan and his men, the immediate danger was closer to home. Rumours started to circulate among radio operators in listening stations set up by G2 of illegal radio transmissions being broadcast from Ireland to Berlin. It seemed someone was already communicating back to Berlin from inside Ireland. Bryan knew this would prove disastrous should the British find out. As he contemplated his next move he received a letter from London. It had been written by Cecil Liddell, the head of MI5's counter-intelligence section dealing with Ireland.

MI5 and G2 had set up a clandestine partnership known as the 'Dublin link' prior to the outbreak of the war. But the liaison was soon to be tested to the extreme by events soon to unfold. Liddell had become aware of the illicit radio traffic coming from Ireland. Faced with the possibility of a pre-emptive British invasion to remove the transmitter, Bryan was left with a stark choice. He could reply to Liddell telling him that he knew about the transmitter, or he could try to buy some time by telling him he was unaware of it. His next actions would prove vital.

II

THE GERMAN LEGATION TRANSMITTER

'The problem of the German Legation Radio Transmitter was one the most difficult issues which arose between Irish Intelligence and MI5, and in fact can be said to have led to a crisis between those relations.'

COL DAN BRYAN, Director of Irish Military Intelligence (G2)

The house was a nondescript and unremarkable building, but it held within its doors a dark secret. Located inside was a wireless transmitter which was being used to covertly send messages back to Berlin. The messages were of a strategic nature regarding British troop movements, weather reports and the impact of German air raids on Britain. Local legend has it that even the innocuous-looking flower pots arranged on the window sills were strategically placed, to enable IRA members who sympathised with the Nazis to pick up and/or decode messages.

The British, through radio surveillance, had discovered the existence of illicit transmissions coming from Ireland in late 1940, but the broadcasts had begun much earlier. There were two possible origins for the transmissions: they were either from Irish republicans with radio sets communicating in Morse code, or from German or other sources in Ireland. Guy Liddell and his older brother Cecil (who served in MI5's Irish section from 1939), in bringing up the transmitter issue with Bryan, delivered him a simple message: find the source of the transmissions or the British would be forced to take action to deal with the wireless set themselves. Realising the gravity of the situation, Bryan immediately set about locating the origin of the illegal broadcasts.

G2's search would lead them to 58 Northumberland Road, the location of the German Legation[1] that housed the German diplomatic mission to Ireland. While G2 were relieved to have located the source of the messages and wished to make the British aware of their discovery immediately, the Irish authorities feared that it would lead to a major diplomatic problem that could inadvertently result in a pre-emptive British invasion of the Irish Free State. Meanwhile, the British fear that crucial information in relation to British troop movements and weather patterns that could be used for military planning would leak out to Berlin through the embassy was palpable, and exchanges between Bryan and the Liddells were tense.

If anything the legation issue proved that neutrality was a double-edged sword for Ireland. While it certainly kept the country out of the horrors of the Second World War, it also permitted the Germans to maintain in Ireland an espionage centre, a window into Britain that operated throughout the war and did incalculable harm to the Allied cause. In many ways Dublin was the equivalent of Casablanca or Lisbon or any of the other wartime centres of espionage. Key to this was the German Legation, headed by the German Minister to Ireland, a man who would prove to be a divisive figure in the events that would follow.

————

Eduard Hempel had been first sent to Ireland as German Minister in 1937. As the son of a Privy Governing Councillor he attended grammar school in Bautzen and the Fridericianum in Davos and graduated from high school in Wertheim. He completed a law degree from the University of Leipzig and following compulsory military service he joined the judiciary

1 In diplomacy, a legation was a diplomatic representative office lower than an embassy. Where an embassy was headed by an ambassador, a legation was headed by a minister. Ambassadors outranked ministers, and had precedence at official events. Throughout the 19th century and the early years of the 20th century, most diplomatic missions were legations. An ambassador was considered the personal representative of his monarch, so only a major power that was a monarchy would send an ambassador and establish an embassy.

of the Kingdom of Saxony, but was conscripted at the start of World War I. During the war he served as a lieutenant on the administrative staff, including in the military administration of occupied Romania.

Hempel joined the foreign service of Saxony in 1920, which was absorbed into the German diplomatic service. He was posted to Oslo in 1928 but soon returned to Berlin to work in the Foreign Office. In 1928 he joined the German People's Party, and following his posting to Ireland was pressured into joining the Nazi Party in 1938. While not a strict doctrinaire Nazi, Hempel was more than willing to carry out party policy. He was an old-school, shrewd and sensible diplomat, who had quite a detailed knowledge of Ireland, Britain and the relationship between the two countries. He was more than adequately assisted by a patriotic and well-organised staff. Hempel's deputy was Legation Councillor Henning Thomsen, a recent convert to Nazism. The rest of the legation staff included Herren Kordt, Müller, Kochner and Bruckhaus. These men ran the legation and kept the books. The staff also included two female secretaries. Unusually, the legation didn't have a military attaché, a common feature in other legations in neutral countries.

At the outbreak of war in 1939, Hempel became more entrenched in the legation as his position came under more scrutiny due to the deteriorating war situation, and he went to severe lengths to protect his secret transmitter. Three of the diplomats in the legation and one civil servant carried pistols, and a fifth armed man slept there each night. Bolts were placed on all the windows and a ferocious guard dog was kept on the grounds to deter any would-be intruders. Hempel was determined not to go down without a fight in the event that the Irish or British were to become aware of the transmitter and attempt to send any agents to infiltrate the legation. And he had every reason to be wary, as knowledge of the transmitter was quickly becoming widespread.

As early as 1939, a Washington press report touched on worldwide speculation about regular secret contacts between the German Legation in Dublin and Berlin. Due to the fact that international law regarding transmitters held by belligerent nations in neutral countries was so vague, Hempel, in order to draw attention away from the legation, began to encourage the use of other means of communication. This ruse was to prove short-lived, however. Despite maintaining an image of being a strict diplomat, Hempel was of course interested in liaising with whatever forces could aid Germany in the upcoming war effort.

In July 1939, MI5 agents operating in Ireland noted that a report had been received through the Czech Consul in Dublin that on 20 July the German Minister, alongside three members of the Dublin branch of the Nazi Party, had travelled to Inver, Co. Donegal to meet with leading members of the IRA. The meeting was said to have been arranged by Theodor Kordt, the Counsellor of the German Embassy in London, who had visited Ireland for that purpose. The meeting took place at the Drombeg Hotel in Inver, which was owned by an old German national named Hammersbach. One thing remained very clear to G2: despite his well-meaning disposition, Hempel was a serious threat to the Irish state following the outbreak of the war.

———

The legation's increased importance as a watch post eventually led Hempel to request extra staff, and Berlin duly complied, albeit with a certain caveat. Fearful of undesirable British interest in the matter, the German Foreign Office compelled Hempel to seek the necessary papers for the extra staff, through the Irish authorities rather than through Berlin. Hempel informed the Irish authorities that he intended to fly in extra staff via a civilian plane, and furnished them with a list containing the names of the new potential staff members.

The names on the list included Hans Böhm-Tettelbach and Major Kurt Fiedler, who was to take up the role of Consul. Böhm-Tettelbach's wife and the three-man crew completed the names on the list. Hempel was apprehensive that the conditions of Irish airports might impede their arrival, and felt that perhaps they might be better travelling by seaplane. Ever the pragmatist, he suggested that once the new staff arrived time should be allowed to pass so that the speed of his communications via the transmitter would not become noticeable. However, despite his forward planning, Hempel's request to increase his staff created a sense of panic among the Irish authorities.

As a result of Hempel's nefarious activities in the legation, de Valera faced a serious challenge to his policy of neutrality. If he were to concede to the Germans it might raise British and American fears, and could lead to the Allies moving against the legation and the transmitter. On the other hand, refusal could sour relations with Berlin, and would violate international obligations. De Valera's major fear was how the American public might react to news reports of a German plane landing in Ireland with legation staff.

Hempel understood the Irish position, and felt that if they were to become aware of the true intentions of the extra staff (to encourage closer involvement between Ireland and Germany), then it would cause the Irish to doubt Hitler's intentions towards neutral countries. Hempel visited de Valera in order to bring the matter to a head, and was told in no uncertain terms by the Taoiseach that he disapproved of the landing of German officials in Ireland.

However de Valera told Hempel that he would accept those arriving by conventional transport. This caused Hempel to try to find other ways of transporting people into Ireland. Sea routes were to prove difficult, as all passenger ships and freighters were obliged to stop at English ports due to cooperation between the Irish and the British. Sending people through another neutral country was also challenging, as Ireland had no diplomatic links with other neutral countries such as Argentina, Brazil or Spain. The idea of increasing the staff of the legation was eventually abandoned.

Despite the fraught political situation, during this period the transmitter was used in the legation on a regular basis. In the spring of 1940, Hempel advised the German Foreign Office that their prompt reporting of events in Ireland might have alerted the British to the fact that the legation had a wireless set. He knew that the British were looking for an IRA transmitter in Co. Wicklow.

His concern would prove to be well-founded. The British learned that Hempel had a quite sophisticated weather station at his house in Monkstown, and that he was able to read and forecast the weather. The fact that the German Minister to Ireland had this sort of equipment in his private residence looked extremely suspicious. However the British had a much deeper reading of the situation in Dublin than the Germans and Irish initially thought.

———

The British first raised the issue of the transmitter with the Irish in late 1940. They believed the transmissions were coming from the area of Laytown near Gormanstown, Co. Meath, and thus began a period of intense surveillance on behalf of the Irish authorities to try to trace the origins of the messages. The British had written to Dan Bryan through 'the Dublin link' between Cecil Liddell and G2, informing him of their suspicions with regard to the transmitter. In response Bryan contacted his colleague, Capt. Richard 'Dick' Green from the Army Signal Corps, and the two men travelled on a bank holiday Monday to Laytown in Co. Meath to scan the area for transmissions. Bryan felt the exercise to be a terrible waste of time, although he had great faith in the abilities of his colleagues in the Signal Corps. In his heart of hearts he realised that in order for any successful trace to take place a monitoring station would need to be set up on a round-the-clock permanent basis. This was mainly due to the erratic nature of the illicit broadcasts.

The fact that the Germans were operating a clandestine radio in Dublin came as no surprise to Winston Churchill, but it did give him great cause for concern. Almost every capital city in the world operated secret radio transmitters during the Second World War. Indeed the British themselves had their own secret transmitters in Stockholm, Copenhagen and Budapest, as well as many other cities in Europe. Ireland posed a problem for the British, however, in that it was the only neutral country with active belligerent legations that shared a land border with the United Kingdom. Among the various diplomatic missions active in Dublin were the Japanese, American, British and German legations. So in Dublin lay a microcosm of the major players in the Second World War. Nazi Germany had many tentacles permeating the various layers of Irish society, with the German Legation being the epicentre and direct link with the Nazi High Command.

If the German Legation in Dublin wished to communicate with Central Command in Berlin, it had a very sophisticated method of doing so, a high-level diplomatic code. The diplomatic messages Dublin and Berlin sent each other had to go through British-controlled telegraph cables, meaning the British could slow these messages down and delay them for up to a week; but they couldn't stop them, for fear the Germans would find out. Britain was equally sending its own messages from European capitals under German control. The danger however was the fact that the legation's radio transmissions were instantaneous, and the fact that the messages were in code made them difficult to read.

British suspicions were well placed, because in November 1940 Berlin contacted Hempel via the transmitter with a view to ascertaining the Irish appetite for German intervention in Ireland, should the British invade. In a conversation on 28 November 1940, Nazi Foreign Minister Joachim von Ribbentrop broached the subject with Hempel during the course of a very long wireless exchange. Von Ribbentrop was astute when it came to the British, having served as the German Ambassador to the Court of St James from 1936 to 1938. During this conversation he enquired whether it was possible for the German minister to arrange to see de Valera, and if so would it be possible for him to

> raise the question whether the Irish would consider it opportune that you should make enquiries in Berlin about the view Germany would take of the possibility of aiding Ireland with material, etc in the case of a British attack. At the same time you could also assure them in the most explicit terms that Germany has no thought of violating Irish neutrality on her own account. But if an English attack should take place, you had personally every reason to suppose that the Reich's government would be able and willing to give Ireland powerful support.

Von Ribbentrop continued his secret discourse with Dublin, and on 5 December he wired confidential information to Hempel asking him to broach with de Valera the possibility of a British invasion of Ireland. He advised Hempel carefully, coaching him in what to say:

You may express yourself in terms something like the following. You had information from Germany that the German government was naturally interested in reinforcing Ireland's powers of resistance against such an eventuality. With the conclusion of the campaign in France, Germany had come into possession of a great mass of English weapons. You regarded it as not impossible in the circumstances that the Reich's Government might be both willing and able to hand over gratis to the Irish Government a considerable quantity of these weapons, which in make, calibre, etc., are identical to those used by the Irish Army. If de Valera shows interest and you see fit you could make appropriate proposals. From a technical point of view we have no doubt, that in agreement with the Irish Government, Irish neutrality would in no case be compromised in the slightest way through this transaction.

Sensing that something was off, de Valera turned down this offer of arms and ammunition in the event of a British invasion, and von Ribbentrop did not pursue the matter any further with Hempel. The crisis was deepening, however, as the British were putting severe pressure on the Irish Department of External Affairs for information as to the location of the transmitter.

Guy and Cecil Liddell visited Dublin in an attempt to elicit more information from the Irish authorities. Sensing the Irish were not being forthcoming and perhaps holding some information back, Guy Liddell quipped to Col Liam Archer, the then head of G2, 'of course, if you would, you could give us lots of information'. The fact that the transmitter issue arose during a period where the Germans had been victorious in the west and were having some success in the east against Russia only further compounded the difficulties faced by the Irish authorities, and left them with a simple choice: they could attempt to break the German traffic or face the wrath of the British.

Time was quickly running out. Not only was neutrality in danger, but so was the very security of the state. Such was the concern of the British that MI5 had agents in Dublin driving around in unmarked cars trying to source the origins of the illicit messages. With little immediate success being achieved, the British attitude to the 'Irish Situation' was becoming increasingly frayed. MI5's efforts in locating the transmitter eventually paid off, though, and after a period of time the British felt they had sufficient proof of an illegal transmitting set being used by the Germans somewhere in the greater Dublin area. On 11 March 1941 J.E. Stephens wrote a letter on behalf of the British Dominions Office to the British Representative in Ireland, Sir John Maffey, imploring him to take the matter up with the Irish authorities:

> The Authorities here now tell me that they have succeeded in obtaining technical proof of the existence of a German wireless transmitting and receiving set operating in the Dublin area.

Such was the extent of the knowledge possessed by the British that they were able to give a detailed breakdown of the broadcast frequency and the enciphering system being used by the Germans. The British knew that the Dublin transmitter was communicating with Berlin via the Grossfunkstelle Nauen transmitter station in the Havelland district of Brandenburg, Germany, the oldest radio-transmitting installation in the world, founded in April 1906. During the war the station was mainly used to broadcast to submerged U-boats via a low-frequency radio signal.

In the course of his correspondence, Stephens gave Maffey a complete technical breakdown of the radio frequency and the cipher which was being used by those operating the wireless set:

> This station replies to Nauen[2] when the latter marked the call A.M.6. The cipher is five figures, frequency 9859kc/s. The station is located in a triangle in an area around Dublin. The signal is very weak in the country and interception is therefore very difficult. A message which the authorities were unable to read was intercepted in a five figure cipher between 1400 and 14.25 on 5/2/41. We should be grateful if you should bring these facts to the notice of the Eire authorities with a view

2   The Nauen Control used a series of operating signals in the AM frequency. These consisted of lettered codes beginning with the letter 'X' in the case of the German Legation Transmitter.

to their taking such steps as are practicable to detect the station and prevent its further operation.

The author of the letter was careful not to draw attention to the fact that the British had a transmitter in their own legation.

You will of course bear in mind that any course of action that the Eire authorities may be asked to take must be in such form so as not to prevent the wireless transmitter that you have at your office. It might be very embarrassing if we were prevented from using this method of transmission particularly in any emergency.

In reality the British authorities in Dublin had three wireless sets and receivers, as well as a direct telephone line to London. Maffey tried to convince the Irish Under Secretary to the Department of External Affairs, Joseph Walshe, that the British would only use their transmitter in an emergency, in which case it would be advantageous for the Irish government, and that in no way could it be used in the war effort against the Germans.

The British knowledge of the German transmitter proved to be quite detailed. The Dominions Office had been informed by MI5 as to the daily frequency of messages. Transmissions were made at intervals of between 30 and 90 minutes, from 0700 up to 1430, with a further transmission at 2100. Ten messages a day on average were being passed from the control station at Nauen to Dublin via a low-powered set using a 'skip' frequency. This made it difficult for the British to intercept messages, though they could prove that Dublin was able to communicate often with Nauen because they would ask for various phrases to be repeated. Dan Bryan suggested that G2 could try to jam the communications coming from the transmitter, a novel approach given the increasing British discontent at what they perceived as Irish inaction.

In a secret document a few days later, on 14 March 1941, the British representative to Ireland warned that 'if the existence of a German controlled wireless in Dublin proved a definite threat to us that the Government of Ireland must therefore be prepared for a most violent reaction if it could be proven that the Germans could transmit secret messages by wireless from Eire.' The communiqué further stated that 'The Eire Government would be well advised to co-operate with us in the detection of this station by asking for expert assistance from England at once.' But the British were only engaging in bluster, and in reality were becoming increasingly anxious, as the situation became more and more fraught with each passing day.

————

With the pressure mounting on the legation, Hempel temporarily stopped using the transmitter except for messages that were of the utmost importance. In an intervention, Hempel had been told by Joseph Walshe that the British had provided the Irish government with details about the wireless set, including a timetable of his transmissions. Believing that the Irish would not act in relation to the transmitter immediately, Hempel set out a number of protective measures to safeguard the legation and the transmitting set.

From the spring of 1941, it was decided that all messages would be sent on secret, predetermined frequencies to avoid giving the impression that the legation was contacting German war units, ships or planes in the vicinity of Ireland. Hempel also ensured that all transmissions were shortened, and that regularly scheduled reports were eliminated if there was no important news, which could be indicated by sending a code earlier the same day. It was also agreed that all transmissions should be scheduled at various times, with the recognition signs changing daily.

In addition to this, more wires were sent to Washington for recoding and forwarding to Berlin. Suspecting that the British knew about the transmitter, Hempel considered moving it to his house in Monkstown, and in a further precautionary measure he contacted Berlin warning them to transmit only in emergencies. When circumstances warranted the risk he assured the German High Command that he could disguise a message by making it harder to decode or confusing the code with signals sent from planes and submarines.

But despite Hempel's best efforts, the Irish authorities were now prepared to act. De Valera had begun to give serious consideration to dealing directly with the German code. Having trained as a mathematician and having taught in various Dublin schools, including Belvedere College and Castleknock College, de Valera had a rudimentary knowledge of the mathematical and cryptographical work that would be involved in breaking the legation's code. After careful consideration, the Taoiseach felt that Ireland should attempt to break the German traffic, because of the severe threat it posed to national security. He was concerned that the Germans might be considering using Ireland as a springboard to attack Britain, but he equally feared that the British would force him to take action against the legation directly. Eager to observe the strict protocols of neutrality, de Valera informed Hempel that the British probably knew about the transmitter. However he did not tell him that the British and Irish had shared this information.

Deeply worried about the situation at hand, the Taoiseach turned to G2 to help provide a solution. The Irish Army had no codebreaking capacity, and indeed felt that breaking the code would be impossible unless it was attempted by a large team, but Dan Bryan had a plan. He immediately put the legation under constant surveillance from Beggars Bush Barracks, which was only separated from the legation by a lane. And, unbeknownst to anyone, Bryan had an ace up his sleeve, one which would come from the most unlikely of quarters.

———

In Sandyford, Co. Dublin, the Director of the National Library of Ireland, Dr Richard James Hayes, answered a late-night phone call from a familiar voice. It was Col Dan Bryan, and as Hayes listened intently, he knew that his life was about to change forever. He hurriedly volunteered himself for the work offered by Bryan, and as Hayes put down the phone his wife Clare turned to him and asked, with trepidation in her voice, 'Is everything alright, Jim?' As he looked at his wife, the enormity of the phone call dawned on Hayes. He, a librarian, aesthete and young father, was now all that stood between Ireland and Nazi Germany.

Bryan felt that Hayes was the best person to lead a unit to attempt to break the traffic coming from the German Legation. Hayes had worked for G2 prior to the outbreak of war in 1939, but it remains a mystery how he had first been recruited by Irish intelligence. It has been speculated that Hayes and Bryan first became acquainted during the War of Independence as active volunteers in Michael Collins's Intelligence section of the IRA. This has been discounted by Hayes's family, though, as they maintain that Dr Hayes would have been a young man studying in Clongowes Wood College in Clane, Co. Kildare, during the War of Independence, and had no involvement in republicanism whatsoever. However it was that Hayes had first become acquainted with Bryan, one thing is clear: Bryan had full faith in the intellectual capabilities of Hayes.

Despite his prominent role in Dublin society, Ireland's National Librarian and soon to be master codebreaker came from very humble beginnings. Richard James Hayes was born in 1902 in Abbeyfeale, Co. Limerick to Richard James Sr, a local bank manager from Co. Clare, and Katherine Hayes, from Ballymahon, Co. Longford. Hayes Jr spent his early childhood in Claremorris in Co. Mayo. His time there had a profound effect on him, and for the rest of his life he considered himself a Mayo man. He had an older brother named Ambrose, named after his grandfather, as well as a baby sister who died at birth.

Richard Hayes Sr died in 1920, when Richard Junior was 18 years old. Unable to avail of any financial compensation, the family lost their house and moved to Dublin. Soon after, Ambrose ran away from home, and was only seen sporadically afterwards. This left young Richard as the sole carer of his mother. Despite such difficulties at such a young age he excelled academically, winning a scholarship to study in Clongowes, where he was a classmate of Tom McQuaid, a brother of future Archbishop of Dublin, John Charles McQuaid. Indeed, the Hayes family became very friendly with the McQuaids as a result, ironic given the fact that Richard was a lifelong atheist.

A distinguished student, Hayes won an academic scholarship to study at Trinity College Dublin in 1920. He studied for three degrees simultaneously, and in 1924 he graduated with first class honours in the three Bachelor of Arts degrees: Celtic Studies, Modern Languages and Philosophy. In 1936 he further bolstered his academic credentials by obtaining a Bachelor of Law degree, as well as a doctorate. Shortly after graduating from Trinity, Hayes was appointed Assistant Librarian at the National Library of Ireland in 1924, eventually succeeding Richard Irving Best, who had been immortalised in James Joyce's *Ulysses*.

Hayes became the fifth Director of the National Library in 1940, and upon taking office he held the distinction of being the youngest man appointed to the post since the library's foundation in 1877. His first major work, *Comparative Idiom: an introduction to the study of modern languages*, was published in 1927. Another work was published in 1938 (co-edited with Bríd Ní Dhonnchadha), *Clár Litridheacht na Nua-Ghaedhilge*, an index to poetry and prose in three volumes that appeared in a series of periodicals associated with the revival of the Irish language. Such was the importance of the index that it is still being used today.

Hayes was also an avid fan of rugby, and wrote a book on the sport. In 1928, Hayes married Clare Columba Keogh from Cabra, and the couple rented a small adjacent flat there, where their first son Bertie was born in 1929. Hayes also rented a small flat for his mother to stay in. The young family soon moved to the south side of the city, settling at 18 Sandford Terrace in Ranelagh. During this time Hayes began editing the *Irish Motorcycle Guide Annual* and the *Irish Rugby Football Union* annual guide. While Hayes had a quiet and reserved manner, he possessed an abounding sense of humour. On the birth of Bertie, Richard jokingly wrote an invoice on *Irish Motorcycle Guide*-headed paper to his mother. His joy and trepidation at becoming a father were evident:

INVOICE: The goods referred to in our letter of December last have been delivered in good condition.

SPECIFICATION: Date of Arrival: 11AM 1st January, Sex: Male, Weight: 7½ lbs, Hair: Long Brown, Face: Chinese Type, Health: Excellent, Lungs: Loud, Observations: Help!

The s.s. Clare was safely brought into port and is now very comfortable at the anchorage 29 Upper Mount Street. The voyage was an exceptionally calm one and was not buffeted by the high seas which are usual at this season. The ship is due to leave her anchorage to sail for Ranelagh within a week.

Signed: Richard J. Hayes (Captain)

Four more children were to follow: Joan born in 1930, Mervyn in 1932, Jim in 1942 and Claire (whom he nicknamed Faery) in 1943. The family eventually moved to Sandyford, where Hayes built a property named Thornfield situated on four acres, building a tennis court and swimming pool for his family on the site. Hayes spoke several languages fluently, including Arabic, French, Italian, Irish and German. Besides his obvious intellect in the field of linguistics, Hayes also had a fondness for mathematics and, according to his daughter Faery, he was excellent at crossword puzzles, recitations and monologues. Always impeccably dressed, he was rarely seen without his beloved Trinity tie and a modest wristwatch. According to Faery he disliked expensive wristwatches, often saying that 'a watch is there to tell the time, that's all'. Hayes always carried with him a small tin of cigarettes and would enjoy a smoke while working on the complicated German codes he intercepted.

His skill at crossword puzzles was useful, as speed at completion of crosswords was used by MI5 as a recruitment method to the Government Code and Cipher School at Bletchley Park, where Alan Turing broke the Enigma code. One of the skills required of codebreakers was to be able to solve a crossword in more than one language in a set period of time.

Dan Bryan knew that Ireland's role was not to outfight the Germans in terms of the transmitter but to outsmart them and to share the crucial information with the British and other Allied Powers. In Hayes he now had a valuable secret weapon.

————

After naming Hayes to lead the unit to break the German code, Bryan and his superiors assigned him a team of people who were thought to have mathematical capabilities, or who were interested in codes. These included a number of individuals, some of whom have been identified and others whose identities to this day remain unknown. Among the men recruited by G2 to help Hayes were a man by the name of Lennon, who was the head of the Patents Office in Dublin, a chief superintendent in An Garda Síochána, and three military personnel (though the two civilian members were soon released from their duties).

The three remaining members were Conn McGovern, who had just been commissioned in the Army and held a master's degree in mathematics; a non-commissioned officer named Plunkett McCormick, who had trained as a solicitor and was later commissioned in intelligence; and Kevin Boland, an engineering graduate from University College Dublin and son of Minister for Justice Gerald Boland who was himself later a government minister and key figure in the Arms Trial of 1970. Such was the clandestine nature of the codebreaking operation that each member of the team was sworn to secrecy. Boland was told to not even tell his father.

The team were given a room to work in at Beggars Bush Barracks, where a wireless unit recorded incoming and outgoing traffic from the legation, and this operation continued for a period of a few months. The legation transmitter issue had caused such consternation between the British and Irish authorities that communications between MI5 and G2 broke down for several months. In the interim a large number of organisational changes took place within the army structure; Col Liam Archer was promoted from Director of Intelligence to Assistant Chief of Staff, and in June 1941 Dan Bryan succeeded him as the head of G2.

Hayes and his team worked feverishly on the legation code, and after a considerable period of time Hayes was able to obtain a highly sophisticated reading of it, but he feared that attempts to break it and read the traffic would prove fruitless. He also felt that the men he had been provided with were slowing him down:

> I asked for two or three men with high University qualifications in science or mathematics. The help requested was not forthcoming and I was instead given three lieutenants of clerical grade ability. These men were useful for tabulating material and compiling statistics but had no special ability for cryptography.

Indeed the bulk of the codebreaking work was being carried out by Hayes alone, as the men assigned to him were really only of basic ability, and were ill-equipped to deal with the sophisticated workings of the German diplomatic enciphering system.

Hayes's attempts to break the system were detailed and arduous, requiring a wealth of knowledge of codes, ciphers and keys. In the field of cryptography a cipher is a mathematical algorithm used for performing encryption, involving the substitution of letters for numbers in a varied sequence. Enciphering has been compared to putting a message in a locked box to which only the sender and receiver have a key, which is usually a number or a word used to transform the message into an incomprehensible sequence of letters and numbers.

Various kinds of ciphers and keys have been used throughout the centuries, and until the computer age it was widely considered something of a black art. Crucially, there would always be a codebook to go with the keys, with which the message could be decoded. The most basic version of a cipher is a substitution cipher whereby, for example, the letter 'A' might be replaced by 'B' and 'B' might be replaced by 'C', and so on, thus making the message incomprehensible. However, despite its advantages such a method wasn't without its faults. For example the letter 'E' is the most commonly used letter in the English language. Therefore a codebreaker need only look for a repeating number or letter in the message until he or she comes to the conclusion that that number or letter likely corresponds to the letter 'E'.

To counter such a weakness, more complicated ciphers were developed. For example one letter could be encrypted using one sort of substitution and the second cipher could be encrypted using a different substitution. That would virtually prevent 'E' from being the most common number or letter in a given message. During the war the Germans took the process a step further, using what is known as a 'polyalphabetic cipher', an encrypted message using multiple alphabets. If such a cipher were used there could be literally thousands of possibilities in terms of solutions. In a further attempt to confuse any would-be codebreakers, the Germans deliberately put in spelling errors into keywords, as well as 'nulls' or spaces. This made codebreaking without the codebook an extremely difficult endeavour.

Ciphers are only successful if the people making them know they're secure, and the Germans were hugely confident that their ciphers were extremely secure during World War II. In the 1920s Germany had moved into mechanised cryptography, the use of encryption machines to generate coded messages – creating the Enigma machine, for example, which had 150 quintillion keys. If they suspected that they were being broken into they could change them ever so slightly to lock the Allies out. Hayes had studied the work of his predecessors in America during World War I such as Herbert Yardley and William Friedman, and he was in many ways more prepared than the Germans were.

He was able to ascertain, starting with the knowledge that diplomatic codes were based on codebooks or machines, that the legation code was very sophisticated in its nature. He felt that it wasn't of the simple dictionary codebook type, and that in the absence of a machine for calculations more manpower would be needed if he were to have any hope of breaking the code. Writing to de Valera, Hayes reported,

> The transmitter messages are so designed that statistics compiled from thousands of telegrams show an almost perfect uniformity of the figures or letters used. Nowadays they are unbreakable unless the instructions for their use are not complied with or from information from inside. The extent to which diplomatic codes are purchased or secretly copied is much greater than is generally believed. We have much to learn in this respect. Matters of this kind must, of course, be prepared years in advance.

Hayes's efforts at breaking the code, though extensive and exhaustive, were unsuccessful, but they were not in vain, as he was able to devise a method for dealing with machine-based codes which he felt could be useful in the future. In a letter to de Valera commenting on his efforts he speculated that

> It is not certain whether the German Diplomatic code is based on a code book or a machine. It is almost certain that it has not been broken by the British or Americans. It is now known that that the contents of many of the cables from the German Legations throughout the world were available to the British or Americans – within three to four days of their arrival to Berlin. This was achieved by accepting the help of

an official in the German Foreign Office who offered his services. The British refused to deal with him, but the Americans made a deal and this source worked every day for them. After checking the information received through this channel for six months and finding it accurate in every respect, the Americans used it to get all the reports of the German Minister in Tokyo. This proved invaluable for the war in the Far East. It was not possible to get all the copies of all the reports of all the legations but at any time any particular report could be obtained. The inside information from the Far East was of such value that instructions were sent to the source to concentrate all his time and efforts on reports from that theatre. It should be noted that on any given occasion or for any special reason, this inside source could have been used to get copies of messages from the German Legation in Dublin.

While Hayes worked on decoding, Dan Bryan and G2 utilised their military powers to further remedy the grave situation. Gardaí were used to protect German diplomats visiting the legation, and this gave G2 extra eyes on the ground. Indeed such was the level of concern that the transmitter would be used to leak information that military intelligence considered approaching a servant who worked in the legation through a newspaper editor, a prisoner of war in Germany during the First World War who was familiar with the personnel and routines of the Dublin legation. However this plan was abandoned when it was feared that the servant would complain to the minister. But someone acting on their own made overtures to a maid who had been recently dismissed from her job at the German Minister's residence in Monkstown. Some newspapers of the day claimed that Intelligence was responsible, and that the maid should be compensated, though the claim for compensation was eventually refused by G2.

Despite his best efforts, Bryan and his men were unable to infiltrate the German Legation, but there were others who *were* able. The London-based Czech government had planted an agent there who succeeded in bugging the building with various listening devices placed in strategic locations. On one occasion at the beginning of the war, German Minister Eduard Hempel and Irish Under Secretary to the Department of External

Affairs Joseph Walshe went into the garden of the legation for a cup of coffee. The Czech agent directed them to a table near a bush. A few weeks later Walshe, to his shock, received a report of his conversation from MI5. Afterwards, the Czechs decided to remove their agent in order to protect Ireland's diplomatic position. G2 also tapped the legation telephone, and some would-be collaborators were apprehended as a result.

One such person was a Dutch fascist named Jan van Loon, who had deserted from the Dutch Navy serving under the British Admiralty. Van Loon had crossed from Northern Ireland into the south, making his way to Dublin. With him he carried sketches of British convoy layouts, which he tried to bring to the attention of staff in the legation. He was apprehended by the Gardaí, and the sketches were used as evidence to intern him until the end of the war. While he was in prison he would befriend other non-nationals who were recently apprehended with whom he shared common cause.

———

Despite the level of surveillance he was under, Hempel was able to keep Berlin regularly informed on military conditions in Ireland. He noted that the Irish were emphasising public instruction in air raid and gas attack defence, and that de Valera wanted to increase the Defence Forces budget in order to modernise the army to deal with the possible threat of invasion. Berlin was also aware that de Valera wished to purchase arms from Sweden and to expand the 6,000-man army, and by August 1940 a recruitment campaign had seen over 170,000 men enlist. While the leakage of sensitive information about the Irish was a problem, any leaks in relation to Allied activities posed a huge threat to the outcome of the war, and G2 became greatly concerned about information leaking out of Ireland that the British didn't want to fall into the hands of the Germans.

In July 1940, the Abwehr held a conference in Kiel in northern Germany, during which it was decided to begin an espionage campaign against Britain involving intelligence gathering and sabotage. German agents were sent to Britain in a variety of methods – some parachuted or landed via U-boat; others entered the country on false passports or posed as refugees. In order to counter this, the British began a system of counter-espionage known as the Double-Cross (XX) system, and they achieved outstanding results from its use. The Double-Cross was an elaborate system of detaining German agents and turning them into double agents who would then be of use to the Allies. Germans or other nationals who were compromised in one way or another were usually selected for the programme.

Ultimately the Double-Cross system became a weapon of deception against the Germans, and the British used it to plant misinformation about British strategic plans among the German agents they controlled. This was of huge significance, as the Americans were working alongside their Allied counterparts with the intention of invading mainland Europe. At this stage Britain had such a control of German espionage that they were able to use compromised agents to spin an erroneous version of events about the Allies' next moves. Therefore Ireland became hugely important from a strategic point of view. The British were adamant that they didn't want information coming out of Ireland that would call into question the information that the German agents controlled by MI5 were relaying back to Germany. Any information, true or false, that the British hadn't generated themselves could have disturbed the very detailed picture that the Allies were trying to paint.

Meanwhile in Germany the Abwehr was making plans to curtail the attention that the transmitter was attracting. By February 1941, the Chief of German Military Intelligence, Admiral Wilhelm Canaris, declared that weather reports were no longer needed. Canaris felt that similar information in relation to weather could be obtained from other sources, and he ordered that all transmission be cut down with immediate effect. Matters worsened when two German battleships, the *Scharnhorst* and the *Gneisenau*, escaped a British blockade of Brest in a snowstorm. The British press claimed that the Germans had acted on intelligence received from Dublin, bringing matters to crisis level.

The Allies contacted de Valera in order to bring the matter to a head. Eager to protect plans for the imminent invasion of Europe, they duly put pressure on de Valera to have the transmitter removed from the legation. Eventually Hempel conceded, and the wireless set was put into a suitcase, which was then placed in a steel casket and deposited in a safe at the Munster and Leinster Bank. Only Hempel had the key to the suitcase, though both Hempel and Justice Minister Gerald Boland could open the steel container. Only the four bank directors could open the safe.

Despite these developments Hempel believed that the radio would be returned to him in the event of an Allied attack. He also tactically decided that it was necessary to move the transmitter as it helped the maintenance of good relations with de Valera, and as such was a necessary evil. During this period Hempel also refused to have another set parachuted in to him, for fear it would give the British and Americans a pretext to invade. The transmitter and presence of the German Legation in general were to prove a huge thorn in the side of Churchill, who wrote in a secret personal minute in 1943:

> I think we must endure this abominable state of affairs for the present. The entry of the United States into the war has changed the picture, and it may be possible to take stronger action against Southern Ireland and force them to dismiss the enemy representatives they harbour. Their conduct in this war will never be forgiven by the British nation unless it is amended before the end. This in itself would be a great disaster. It is our duty to try and save these people from themselves. Any proposals which you make to terminate the enemy representation in Dublin will be immediately considered by me. We ought not to shirk the difficulties unduly for the sake of a quiet life. There seems to be a very strong case for doing what is right and just and facing the usual caterwaul from the disloyal Irish elements in various parts of the Dominions. I shall take advantage of my visit to Washington to discuss the matter again with the President. I am quite sure that the opinion of the House of Commons would be overwhelmingly favourable.

Churchill's attitude was to place considerable pressure on Bryan and the Irish authorities who, perhaps more than de Valera, realised the increasingly alarming state of affairs that the Irish nation was facing. The unfolding events were to strengthen Bryan's resolve that it was in Ireland's best interest to cooperate in the sharing of information with the British in order not only to preserve neutrality but to protect the very sovereignty of the state itself. Ultimately the British authorities saw two courses of action available to them to solve the legation issue: they could either seek the expulsion of the German Legation from Éire or compel the Irish government to seek the removal of the wireless set from the safe, to which Hempel had a key.

The British assumed that de Valera would seek proof that the Germans were engaged in espionage before he would seek to expel the legation from the country, and while the British thought that they did have proof, they felt that revealing it would compromise their most secret material. The only course of action available to the British was to prove that the legation had used its transmitter at a time of impending British operations, where it could be surmised that the legation was sending urgent intelligence to Germany. The British were aware that Hempel sought to recruit another wireless operator whose 'touch' would be unrecognisable to the British. The gentleman in question was Feldwebel Hans Bell, and alarmingly the British speculated that the Irish authorities had agreed in principle to Bell working in the legation as an assistant at cipher work. The British thought that if he was employed and his qualification as a wireless operator became known, this would give them a pretext to make a démarche through the British representative in Ireland. In any case the situation was now becoming very serious.

By 1943, plans were already underway for the invasion of Europe, and both the American and the British authorities were concerned that any information leakage from Dublin could have a detrimental effect on invasion plans. Hempel continued informing Berlin of various details in relation to the Air Force and Navy. He estimated that the Air Force had been increased from 40 planes to 170 regular aircraft and 12 seaplanes. Despite the fact that Ireland possessed a few armed patrol boats rather than a fleet, harbour forts had been strengthened with heavy artillery and a new coastal defence force consisting of experienced seamen.

The Irish defences were lacklustre at best. All forces lacked light weapons such as hand grenades, which the Irish could not manufacture and the British could no longer provide to them. Hempel was able to provide the German High Command with information about the British, however. In July 1942 he reported that a Vauxhall tank factory employing 15,000 workers was operating 50 km from London. Adjacent to this was the Percival Aircraft Company, with 3,000 workers and 200 inspectors, as well as various factories which manufactured arms and munitions for the British war effort. Hempel estimated that that about a million Englishmen and 100,000 Americans were stationed in southern England in June of 1942, and that 60,000 or so Americans had remained in Northern Ireland after almost all of the British had left.

Hempel further informed Berlin that the Americans were producing planes on a large scale. These were mainly Liberators, B-24s flying across the Atlantic to Foynes, Co. Limerick, on the Shannon estuary, then continuing on to England or Lisbon. During the war the Liberators were the only air contact that Ireland had with the rest of the continent, and Berlin requested that Hempel obtain more detailed information on the planes. He deduced that they were produced by Ford and Kaiser, and were likely to see bomber duty as well as transporting passengers between Canada and Britain. He also relayed that England was building poison gas-proof shelters as England feared German gas attacks, but despite this sign of trepidation he also reported that the general English population seemed confident that the Allies would eventually win out. This was generally attributed to Allied victories in North Africa and Sicily, and the British and American capacity to wreak large-scale destruction on German cities.

Hempel gave detail as well on the activities of the British Eighth Army. He garnered much of this information through conversations with indiscreet members of the Eighth Army who were on leave in Ireland. In one case a sergeant major gossiped to a friend who held radical nationalist views, and the information was then passed to Hempel through an intermediary. More tellingly, Hempel became aware of reports that an artilleryman on leave from the Eighth Army in Ireland spoke of preparations for a great battle in Italy. The gentleman recounted:

> As regards the forthcoming invasion of the continent, while preparing for a breakthrough in Italy men were suddenly embarked for England

with the greater part of the British contingents of the 8 Army. The attack from England is to begin in February. Heavy losses are expected.

Other items of information sent to Berlin resulted from conversations with a Canadian pilot on leave in Ireland who was member of a parachute brigade transferred to England from Italy.

How much value can be attributed to Hempel's information is debatable. He was closely monitored by G2, and the British kept feeding him false information. It is believed, however, that he was aware that he was being watched, given his extreme caution in dealing with people who offered their services to him. While the British were able to slow down and read cable communications, the transmitter was seen as an uncontrollable source of information leakage which they sought to compel the Irish authorities to deal with conclusively. To that end it was decided that the transmitter would be removed from the bank by G2. The job was given to one of the Signal Corps' most trusted recruits.

———

The transmitter was eventually picked up by a Junior Military Intelligence Officer named John Patrick O'Sullivan, a native of Valentia Island in Co. Kerry. O'Sullivan had previously worked with the Marconi Company before joining the army, and was therefore adept at the intricacies of wireless communication. In 1915 O'Sullivan had trained a young Michael Collins in telegraphy in the Marconi School in Cork and had joined the Army's Signal Corps many years later at the invitation of his old pupil in July 1922. Prior to joining the army he had an extensive career with the Mercantile Marine as a telegraphist and radio officer. In 1917 his ship had visited Halifax, Nova Scotia, and had a narrow escape when a French ammunition ship exploded in the city's harbour just as his ship dropped anchor outside the bay. The disaster claimed 2,000 lives and destroyed much of Halifax.

O'Sullivan had been transferred to Military Intelligence at the beginning of the war, and he and others set up a monitoring station at GHQ in Collins Barracks to listen in to illicit transmissions and to record them for deciphering. The group that reported directly to Dan Bryan included O'Sullivan, Commandant Seán Nelligan, a school teacher called Joe Sweeney and Eugene O'Connor, a former Jesuit priest seconded from the Department of Defence. The group were also aided by a professor of Spanish at University College Cork, Joe Healy, who had himself been seconded to Military Intelligence for the duration of the war. By this stage G2 had developed a system for the detection of illegal transmitters in the Dublin area. Frame aerials were attached to vans which were then driven around areas which were suspected to contain illegal wireless sets. The aerials were able to detect signals within a three-mile radius, and by using separate vans in up to 17 different locations in the city, G2 were able to triangulate the location of illegal transmissions and subsequently act on them.

O'Sullivan also volunteered to set up another monitoring station at his home in Chapelizod, where he worked 'off duty'. As a result his home was protected round the clock by two military policemen, who routinely kept an eye on the listening equipment he stored in a shed at the back of the house.

Such was the group's success that most if not all of the illegal spy stations in Ireland were intercepted, and the equipment being used by belligerents was also confiscated. After the legation transmitter was confiscated O'Sullivan and his officers placed Hempel under house arrest.

Using his expertise in telegraphy, O'Sullivan discovered that messages were being transmitted from a station near Berlin to Ankara, Madrid, Lisbon and Tokyo. O'Sullivan gained such an understanding of the transmitter that he was able to spot even the slightest variation in the broadcasts being sent, allowing him to deduce, in one instance, that Berlin had been hit in a bombing raid. This was later proven in statements sent out by the German Foreign Office, confirming that a thousand-bomber raid had taken place the previous night.

O'Sullivan shared this crucial knowledge with his colleagues in G2, and it would later prove invaluable to Richard Hayes and MI5 in their efforts to break the legation code. O'Sullivan's group's most notable success was the breaking of the 'Barbarossa Code', which was being transmitted in geometric progression using a polyalphabetic substitution system. The coded transmissions outlined plans for Hitler's invasion of Russia, and while G2 shared this information with the Allies they did not accept this until the Germans invaded Russian territory on 22 June 1941. They continued to supply crucial information to the Allies, and such was the success of their work that in 1945, at the end of the war, both Truman and Churchill thanked de Valera for the work carried out by O'Sullivan and his group. John Patrick O'Sullivan retired from the Army in 1946, having reached the compulsory age for retirement at his rank, and went on to a successful career with Kenny's advertising agency in Dublin and the Lep Transport Company in London. He died in 1977 and is buried in Palmerstown Cemetery in Lucan, alongside his wife Mary.

By August 1944, Hayes had carried out a detailed investigation of the German diplomatic code. This investigation was founded on the idea that the code being used was based on a machine. Hayes worked out a mathematical system that allowed the code to be tested for the more probable possibilities. Each test involved the solution of 219 equations for nine unknowns, and from this Hayes concluded that it was theoretically possible to break the code. The nine tests also each necessitated three weeks of intensive work, which could not be interrupted for more than a few hours if the mathematical thread of the argument was not to be broken. To further complicate matters, any mistake rendered the whole operation useless, and it would have to be started all over again from scratch. Hayes felt a staff of five competent mathematicians might have achieved a result in three to six months.

Eventually, towards the end of the war, Hayes and his staff, working with G2 in conjunction with MI5, managed to break the legation code using a myriad of resources. Such was the fear of information leakage that the British prioritised the breaking of the Dublin code over that of other embassies and legations active during the war. While it had taken a considerable amount of time to break the code, Hayes's attention in the interim was elsewhere. He and G2 were busy dealing with an even greater threat.

III

A SPY IN MEATH

'I developed a plan without prejudice to the preparations of Operation Kathleen to organise a minor war in Northern Ireland.

DR HERMANN GÖRTZ, Abwehr agent, May 1940

On 12 May 1940 the war seemed a far and distant prospect to the residents of the sleepy village of Ballivor. Nestled halfway between Mullingar, Co. Westmeath and Trim, Co. Meath, the townsfolk adhered strictly to the government's neutrality policies, and no lights were lit after dark in an effort to deter any hostile aircraft. As the townsfolk settled into their beds, a Luftwaffe aircraft was preparing to depart Jever Airfield in southern Germany; its destination: Ireland.

The pilot of the Heinkel He111 plane, Karl Eduard Gartenfeld, took off just after nine o' clock, and began gently climbing to an altitude of 30,000 ft. He had been tasked with a top-secret mission, and carried on board a most secret cargo. In the back of the plane an Abwehr agent dressed in full Luftwaffe uniform and wearing his World War I medals was preparing two parachutes, one for himself and another for the 'Afu' transmitter he would use to communicate with Berlin after landing on Irish soil. The agent's name was Dr Hermann Görtz, the most formidable Nazi spy to be sent to Ireland during World War II, and the real face behind the mysterious Dr Schmelzer mentioned to detectives by Ernst Weber-Drohl.

Hermann Görtz deliberately dressed in his Luftwaffe uniform as, due to international law, he could have been summarily executed if he had entered Ireland in civilian clothing. Both Görtz and Gartenfeld were anticipating enemy interference as they flew over England, but were relieved to find a thick blanket of cloud over most of England, giving them sufficient cover. As the plane passed over Scarborough, Görtz's fear of being spotted by enemy searchlights faded, and he calmly watched the cloud break up as they passed over the Irish Sea. Soon he would make his jump and land in what he thought was Co. Tyrone. There he would meet with the IRA and help facilitate an uprising, giving Germany a pretext to invade Ireland. If his plan proceeded as he hoped, he would go down in German history as a daring spy and perhaps even be decorated by the Führer himself.

Without having a clear indication of where they were, Gartenfeld encouraged Görtz to jump, assuring him that he would throw the parachute attached to the transmitter after him so that they would reach the ground at the same time. Görtz carried with him $26,000, a Belgian Browning 9-mm pistol and a dagger. The parachute with the transmitter contained two shovels which he would use to bury the parachutes before he went on his way. Gartenfeld gave the signal and Görtz prised open the Heinkel's door. He braced himself and jumped into the darkness.

As he descended from 1,500 metres, Görtz was unaware that he was severely off target directly over Ballivor, Co. Meath, in neutral Éire. Gartenfeld hastily threw the transmitter out of the plane and returned to the cockpit. On his way back to Germany he was attacked by an RAF night fighter and had no idea if Görtz had landed safely on Irish soil or had been dropped in the Irish Sea. Gartenfeld battled the RAF fighter, eventually losing it in a thick blanket of cloud. He made his way back to Germany and briefed his superiors about the botched drop. Meanwhile Görtz braced himself for landing. As soon as his feet touched Irish soil he went to look for the transmitter, but he couldn't find it. Utterly dismayed, he searched frantically throughout the entire jump zone for several hours before eventually giving up. To make matters worse he had also lost the shovel to bury his parachute, and eventually decided to hide it under a bush.

Eager to avoid detection, Görtz managed to stay hidden until daylight, when he aroused the suspicions of two local farmers: an elderly man named Andrew Gooney and a younger man named Christopher Reilly, who Görtz would later describe as 'a half-idiot'. Reilly suffered from a mental disability, and it was he who first discovered Görtz in a dishevelled state lying in a roadside ditch. Gooney later told Gardaí that he saw Reilly cursing at the ditch and beating it with a pitchfork. Afraid that Reilly was 'having one of his fits', Gooney chose to keep a safe distance. Eventually Reilly stopped swinging the pitchfork and shouted at Gooney, 'Come here till you see this old bowsy.'

When Gooney went to investigate he discovered Hermann Görtz lying in a state of distress, attempting to shield himself from another volley of blows from Reilly's pitchfork. Far from being perturbed by a fully uniformed Nazi lying in the ditch of a local farm, he later told Gardaí he was more afraid of Reilly wielding the pitchfork and shouting in what he described as 'a most terrifying fashion'. After Reilly ceased his attack Görtz got to his feet and dusted himself off. He gave Reilly a £1 note to calm him down, and promptly asked Gooney for directions to Co. Wicklow.

Görtz decided that since he had missed his landing zone he would have to find somewhere safe to stay, and he knew that he would have a bed for the night if he made his way to Francis Stuart's house in Laragh, from where he could later arrange to meet with the IRA. Gooney later claimed that Görtz offered him £100 but he turned it down. The authorities found Gooney to be an obstinate and difficult man to interview. G2 officers suspected that he had taken the money and, unbeknownst to Görtz, had hidden his transmitter in a shed on his farm. In fact the transmitter was never seen again. In an interview with Gardaí Gooney 'remarked someone may have buried it'; it is likely that the transmitter is to this day somewhere in the vicinity of Ballivor.

After this bizarre incident Görtz set off on the long walk to Wicklow, a distance of approximately 90 km. Feeling shaken after his unfortunate encounter with Gooney and Reilly, he decided that he would only travel by night and rest during the day. Passing Kinnegad, Co. Westmeath, he crossed a tributary of the Boyne, and after marching a further considerable distance he discovered that Gardaí had mounted a checkpoint on a bridge crossing the river Boyne itself. Görtz decided to swim across the river to avoid detection by authorities, but in the heat of the moment he forgot that he had 'G-Tinten' invisible ink hidden in the shoulder pads of his Luftwaffe coat.

'G-Tinten' invisible ink was used for writing by spies. It is invisible either on application or soon thereafter, and can later be made visible, usually by applying a chemical solution to the writing by means of an eye drop or other apparatus. Görtz's sudden decision to jump into the river was a costly one, as his invisible ink was soon washed away when he entered the water, an unfortunate event, since it was his only supply. After he got out of the water he had a period of fainting spells before eventually making his way to Ballinakill Bog in Carbury, Co. Kildare.

When he reached the bog he decided to remove his uniform tunic, which was eventually recovered by Gardaí. Oddly, Görtz chose to keep his Luftwaffe cap as something to drink out of, as well as his World War I medals. Clad in a sweater, the riding boots he had made the jump in and a black beret, he continued on his way to Laragh, and amazingly arrived there at 10 a.m. on 9 May undetected by the authorities, despite having walked through Newbridge in his bizarre outfit during broad daylight. Legend has it he even stopped in the Garda station in Poulaphouca, Co. Wicklow to ask for directions, and was sent in the right direction by an obliging Garda. Görtz was received in an exhausted state after his long walk by Francis Stuart's wife, Iseult, who surely wondered who exactly this strange German spy was, and what had brought him to Ireland.

––––

Hermann Görtz was born on 15 May 1890 in the Hanseatic City of Lübeck in Schleswig-Holstein in northern Germany. The fourth of seven children, his father was Heinrich Görtz, a well-known solicitor and later judge, who would foster in his son an interest in the legal profession. Classically educated, the young Görtz developed a love of music, literature and art which was to stay with him for the rest of his life. He studied ancient languages, eventually moving to Gymnasium to study English and French. This was to have a profound effect on him, and he spoke fluent English for the rest of his life.

Hermann Görtz's introduction to the military came at the age of 20, when he enlisted as a reserve soldier in the Fifth Foot Guards Regiment in 1910. Wishing to follow in his father's footsteps, he completed a law degree in the University of Heidelberg, and also studied for brief periods in Berlin, Kiel and Edinburgh. The young Görtz was particularly taken with the beauty of the Scottish Highlands, which he visited on a study break. Passing his final legal exams, he qualified as an attorney in June 1914, and secured a job in his native Lübeck just before the outbreak of the Great War.

Görtz was steadfastly dedicated to his career in the military, having been imbued with a deep sense of patriotic duty during his training. He became a highly decorated lieutenant during the war, fighting on both the western and eastern fronts, and he was awarded the Iron Cross Second Class in 1914. However, battle wounds and a respiratory illness led to his transferral to the Army Air Service, and he eventually graduated from flight school in 1915. Görtz would stay with the Air Service until the armistice in 1918, and during this period he also allegedly became acquainted with Hermann Göring, the ace fighter pilot who would go on to lead the Luftwaffe and become number two to Hitler.

During the course of the war he married Ellen Aschenborn, the daughter of German Vice Admiral Richard Aschenborn. Ellen bore him three children, Wiebke, Rolf and Ute. After the war Görtz returned to Lübeck, his sense of duty to his country further deepened by the loss during the conflict of one of his brothers and the severe disabling of the other. Like many German men of the period Görtz prided himself on his patriotism and his devotion to the fatherland; however the economic downturn of the 1920s affected him severely.

The family law practice began to suffer, and eventually closed down, prompting Görtz to move to the United States. In 1927, he and his wife visited Ireland for the first time, touring Dublin and Wicklow. During the visit the couple observed the funeral of Minister for Justice Kevin O'Higgins, who had been assassinated by the IRA on 10 July 1927. It is perhaps here that he first gained an understanding of the intricacies of Irish politics. Görtz returned to Germany and resumed his law career, this time in the private sector. Politically conservative, he eventually joined the Nazi Party in 1929 shortly after the Wall Street Crash. Owing to a number of legal cases that resulted in him suffering financially, he found himself nearly bankrupt. He applied to join Hermann Göring's new Luftwaffe, but was turned down for lying on his application form. In 1935 Görtz applied to be a civilian volunteer for the Abwehr, and was given a mission that would see him sent to England and ultimately spend three years in prison there.

Despite the fact that Hitler had strictly forbidden espionage in Britain, Görtz travelled there in an effort to spy on the Royal Air Force. Before he left he resigned his Nazi Party membership lest he provoke an international incident if he were caught. Görtz planned to masquerade as a writer as part of his cover story, even going as far as carrying an uncompleted manuscript with him in an attempt to sell his story. His book was to be a family history, and would include details about aeroplanes, giving him what he thought was the perfect cover story to observe RAF bases.

Görtz travelled to England with 19-year-old Marianne Emig, who had worked as the stenographer in his law practice in Lübeck, and he soon developed an extramarital relationship with her. The couple spent a few weeks in Suffolk, and they eventually moved to a rented house in Broadstairs in Kent. There they befriended a British airman named Kenneth Lewis, and through him began to collect information about the RAF Manston Air Base. Emig asked for letters on Royal Air Force stationery and photographs of the planes and aerial views. When Lewis became concerned that he might be passing on military information, she assured him that Britain and Germany would be on the same side in the next war.

Near the end of their six-week tenancy Görtz visited Germany, telegraphing his landlady, Mrs Johnson, that he would be gone for two days, and asking her to take care of his belongings in the outhouse, including his 'bicycle combination'. Görtz had meant his overalls, but Mrs Johnson thought he was referring to his Zündapp motorcycle. Mrs Johnson checked the outhouse, did not find the motorbike, and reported to police that it had disappeared. When police investigated the apparent theft, they found sketches and documents about Manston airfield. When Görtz returned to Britain three weeks later, police arrested him at Harwich Harbour in Essex. Emig had wisely stayed behind in Germany, but Görtz was detained in Brixton Prison, and accused of offences against the Official Secrets Act.

The trial at the Old Bailey began in March 1936 and attracted much publicity in the British press. Görtz pleaded not guilty, claiming the documents were part of his research for an intended book about the enlargement of the British Air Force. Marianne Emig refused to come to Britain to testify for Görtz' defence, fearing that she would be tried as well. In her absence Görtz was convicted and sentenced to four years in prison for espionage, serving his sentence in Maidstone Prison.

In February 1939 he was released and deported to Germany. German military intelligence eventually did employ him, however the publicity surrounding the Görtz case was to prove a major source of displeasure to Hitler. Despite his obvious lack of competency as a spy and possible psychological damage arising from his incarceration, Görtz was reintegrated into the Abwehr, and on 19 January 1940 he was selected for his mission to Ireland, which was given the codename 'Operation Mainau'. In keeping with his tendency to exaggerate, Görtz claimed full credit for the planning involved for his mission to Ireland:

On my release I returned to the German Air Force, I suggested to my command that it might be possible to make use of the IRA in Ireland for intelligence purposes when the now inevitable war broke out. I urged that the astonishing fact of their having declared war on England should be taken seriously, and pointed to the possibility of starting a revolt in the Six Counties – or as we in Germany generally call it, Ulster. My suggestions, no doubt, had some influence.

Before departing for Ireland, Görtz made an unusual request of his superior officer. He asked for a phial of cyanide, which he reasoned would allow him to take what he thought an honourable course of action if he were caught. The request drew the ire of Abwehr Chief Admiral Canaris, who told the officer dealing with the request, '[W]e don't work with poison'. When Görtz persisted in his request it was eventually agreed to by OKW Chief General Wilhelm Keitel. The request for poison alone should have alarmed the Abwehr, but they allowed Görtz to continue in his mission.

Görtz felt strongly that the IRA would be a useful ally to Germany; however, his perception of them couldn't have been further from reality. He believed they were an underground army ready to rise when he gave the order, and in many ways he hoped that they would be in awe of him as a German officer. Instead, he was to find a disorganised rump of extremists, ideologues and opportunists. Nonetheless, his determination was evident:

> I was to try to stir up a partisan war in Ulster. It would certainly signify a great success if, in consequence of this, the English were forced to send additional troops to Northern Ireland. But I was not on any account to set any action in train unless it was certain that there would be a definite initial military success. If the action did not go well, then I was to call it off, because a setback at the beginning of a rising could have very serious military and political consequences. For this reason they would send me an experienced parachute officer trained in guerrilla warfare and not a young one – an officer of the Brandenburg Regiment must have been intended.

The Abwehr saw Görtz as more of a liaison officer with the IRA than a serious subversive, and in many ways they treated him with a sort of contempt. Curiously, there is only a brief mention of Görtz's mission in the war diaries of Maj. Gen. Alfred Jodl, the then head of the Wehrmacht Planning Staff. It seems likely that Görtz's mission was personally sanctioned by Admiral Canaris, and was kept from the rest of the Wehrmacht. Despite the clandestine nature of the operation Görtz had a clear idea of what his mission to Ireland entailed, and he was prepared to link with the IRA once he made contact with them.

Görtz planned to direct his mission against Northern Ireland and use resources gathered in the Irish Free State to establish a secure communications link between Ireland and Nazi Germany. He also hoped to consult with the IRA on the prospect of reconciliation between the Irish state and the republican movement; to help direct the military activities of the IRA towards British military targets (specifically naval installations); and to report any incidental items of military importance. It was a mission that was to begin in the most unlikely location: Laragh Castle in Co. Wicklow.

——

It took a dishevelled Hermann Görtz several attempts at reasoning with Iseult Stuart at the entranceway to Laragh Castle before she believed him that he was a German officer and a friend of her husband. Francis Stuart had agreed for a prearranged signal to be used where a 'four-leaf clover' would be mentioned by Görtz and therefore recognisable to Iseult. Once he mentioned the clover Mrs Stuart relented, and gave Görtz a bed where he rested for a full day. Within a few days Görtz began to work his charm on her, and Iseult became quite taken by the dashing German officer. Remarkably, the relationship became romantic, and the two began an affair behind the backs of both their spouses.

Writing in her diary, Iseult spoke of her attraction to Görtz with great enthusiasm: 'No voice has ever caressed my ears like one which I may never hear again, no voice has so enveilghed [sic] me.' She wrote of running away with Görtz and marrying him. Indeed Görtz kept in contact with her during his time in Ireland, writing letters to her often. In one exchange he lamented, 'I would have risked to touch you if he had known anything'. But their liaison was to cause trouble for the impressionable Iseult.

While Görtz slept, Iseult drove to Dublin accompanied by her mother, Maud Gonne. The two ladies went for coffee, and debated what they would do with their new visitor. After some time the pair decamped to Switzers department store, where Iseult bought Görtz a new suit so that he would be in civilian clothes and therefore wouldn't attract unwarranted attention to himself. The two ladies then hurriedly left Switzers and made their way to Shankill to the home of Jim O'Donovan, to tell him of Görtz's arrival. He got into their car and the trio made their way to Laragh to meet their guest.

In Laragh Castle, Görtz awoke to the sound of a car crunching along the gravel outside. Convinced it was the authorities, he dressed himself quickly and escaped out a nearby window. He was halfway up a nearby field when he realised it was Iseult, though she was accompanied by a man he didn't recognise. Making his way towards them, Görtz asked Iseult who the man was. The gentleman insisted he was a friend. When Görtz looked as though he might run off again the man introduced himself as Jim O'Donovan. He explained to Görtz that he knew he was a German agent as the Abwehr had alerted the IRA that one had landed in Ireland and was most likely making his way to Co. Wicklow.

Once O'Donovan gained Görtz's confidence the two men departed for Dublin, eventually making their way to O'Donovan's house, Florenceville in Shankill, on the outskirts of the city. Before he left, Görtz promised Iseult he would write to her, and that he would come back to see her when time allowed him to do so. He spent two nights with the O'Donovans, where he slept in the loft in their garage. During the day he spent time in an orchard behind the house. O'Donovan told Görtz that the IRA would be happy to receive him, and that he would even get a chance to meet the Chief of Staff. Görtz was delighted that he would meet the leader of the IRA, somewhat lessening his displeasure at his less than salubrious accommodations. Little did he know that his sojourn at Florenceville would be for him the proverbial calm before the storm.

On 11 May, four young IRA men arrived at O'Donovan's house to take Görtz with them. The men behaved aggressively, demanding Görtz hand over his money to them. O'Donovan, who at this stage had distanced himself somewhat from the IRA, intervened, insisting that the two parties reach a compromise. He suggested the money could stay with him and they could take Görtz, or vice versa. When the IRA men began threatening him, Görtz agreed to go with them so as not to cause any further difficulties for the O'Donovans. As he got into the car he had no idea he where he would be going.

Two of the IRA men, Stephen Carroll Held and Patrick McNeela, moved Görtz to 11 Winston Avenue, Rathmines, the home of IRA member J.J. O'Neill. En route, the men again demanded money from Görtz. Eventually, to avoid any more trouble he handed them over $15,500, keeping $10,000 for himself. The fact that Görtz was carrying US dollars, with no means of converting large sums of money, perhaps illustrated how ill-equipped he was for his mission. While staying with the O'Neills Görtz acquainted himself with Mrs O Neill, who brought him up to speed with the political situation in Ireland.

He was also introduced to the Acting IRA Chief of Staff, Stephen Hayes, and a further meeting was set up between the two at Hayes's house at Auburn Villas in Donnybrook. Görtz also sent a postcard to Germany, alerting his family to his safe arrival in Ireland; this was lost by the postal service before it could be examined by G2. Dan Bryan had been notified of two suspicious-looking postcards that had come through a Dublin sorting office, which aroused his suspicion that a parachutist had entered Ireland illegally.

During his meetings with Hayes, Görtz was informed of the strength of the IRA, which he was told consisted of 5,000 sworn-in members, 1,500 of whom were based in Northern Ireland. Hayes assured Görtz that he could call upon 10,000 extra volunteers in the north and 15,000 in the South should an armed revolt occur in Northern Ireland. Görtz didn't know that the numbers were highly exaggerated, but he was unimpressed by Hayes, describing him as 'an upright patriot, whose roots are in the people, quiet, almost passive. Not outstanding as a natural leader.' He also struggled to understand his Wexford accent, something which would cause difficulty for Görtz at a later stage during his time in Ireland.

One issue had been troubling Görtz ever since his arrival in Ireland, and when given the opportunity to address it he did so, asking Hayes to retrieve his parachute, radio and uniform from the places he had hidden them near Ballivor. Hayes dispatched an IRA team to retrieve the items. Masquerading as men from the Board of Works, the IRA men drew much attention from local farmers, who noticed them searching the nearby fields at night. The IRA recovered one of Görtz' parachutes, but the other was eventually found by Gardaí, along with Görtz's uniform, in Carbury, Co. Kildare. It was then passed on to G2 and stored behind a shed in Collins Barracks. Noticing the Luftwaffe badges, they sensed that their worst fears were true, that a German agent had indeed entered Ireland via parachute. The IRA were unable to find the radio, and Görtz foolishly suggested they put up posters offering a £10 reward for the safe return of it; however this plan was wisely never put into action.

During his meeting with Hayes, Görtz attempted to get a general consensus about the future of the IRA and the attitude of the Irish people to Germany. Hayes assured Görtz that only a British invasion of the Irish Free State would galvanise popular support for a German intervention. Görtz stressed that the Germans didn't wish to invade, but to instead offer financial and logistical support. Hayes asked for automatic weapons for the IRA, much to Görtz's dismay. He informed Hayes that should such weapons arrive they could under no circumstances be used in the Irish Free State. Showing his ignorance of Irish politics, Görtz then suggested that the IRA could be incorporated into the Irish Army, pointing out that the Sturmabteilung had been assimilated into the Wehrmacht in Germany. The idea was of course laughed off by the IRA Chief of Staff. In a final meeting Hayes introduced Görtz to a man named Liam Gaynor, the author of the proposed Nazi/IRA invasion of Northern Ireland, codenamed 'Plan Kathleen'.

———

Liam Gaynor lived at 117 Home Farm Road in Drumcondra, Dublin. Originally a native of Belfast, he worked as a civil servant in Dáil Éireann. At 60 years of age Gaynor was a loquacious character, who apart from his keenness in subversive activities also had a burgeoning interest in debating, and was an active member of St Vincent de Paul, Catholic Action, Catholic Sociology and the Irish Industrial Development Group. Gaynor first became acquainted to the IRA through Stephen Carroll Held, one of the men who had picked up Görtz from Jim O'Donovan's house.

Gaynor first met Held at a lecture they had both attended, concerned with industrial development in Dublin. On the final day of lectures Held took Gaynor for a drive in his car to Bodenstown, Co. Kildare, where the two men discussed Wolfe Tone and the various facets of Irish republicanism. During the conversation Held made derogatory remarks about Tone being Protestant, to which Gaynor expressed his unhappiness at such a bigoted view of religion. At the outbreak of the war the men met again. Held was accompanied this time by members of the IRA, and the group discussed the impact the border would have on the war.

At the conclusion of the meeting Gaynor agreed to compile an invasion plan for Northern Ireland that would involve help, if it could be acquired, from Nazi Germany, be it in terms of financial aid or troops. The plan would be supervised and signed off on by Held and the IRA. When Gaynor delivered the final plan Görtz was dismayed. Plan Kathleen consisted of a map, on which was the suggestion of a German invasion by way of an amphibious assault in the vicinity of Derry. The aim of the plan was the conquest of Northern Ireland via a simultaneous IRA insurgency and use of German forces.

The IRA would be concentrated in Co. Leitrim, on the border facing lower and upper Lough Erne, to await the arrival of German forces in Northern Ireland. IRA units in Ballyshannon, Co. Donegal and Dundalk in Co. Louth would also assist in the operation. The general line of thinking of Gaynor's plan was that the British would be forced to intervene at Carlingford Lough, thereby breaking neutrality and creating the conditions for a German intervention. However, the IRA plan gave no thought to how German troops were to be brought to Derry, how control of the sea approaches was to be obtained or where and how the coast of Northern Ireland was fortified.

Görtz described the plan at the time as 'completely useless'. He went further, saying, 'It nearly broke my heart, since it came from the IRA Chief of Staff'. Görtz was slowly learning that his faith in the IRA was deeply misplaced. Plan Kathleen envisaged a landing in Derry in the manner of the German assault on Denmark and Norway, calling for the deployment of 50,000 German troops. The bait for the Germans was supposed to be the chance to neutralise the RAF's use of Lough Erne as a tactical base against the U-boat fleet. Gaynor believed that it would turn public opinion in the 26 counties against the British, and that the general population would rise up against the 'occupying forces'. The practicalities of successfully carrying out the plan, however, were slim.

In reality the plan was poorly constructed, and not treated with any seriousness by the Abwehr or German Foreign Ministry. Görtz was hugely underwhelmed by the IRA, describing them in unflattering terms: 'I know that thousands are willing to die for Ireland, but very few dare to think bold'. It is not known whether any serious planning was done for Plan Kathleen, although the operation appears to have been widened in scope by Görtz, who was determined to try and make it work.

MI5 and G2 feared that as part of the plan Görtz and the IRA would set up a mobile transmitting station in Ireland which would be used to communicate with another transmitting station to be set up in Belfast. This station would communicate troop movements and weather reports to Görtz, who would then communicate this crucial information back to Central Command in Berlin. Görtz also hoped to install an automatic weather transmitter that could communicate directly with Germany. Despite the ramshackle nature of his arrival into Ireland, Herr Görtz still posed a serious threat.

———

Hermann Görtz stayed with the O'Neills until 19 May. Eventually he was brought to Stephen Carroll Held's house at 245 Templeogue Road on the south side of Dublin. As Görtz approached the house he became apprehensive. The name on the property was familiar. It read 'Konstanz', and it reminded him of the German Lake Constance on the Rhine at the northern foot of the Alps. The Templeogue house was colloquially known as the 'Nazi House', as it was erroneously believed that the house was in the shape of a swastika when looked at from above.

Local lore also had it that Hitler had selected the property as a safe house should he have to escape Berlin. A swastika was allegedly painted on the roof so that it could be identified from the air, though this story has never been proven one way or another. The house did, however, have a large swastika motif painted in its entrance hall. As he passed through the gates Görtz questioned the safety of his lodgings, given the fact that it only had one entrance and could be easily sealed off by the authorities should they get wind of his location. However his fears were assuaged and his anxiety temporarily subsided as he felt he now recognised one of the men driving the car, the gentleman with the unusual surname whom he had first met in Jim O'Donovan's house.

Stephen Carroll Held was the adoptive son of a German national, Michael Held, who in 1890 had travelled to Ireland where he founded a successful sheet metal business. Held senior met and married Stephen's mother and adopted him, giving him his own surname. As a German citizen, Stephen Held had been interned for the duration of World War I. He eventually emigrated to America, where he married and settled down. He returned to Ireland to work for his adoptive father in the 1930s. Despite his background he never learned to speak German.

He eventually joined the IRA and because of his German background was selected to travel to Hamburg as a representative of the IRA. There he met with the Abwehr who were sceptical of his credentials and initially believed that he was a British plant. In an attempt to show the Abwehr his bona fides, Held produced 'an invasion plan for Ireland' which could be of use to the Germans. The plan would become known to the Germans as the 'Artus Plan' and to the IRA as 'Plan Kathleen'. After describing the plan to the Abwehr, Held asked for a German officer to be sent by the German High Command to help in its coordination.

Unbeknownst to Held, Görtz had been present at the meeting, and observed him briefly from a distance. Held arranged the second meeting with Görtz at Konstanz, where the men could discuss the use of a transmitter to allow Görtz to communicate with his superiors; IRA Chief Stephen Hayes was also present at the meeting. Görtz told Hayes that a communication between Ulster and Germany was essential, and that a transmitter should be located in an area where 'one intended to stage operations'.

Görtz felt that a transmitter located a considerable distance away was a waste of time. Hayes assured him he would get one, and a transmitter was delivered to the house on the second day of his stay there. However the transmitter was soon to prove unfit for purpose. It was large and cumbersome, and was not powerful enough to transmit the required distance to Germany. Also, owning such a transmitter was a criminal offence in Ireland during the war – a point lost on Görtz, who thought Ireland was similar to other neutral countries such as the USA and Sweden, where transmitting was legal. Görtz noted that even the most trustworthy citizens in Germany were not permitted to own wireless sets, and he eventually put the confusion about the set down to his inability to understand Hayes's 'thick accent'.

Far from a secure location to plan covert operations, the house was easily accessible from the Templeogue Road. Held lived there with his mistress, Elizabeth Hall, their son and his mother, who soon began to question the identity of the German visitor. Görtz was right to be apprehensive about his safety, as MI5 had been covertly watching the house from a nearby road, and had taken photographs of Held, as well as his mistress and child.

G2 were also monitoring the house, and keeping tabs on those who visited it. Dan Bryan had a wiretap placed on Held's phone, and G2 had approached the maid working in the house in order to get more information about who was staying there. The net was closing in on Held and Görtz but, oblivious to this, another meeting was scheduled between them for the evening of 22 May. Görtz spent the morning preparing notes for the rendezvous when he suddenly received a message telling him the meeting was cancelled.

To kill some time, Held and Görtz decided to go for a short walk, and while they were gone a Garda car suddenly stopped outside the front of the house. Gardaí and G2 burst into the house and began to search it from top to bottom. They noticed the top room was locked and the occupants were nowhere to be found. The officers decided to bide their time and wait for whomever lived there to return home. As they returned from their walk Held and Görtz noticed the authorities outside the house. Görtz hid behind a shrub, where he watched the raid before eventually fleeing; he had known it was the Gardaí, as their screeching brakes reminded him of the ss.

Held, on the other hand, walked straight into the house, deciding he would rather face the authorities head on. As he walked in the front door he was immediately taken into custody and questioned by detectives about the locked room. Held told them a guest had been staying, and that they had locked the room and left. Gardaí felt that Held was not telling the truth, and broke the door down. To their amazement they found a typewriter with several documents lying beside it. The documents contained files and maps with military details about Irish harbours, airfields, bridges, roads and landing grounds. They also had information about the distribution of the Irish Defence Forces around Ireland, as well coded wireless traffic and a breakdown of the enciphering system used to code illicit messages to be communicated to Germany at an appropriate time.

As detectives continued searching the house they discovered a parachute and a wireless transmitter and receiver, as well as nearly $20,000, all of which were stored in a locked safe. In one of the bedrooms they found Görtz's World War I medals, along with a Luftwaffe badge and a black tie with the word 'Berlin' printed on it. Some notes were also discovered that had been written by Görtz in preparation for his meeting with Stephen Hayes. As they sifted through the papers the detectives were shocked to discover that Ventry Harbour in Co. Kerry was being touted as a possible location for a weapons dump. The note read: 'Ventry Harbour as operations base, Fishing Boat Motor – where to get – provisions, crew, harbour.'

As G2 examined the notes, which contained references to 'Leg' (legation) and L.H. (Laragh House), Dan Bryan became convinced that there was some sort of connection between the Stuarts in Laragh, Dr Hempel, the German Legation and the mysterious parachutist. When the notes were further examined it became clear that Görtz planned to send them to the OKW in Berlin, as he had written down an outline of what he had been up to in Ireland since his arrival. Detectives asked Held about the various items they had discovered. Fearing that the IRA's plot with the Germans would be discovered, Held concocted a story that the items belonged to a Heinrich Brandy, whom he maintained had arrived at the house the previous night begging for lodgings.

According to Held, the fictional Mr Brandy was a relative of a Dublin businessman, and he had let the room out to him for £2 and 10 shillings per week. Held told detectives that Mr Brandy had asked him out for a drink but that he had declined, as he had work to do in his metal-engraving workshop. He claimed that he and Brandy then separated, that he hadn't seen him since and he had no idea why he was out and had his room locked. Held's explanation failed to impress G2, and he was subsequently arrested and brought before the Special Criminal Court in Beggars Bush Barracks on May 24.

Held was charged with breaches of Articles 26 and 28 of the Emergency Powers Order, and of offences against the Emergency Powers Act. He was accused of being in possession of a code and had given shelter to an as yet unidentified person who might be of immediate danger to the state. On 8 June, Held was further charged with having the keys of the safe in the house, as well as the keys to 'Mr Brandy's' room. Held had forgotten to take them off his key ring when he returned home with Görtz. The most incriminating item, however, were the plans for an IRA rising against the Irish government, and these ensured that Held would not be a free man for much longer.

Held was tried and sentenced to five years' imprisonment on 26 June 1940, and as a result of his arrest G2 organised a round-up of suspected IRA members and other politically suspect individuals. By 7 June over 400 suspected IRA members had been arrested and put into internment camps after being subjected to interrogation. Many of those arrested were not released until after the end of the war.

When news of the raid reached de Valera he became very concerned, and issued an appeal to Irishmen to join the Army and defend their country from all attackers, both foreign and domestic. Dan Bryan contacted the Department of External Affairs and urged them to contact Britain to make them aware of the Held raid and subsequent arrests and trials. In Washington the German ambassador reported back to Berlin that the Held raid had been reported on in a number of newspapers.

The whole fiasco caused huge difficulty to the German Legation, and Dr Hempel decided that the best course of action was to pretend publicly that he knew nothing of Görtz or the raid. However, secretly Hempel sent a coded telegram to Berlin saying that he had warned them of the dangers of using Held as an agent. The German High Command reasoned that a policy of not getting involved was the best approach, so as not to cause a diplomatic incident. As the furore over the raid continued, Hermann Görtz was making his way back by foot to what he thought was the safety of Laragh Castle and Iseult Stuart. Little did he know that the G2 were in hot pursuit.

———

Görtz's trek back to Laragh was long and arduous. Having no supplies, he was forced to survive on a diet of wild berries. Meanwhile Gardaí had identified Iseult Stuart as the purchaser of the clothes from Switzers which were found in Held's house. G2 had gone to the department store and questioned staff, who remembered Mrs Stuart and thought it was curious that she was buying a suit when her husband was out of the country in Germany.

Gardaí arrived at Laragh Castle and arrested Iseult Stuart, charging her under Section 5 of the Emergency Powers Act of 1939. She was accused of interfering with apprehension of a person who had committed an offence, as well as refusing to give all information in her possession relating to the commission by another person of a scheduled offence. Iseult Stuart was put on trial on 2 July 1940, and while there was more than enough evidence to convict her she was strangely acquitted on all charges. Newspapers speculated that this was because of the status of her mother, Maud Gonne, but the real reason was much more ingenious. Bryan and G2 felt that if she were let go then it would be possible to put surveillance on her and see if the 'fugitive parachutist' would contact her.

When he eventually reached Laragh after the 24-mile hike Görtz hid in the bushes near the castle, and was brought food by the Stuart children. Eventually he was met by a strange woman, who informed him that Iseult Stuart had been arrested and was in custody. The woman was Helena Moloney, secretary of the Women Workers' Union and a lifelong socialist with republican sympathies who had fought in the Easter Rising. She brought Görtz to Jim O'Donovan's house, where the two of them stayed overnight before moving to Maeve Kavanagh McDowell's house at 57 Larkfield Grove, Harold's Cross. From there Görtz stayed in a number of houses, moving between them usually under cover of darkness.

In June 1940 he stayed in Mary Coffey's house in 1 Charlemont Avenue, Dún Laoghaire, where he was known as Mr Henry Robinson, pretending to be a commercial traveller. He claimed that he was visiting customers when asked to explain his absences; in reality he was staying in a second safe house, St Alban's in Nerano Road, Dalkey, which had been rented by Moloney and her friend Maura O'Brien. For a short period a radio transmitter was installed at the house for Görtz's personal use. During his stay here Maisie O'Mahony acted as his chauffeur, driving him between Dún Laoghaire and Dalkey at night. An employee of the Dublin Hospital Bed Bureau, she was arrested on 20 October 1941 and later released from detention on 24 January 1942, after which her employment with the bureau was terminated. When Mary Coffey was later questioned by G2 she maintained that she was unaware of Görtz's true identity, despite evidence to the contrary.

During his stay in Dalkey Görtz began to ingratiate himself with prominent members of Dublin society. Often many of these visited him, and one visitor to Görtz's safe house in Nerano Road was Maj. Gen. Hugo MacNeill, commander of the 2nd Division of the Irish Army, who enquired of Görtz if Germany would come to Ireland's assistance if the British forces in Northern Ireland invaded the country. MacNeill was treading on very dangerous ground and risked being court-martialled had the government become aware of his dealings with the German spy. The British believed that MacNeill, as the leader of the anti-British faction of the Irish Army, was prepared to collaborate with Gen. Eoin O'Duffy in the formation of a new fascist organisation in Ireland, and that it was probable that Görtz convinced them he could be of assistance.

Also while in Dalkey Görtz met a large circle of people including politicians and Dr Brennan, City Coroner for Dublin, who treated him for the recurring problem of a duodenal ulcer that had been troubling him for some time. When Hempel, the German Minister to Ireland, became aware of what was going on, he indicated to his superiors in Berlin that de Valera would have nothing to do with what Maj. Gen. MacNeill was proposing. Hempel was reluctant to meet with Görtz in case the Irish authorities became aware of any contacts or meetings between them. He was also afraid that Görtz was competing with him for control of German policy in Ireland, but at the same time realised that the Irish feared a British invasion, and that the Irish Army needed support.

Görtz made the first move to rectify the situation by proposing to meet Hempel, but the minister was reluctant to take the risk of being caught in the company of the parachutist, especially given the fact that he himself was under surveillance by G2. Hempel devised a novel way for Görtz to meet him safely – he arranged a party for members of the German community in Dublin as cover at his personal residence, Gortleitragh, in Monkstown, Co. Dublin. Görtz attended the party in the guise of a guest, and went unnoticed by the G2 men on duty outside.

On arrival at the front door he uttered the prearranged phrase 'Where is the WC?' to the maid who opened the door, in accordance with prior instructions made with Hempel. She ushered Görtz into a study, and informed Hempel of his arrival. Görtz remained out of sight from everyone while at intervals during this party Hempel excused himself from his guests and held brief conversations with him. During their exchanges Görtz indicated to Hempel that he wished to return to France as soon as possible to make his report on his activities in Ireland. He felt that if he could organise passage by sea he could reach the safety of SS headquarters at Brest harbour in the French département of Brittany.

Görtz informed Hempel that he intended to leave as soon as possible, and that if he could leave on a solo trip due to weather he was happy to be dropped off on Inishduff, an uninhabited island off the coast of Donegal, where he would wait for transport to France. He told Hempel that he hoped to return to Ireland someday to help persuade the IRA to not act so rashly and to behave in a more professional manner. This news delighted Hempel, as he thought that Görtz's activities threatened his mission to Ireland, and that Görtz's contacts and intrigues with Maj. Gen. MacNeill posed a huge threat to Irish neutrality.

Hempel was also concerned that the Allies might use the presence and activities of Görtz in Ireland as a German intelligence gatherer to force de Valera to abandon his stance of neutrality and enter the war on the Allied side. It also appears that on several occasions the German embassy was used to relay reports by Görtz to Germany. Hempel suddenly found himself in a difficult situation – his mission was to keep Ireland from joining the Allies and to prevent the country giving direct assistance to them, as well as to ensure that the country remained neutral and if at all possible to try and get Ireland to align itself with Germany, however unlikely this might be. With Görtz now in the picture he was left walking a diplomatic tightrope.

While he was on the run Görtz also grew increasingly frustrated with Acting IRA Chief of Staff Stephen Hayes, who he felt had caused him to make tactical decisions that scuppered his mission. He also accused Hayes of having betrayed him to the Gardaí in the Held raid, despite the fact there was no evidence to support his claim. Meanwhile Görtz grew increasingly anxious that he had no means to contact Germany. Helena Moloney and others sourced radios in Donegal to help Görtz, but they were of an amateur nature, and proved to be of no use in his attempts to communicate with the Nazi High Command.

Görtz continued to test various transmitters at several sites around Dublin, but to no avail. He then set about training two part-time Morse operators to aid him. When the two men proved to be incompetent he was provided with an IRA member who turned out to be very adept at the use of radio. However his experimentations with the radio sets had dwindled his resources, and as a result Görtz found himself under severe financial strain.

These events further deepened his anger with the IRA, and strengthened his determination to get back to Germany as soon as possible. Despite his feeling of abandonment, the Abwehr were planning on alleviating Görtz's financial situation. Admiral Canaris sent two Spanish fascists to London with the address of an IRA safe house and money for Görtz. Despite these efforts Görtz never received the money, so the Abwehr tried to send money to him via different means.

The Abwehr chose to utilise a most secret agent, an Irish woman named Mary Mains who lived in Madrid under the pretence that she worked as a governess to elderly ladies. In reality she was an agent for the Abwehr, with links to the Irish Minister in Spain, Leopold Kerney. Kerney had been keeping an eye on Mains's whereabouts due to requests from her family through the Department of External Affairs. In November 1940, Kerney asked Dublin that Mains be allowed to enter Ireland aboard a ship that had been transporting displaced Japanese nationals.

She arrived in Galway the same month, secretly carrying $10,000 and a new supply of 'G-Tinten' invisible ink for Görtz. She also supplied Görtz with a new keyword for radio transmissions. With her mission complete she returned unhindered to Spain. Kerney's request for preferential treatment for Mains caused considerable levels of suspicion among G2, who at a later date sent Dr Richard Hayes to Spain to investigate the links between Kerney, Mains and the Abwehr. Hayes travelled to Spain, along with G2 agent and Professor of Spanish at University College Cork Joe Healy, under the guise of being on a research project for the National Library of Ireland, examining manuscripts at the archive in Simancas in central Spain. Dan Bryan urged that action be taken against Kerney, though this never came to pass; however customs officials were circulated information on Mains lest she attempt to return to Ireland.

The Abwehr assumed that Görtz was now able to resume his mission, and had no need to return to Germany; however he grew increasingly anxious at his situation in Ireland, something which he confided to his many female friends. In an attempt to ingratiate himself with Dublin society, Görtz contacted various politicians after the abandonment of his escape attempt. He asked that his friends no longer keep his identity a secret, and began a series of meetings with various interested parties he felt respected him as a German officer. Members of the Dáil, such as TD Criostoir O'Byrne, Minister for Agriculture Dr Jim Ryan, Minister for Posts and Telegraphs P.J. Ryan and Minister for Coordination of Defensive Measures Frank Aiken, are reputed to have visited Görtz during this period.

Despite his dealings with politicians and well-known faces in Irish society, Hermann Görtz's mission to date in Ireland was an abject failure. His liaisons with the IRA had proved fruitless, and he was growing increasingly disillusioned. His relationship with the IRA was strained, given the arrests that had depleted their numbers following the Held raid, with many of their best men now languishing in jail. Some members of the organisation openly despised Görtz as a result of this, and blamed him for attracting unwarranted attention to their ranks and for not acting on promises he made to supply them with much-needed arms for the campaign against England.

Despite the strained relationship, contact between Görtz and Stephen Hayes was eventually re-established. Görtz's chauffeur, Maisie O'Mahony, was to attract considerable attention to his case. O'Mahoney was the daughter of Fianna Fáil TD Seán O'Mahony, and her romantic liaisons with Görtz were to cause quite a stir. Hayes had stayed with O'Mahony on several occasions, and her home was used as an IRA safe house at various stages. As a preventative measure G2 began to monitor O'Mahony. She was eventually arrested in October 1941, having been identified as a security risk for aiding a German agent in Ireland.

By 1941, Görtz's fortunes had changed entirely. The Abwehr came to the realisation that the IRA would be of no use to them, and subsequently decided to leave him to his own devices. Görtz decided to focus on the ill-conceived idea that he could foster reconciliation between the Irish government and the IRA. He believed such a course of action would prove fruitful if it led to a military intervention in Northern Ireland. Görtz wrote to Jim O'Donovan asking him to contact someone in the Irish government to broach the idea, but this came to nothing. Görtz may also have been trying to contact German Legation Counsellor Henning Thomson or Taoiseach Éamon de Valera directly. When these endeavours proved futile, Görtz started to feel that his luck was running out, and wished to return to Germany at the nearest opportunity:

> All this time, too, I was anxious to return to Germany. I had seen very early that the main purposes of my mission could not succeed and that the German Supreme Command could not hope for anything in the shape of serious military action by the IRA. Clearly my instructions needed to be rewritten if any considerable military diversion was to be created by the Six Counties. All my original plans for landing grounds, all the money I had hoped to spend quietly, but effectively, on building up equipment for German troops when they should come; all this was useless when I could not find sufficient solid support among the one body in Ireland out to fight Britain. Events have developed in such a way that I have decided to go home.

In February 1941 Görtz made a another attempt to escape, this time to France by boat from Fenit, Co. Kerry. The crew were arrested by the authorities but Görtz evaded arrest with the assistance of a sympathetic member of An Garda Síochána, who was later disciplined and sentenced to five years' imprisonment. Görtz returned to Dublin and stayed with sisters Mary and Bridie Farrell in 47 Spencer Villas in Glenageary; with their assistance and that of Maisie O'Mahony he purchased a boat which he later described as a canoe with an outboard motor.

In July, Helena Moloney rented a hut in Brittas Bay, Co. Wicklow, where Görtz spent August preparing for his departure. She also checked out a number of books from Rathmines Public Library in order to aid her German comrade. These included *Navigation and Astronomy*, *Amateurs Afloat* and *Practical Navigation for Yachtsmen*. However despite her good intentions, Moloney only attracted further attention to Görtz. When she failed to return the books the head librarian became suspicious. An overdue book notice was mailed to her and postal censors immediately contacted G2, who put Moloney under surveillance.

Undeterred by the unfortunate turn of events, Görtz made his first attempt to escape on the boat on 13 August, but his motor failed and he had to return to Brittas Bay by sail. Bad weather during the remainder of the month prevented any further attempts. A second attempt was made on 2 September, and he made it as far as Tuskar Rock lighthouse before his motor flooded and his boat began to take in water; again he managed to make it back to Brittas Bay. It was also planned to try and get him on board a Japanese ship scheduled to call at Dublin to collect Japanese nationals stranded in Ireland due to the outbreak of war, but these plans also fell through. In late autumn 1941, the Garda Síochána, working with G2, rounded up nearly all of those who were assisting Görtz, including Jim O'Donovan, having obtained information on the location of most of the safe houses used by the IRA from files and documents seized in the raid on Stephen Carroll Held's home.

In September 1941, eight Garda cars under the command of Superintendent W.P. Quinn, who headed the Bray Garda District which Shankill was part of, and Sgt Michael Wymes arrived at Florenceville and arrested Jim O'Donovan, who refused to divulge anything about all the activities that had taken place. The house was raided from top to bottom, but nothing incriminating was found. O'Donovan was subsequently taken away by the Garda Síochána and ultimately interned in the Curragh Camp, where he was held until his release in 1944.

When he got out of prison he returned to his job with the Electricity Supply Board, his employer before internment. Curiously, the ESB took no notice of his activities, which had no major impact on his subsequent career. Despite this, however, his relationship with his family never recovered, and for many years afterwards they held much antipathy towards him for getting involved with Görtz and the IRA.

———

Görtz knew that the Irish authorities were closing in on him, and that it was vital for him to reach France to report his belief that the Irish Defence Forces would support Germany if the British attempted to seize Irish ports. He knew the ports were of huge strategic importance in the Battle of the Atlantic; he also saw it as a chance for him to prove his worth to his superiors. Unbeknownst to Görtz and the Abwehr, his arrival into Ireland had caused a stir, particularly in Dublin, where new Nazi sympathisers had begun to fill the void left by Adolf Mahr and the Dublin branch of the Nazi Party. Pro-Nazi gatherings were held in Wynn's Hotel off O'Connell Street, and were attended by several well-known personalities in Irish life. Many of the figures spoke of their admiration for Hitler and their hope that Germany would win the war. Heartened by this, Görtz decided to take refuge in Dublin, feeling that he would have a better chance at anonymity in a large city than in the countryside.

The Abwehr had been informed by Hempel that Görtz had tried to escape from Ireland unsuccessfully, and that most of his IRA companions had been arrested. He also contacted Germany from the legation to say that he had no direct dealings with Görtz, and did not wish to act as a middle man for him and the Abwehr. Also, because he had no working transmitter, the Abwehr felt they had no reasonable means to facilitate Görtz's escape from Ireland. This was compounded by the fact that coordination for an airdrop through the legation was now impossible. Görtz now found himself alone and cut off from both the Abwehr and the IRA.

With Görtz still on the run, matters were about to take another turn for the worse. G2 had become aware of rumours of U-boats being spotted in the vicinity of Co. Kerry. It was feared that the Abwehr were planning on sending more agents to Ireland. The threat was now severe, and Dan Bryan feared that the British would grow increasingly impatient with Irish attempts to rectify the situation. He travelled to London to brief MI5 in relation to the transmitter and Görtz, assuring them that he would be apprehended quickly and that the matter would be brought under control soon.

In Berlin the German High Command had begun compiling official invasion plans for Ireland, to be used in the event of a victory in the Battle of Britain. With London, Belfast and Coventry under heavy bombardment by the Luftwaffe, Bryan felt that it was time to mobilise all the weapons at his disposal. Görtz had to be apprehended, and any communications that he had been making had to be deciphered. It was undoubtedly a job for Dr Hayes, but little did Bryan know that before they found Görtz and broke his code, G2 would have to decipher coded messages being used by other German agents who had been operating in Ireland, right under the noses of the authorities.

The Abwehr were determined to make a breakthrough in Ireland, and decided to send more agents in order to link with the IRA and report back crucial weather and security information. Bryan and others in G2 knew the danger posed by this, to neutrality as well as the wider war effort. While de Valera and others worried about keeping neutrality intact, Bryan, Hayes and others in G2 saw the bigger picture. Germany was winning the war, and with the fall of France Britain would soon stand alone in the battle against Nazi Germany.

Day by day other neutral countries were falling under Hitler's control, and G2 was being inundated with security alerts. The war, which had seemed so distant and unreal to the Irish population, was rapidly becoming a clear and present danger. G2 was the last line of defence to protect the country; if they didn't act to stop the threat, nobody else would.

IV

U-BOATS IN KERRY

'Ciphers have been of far greater importance in the present war than ever before in history.'

DR RICHARD J. HAYES

On 23 August 1939, representatives from Nazi Germany and the Soviet Union had met to sign the Nazi–Soviet Non-Aggression Pact, which guaranteed that the two countries would not attack each other. In ensuring he would not have to fight a war on two fronts, Hitler was left with one logical enemy standing in the way of his domination of Europe: Britain. Following the fall of France, Hitler hoped the British government would seek a peace agreement, and he considered invasion of Britain only as a last resort, if all other options failed.

By late May 1940, the British Expeditionary Force had been driven to the sea at Dunkirk by Hitler's Panzer Divisions, and the British War Office made the decision to evacuate British forces on 25 May. In the nine days from 27 May to 4 June, 338,226 men escaped, including 139,997 French, Polish and Belgian troops, together with a small number of Dutch soldiers, aboard 861 vessels, 243 of which were sunk during the operation. The last of the British Army left on 3 June, and in a spirit of solidarity Churchill insisted on coming back for the French. The Royal Navy returned on 4 June to rescue as many as possible of the French rear guard. Over 26,000 French soldiers were evacuated on that last day, but between 30,000 and 40,000 more were left behind and forced to surrender to the Germans. With Britain in a weakened state Hitler felt now was the opportune time to strike. The planned invasion of Britain was to be codenamed 'Operation Sea Lion', and given its close proximity, Ireland was to be of huge strategic importance to the success of the operation.

In order for Operation Sea Lion to be a success, weather reports were crucial, meaning Ireland once again became of significance to the Führer. Any information from spies such as Görtz would have been a huge asset to German preparations. In order for the plan to proceed smoothly, Hitler put two of his most trusted lieutenants in charge of preparations. Großadmiral Erich Raeder of the German Navy and Reichsmarschall Hermann Göring of the Luftwaffe were given primary responsibility for Operation Sea Lion, and the planned invasion of Ireland, 'Fall Grün', or Operation Green, was a major part of its remit. Implementation of Operation Green was the responsibility of Leonhard Kaupisch, commander of the 4 and 7 Army Corps. The instigator of Operation Green was the newly promoted Field Marshal Fedor von Bock of Army Group B, who compiled Operation Green into five separate volumes which looked at Ireland from every conceivable military viewpoint.

One volume, entitled *Militärgeographische Angaben über Irland*, contained 78 pages of military and geographical data on Ireland, including historical data as well as information on Irish industry, transport, infrastructure, climate and weather. It also included 17 pages of maps and sketches of major Irish cities and towns. Chillingly, some of the detail included was more advanced than the contemporary Ordnance Survey maps of Ireland. The information was intricate enough to include details of hotels, important buildings and petrol stations in many towns. In addition to this, a highly detailed map at a scale of 1:250,000 was drawn up. Tourist photographs were included alongside the maps to give visual representations of some of the towns identified. Operation Green also included details on spring tides, geographical formations and projected invasion beaches.

The Germans identified Wexford as the most ideal point of invasion, as the west coast had a largely unsuitable coastline for carrying out a successful sea landing due to rocky inlets and islands obstructing landing points. As part of the reconnaissance for the plan, the Luftwaffe carried out surveillance flights over Ireland, taking photographs from 30,000 ft. Such was the level of detail in the photographs that individual houses could be identified. Much of the reconnaissance work had been relayed by members of the German community who had lived in Ireland in the years leading up to the outbreak of the war, helping to paint a vivid picture of Ireland for the German High Command.

In response to the perceived threat from a German invasion of Ireland, both the Irish and the British governments designed a series of contingency measures known as 'Plan W'. The first meeting on establishing a joint action plan in the event of a German invasion was on 24 May 1940. The meeting was held in London and had been convened to explore every conceivable way in which the German forces might attempt an invasion of Ireland. At the meeting were Joe Walshe, Irish Secretary of the Department of External Affairs, Col Liam Archer of G2, and officers from the Royal Navy, the British Army and the RAF.

By May 1940, Irish troops were already organised in mobile columns to deal with parachute landings. By October 1940, four more regular army brigades had been raised in the State and Local Defence Force, and recruiting figures were increasing. While the Irish and British governments attempted to curb the growing threat, a new German agent arrived by U-boat in Co. Kerry in June 1941. Nazi Germany now had everything working in its favour in Ireland, and it would take all of G2's resources to thwart it.

————

The man who landed in Kerry was far from a typical German spy. Walter Simon was born on 12 December 1881 and was almost sixty years of age when he was sent as an agent to Ireland. Simon had a background in seafaring and could boast a considerable amount of experience to his superiors in this area when the gaunt well-built German was selected to be sent to Ireland. Simon spoke in a very harsh and rough tone due to an operation on his larynx in his youth. Wearing the uniform of an officer in the German Navy, Simon arrived on board U-boat U-38 in Dingle harbour on the night of 12 June 1940.

Using the alias 'Karl Anderson', Simon rowed ashore on a dinghy by bright moonlight. When he reached the shore he buried a small suitcase containing his wireless set. He planned to travel to Dublin to find an adequate location from which to operate the transmitter and send reports back to Germany. He hoped to return to Dingle to pick up the wireless set at a later date. Simon was tasked by the Abwehr to report back to Germany on British escort vessels and any other incidental items that might be of interest.

After burying his wireless set, Simon marched on foot towards a disused railway. Not realising it was out of use, he asked two local men what time the next train was at. Trying to contain their laughter, the men informed him the railway had been out of operation for 14 years. Simon's next move would prove to be a costly one. One of the gentlemen who Simon asked about the train was a publican, and he asked him back to his establishment. With a few hours to wait until the next train to Dublin, Simon thought this a welcome way to spend the time, and followed both men to the public house.

After several glasses of whiskey Simon began to curse Neville Chamberlain and Winston Churchill, and remarked to the bewildered patrons of the pub 'that the poverty of Ireland will change when Hitler comes to this country'. The patrons of the bar were understandably alarmed as Simon finished his drink and left, making his way to Tralee railway station. As he walked to the platform he noticed that he was being observed by a number of gentlemen he believed to be special branch detectives.

The men were in fact plain clothes detectives; sensing something was up, they struck up a conversation with Simon and eventually boarded the train with him. One of the detectives jokingly asked Simon whether he knew anyone in the IRA. Simon drunkenly asked the men if *they* were in the IRA. While one of the detectives kept Simon busy with idle conversation, the other quietly slipped away to place a call to Dublin. When the train arrived at Kingsbridge (Heuston) Station, Simon, in the company of the two detectives, was met by Gardaí and promptly arrested.

Simon was brought before a sitting of the Special Criminal Court in Collins Barracks in Dublin. One of the detectives on the train had noticed that Simon was carrying a paper bag with him on the train, and when this was examined it was found to contain 120 one-pound Bank of England notes which on further examination were discovered to be counterfeit. Along with other currency Simon had in total £215 on him. He was also carrying fake identity papers in the name of Karl Anderson. Simon told the court and the arresting officer conflicting stories, maintaining to the detectives that he was a British national.

In another exchange, he claimed that he was visiting a sister in Annascaul, Co. Kerry, who he said had the surname O'Sullivan, but that he had a fight with her in the middle of the night and was making his way home to his wife and children in Dublin. In another bizarre story, he told detectives he was a Swedish native who having grown tired of life in Nazi-controlled Europe had boarded a fishing boat in Dover and given the skipper £50 to take him to Ireland. Owing to his conflicting stories the authorities suspected Simon of being involved in espionage, and decided to hold the proceedings against him in camera. Much like Weber-Drohl, the court believed his story despite the fact he gave differing accounts. It looked as though he might be released when information came from England that turned his many alibis on their head.

When he eventually appeared before the court Simon was accused of entering Ireland illegally, and during the case a police officer gave evidence that Simon had been convicted of a similar offence in England in 1939. Also detectives in Kerry had noticed his footprints on the beach in Dingle and had subsequently dug up his transmitter, which was transported to Dublin and used in evidence against him in court. Acting on information supplied by MI5, Commandant Éamon de Buitléar of G2 held up a picture of Simon in prison in England for his previous offence.

With a considerable amount of evidence against him, Simon pleaded guilty to illegally entering Ireland. He was sentenced to three years' imprisonment and was transported to Mountjoy Prison to serve his sentence. Simon was the first German agent to be detained in an Irish prison, and despite his attempts at evasion he had given G2 plenty of material to study. His wireless set was examined thoroughly, and the authorities now had a much clearer picture of how German agents were going about their business in Ireland. This would come in useful for G2 when the Germans sent another agent a few weeks later to the same location as Simon, near Dingle.

―――

Up until this point Dr Richard Hayes had been busy working on the German Legation transmitter code. However a much graver situation now presented itself. German Abwehr agents were being equipped with hand ciphers known and ISOS[3] ciphers, which they used to communicate in paper-based messages. G2 knew that these posed a very significant threat to the security of the state, and Dr Hayes was tasked with breaking them. Such was the threat posed by these codes that Bletchley Park, the location of the British Government Code and Cipher School, had an entire hut with 16 staff working on breaking these messages. Ireland would have to survive with just Dr Hayes to attempt to break the codes. It was a seemingly impossible task, and one which became graver when Walter Simon's successor arrived in Kerry.

Wilhelm Preetz was a far more nefarious character than Walter Simon. An unapologetic Nazi, Preetz was a native of Bremen in north-western Germany. Born there in 1906, he worked as a crewman on a private yacht in New York in the early 1920s, where he met a young Irish girl named Sarah Josephine Reynolds, known as Sally, from Tuam, Co. Galway. By 1933 Preetz had returned to Bremen and joined the Nazi Party when Hitler took power in Berlin. Preetz was taken with the policies of Hitler's NSDAP, and in 1933 he also became a member of the SA, Hitler's brownshirts.

Preetz married Sally Reynolds in Bremen in 1935, and the couple travelled to Tuam to meet her parents in 1937. Having married an Irish girl, Preetz was approached by the Abwehr, who sensed an opportunity to use him as an agent. He entered Ireland on board a U-boat, arriving at Minard near Dingle, and unlike Simon he didn't make his way to the nearest railway. Instead, he chose to wade through shallow water in the dead of night once he had disembarked from the U-boat. He walked across the beach and traversed a few roads before he found a secluded place and fell asleep behind a stone wall.

3   Illicit Services Oliver Strachey. The section derived its name from Oliver Strachey CBE (3 November 1874–1814 May 1960), a British civil servant in the Foreign Office who was a cryptographer from World War I to World War II. During World War II he was at Bletchley Park, and headed the ISOS section deciphering various messages on the Abwehr network involving turned German agents (part of the Double-Cross system), with the first decrypt issued on 14 April 1940. Initially codenamed Pear, the decrypts became known as ISOS.

When Preetz awoke he buried his transmitter before making a plan to get to Dublin, where he planned to blend into the large population and avoid detection. Given his intimate knowledge of Ireland he knew that it would be market day the next morning when he woke up. He waited until a cattle truck was passing by him, and when nobody was looking he climbed aboard. Having spent some time in Ireland with his wife, Preetz was dressed in typical Irish clothes, and therefore did not arouse any suspicion in the driver or anyone else he interacted with.

Preetz was also smart enough to speak in an Irish accent and use some colloquialisms native to the area in order to avoid attracting unwarranted attention. Prior to his visit Preetz had obtained a false Irish passport which identified him as 'Paddy Mitchell' of Eyrecourt in Co. Galway. In later investigations G2 came to the conclusion that a member of Preetz's wife's family in Co. Sligo had helped in the forging of the passport. When Preetz and the farmer reached the next small town they parted company and Preetz went to a local pub for a drink before making his way to Dublin by taxi.

Arriving in Dublin he hid around the port before eventually renting a small shop at 32 Westland Row which he planned to live above. He returned to Minard by train, staying overnight in Limerick, and picked up the transmitter before returning with it to Dublin. From his flat above the shop Preetz sent messages back to Berlin undetected for several weeks. During his time in Dublin he drew a considerable amount of attention to himself, soliciting prostitutes and at one stage buying a flash Chrysler saloon sports car, which he drove around Dublin city centre at speed.

Preetz's indiscretions, as well as the frequency of his broadcasts from Westland Row, were to prove to be his downfall, and G2 soon triangulated the area from which his transmissions were being made. For a period of a few weeks they listened in to Preetz's broadcasts from a listening station at Collins Barracks, and such were the frequency of his transmissions that G2 put staff at the listening station on 24-hour duty to record his messages. A smarter agent would have made more infrequent broadcasts in an effort to thwart the security services, but Preetz's arrogance had gotten the better of him.

Detectives made notes on the messages, as they were not able to fully decipher them. However, the authorities were able to estimate that Preetz was transmitting 14 words per minute, and that he was making frequent mistakes with his use of Morse code, which required him to make multiple broadcasts in order to convey his information to Berlin correctly. This gave G2 a second opportunity to record Preetz's transmissions. They also noted that he frequently used the call sign LMR, as well as other call signs composed with the letters of his name. The net was closing in on Preetz, and when G2 and Gardaí raided his Westland Row lodgings they found a treasure trove of incriminating material including a Morse key, a transmitter and a receiver.

Sensing that time was up for him, Preetz immediately disclosed his real identity to detectives before giving himself up for arrest, and he was brought to Arbour Hill prison for interrogation. Detectives had also found pages of notes in the apartment that Preetz had used for enciphering, and these were immediately brought to Dr Hayes for deciphering. After studying the documents carefully for several days Hayes began to break Preetz's system:

> Preetz's cipher was a transposition in a cage twenty spaces wide based on the pages of a novel. The page was determined by adding the day of the month, the month and a constant. The preamble to his message was based on a numbering of the letters on the first unindented line of the page and the letters at the beginning of each line for twenty lines down from the top formed the keyword for the transposition of the cage. A certain number of x's were also used as nulls placed in a pattern in the cage. This letter was also employed as a full stop and an emphasising sign with names.

Confident in his fluent German, Hayes was able to break the Preetz cipher without much difficulty, noting that the use of the letter 'q' was the key to breaking the code:

This kind of Cipher is not difficult to break. If the language is German the c's and the h's and the c's and k's can be tested in different links. In fact an even easier method was available because of a few of the messages contained the letter 'q' in the word 'frequenz'. The fact that 'q' was present made it clear that unless 'q' was a null it must form part of the sequence 'equen' as was in fact the case. Preetz made the foolish mistake of ending all his messages with the same word 'gruesse'.

Hayes was able to decipher Preetz's coding system, theorising that it was simple in its origins. Using frequency analysis[4] he was mathematically able to extrapolate one of Preetz's keywords, 'ANALECTA HIBERNICAMUR'. Once Hayes had figured out the keyword he was able to read all of Preetz's messages.

Hayes also discovered that Preetz was carrying an emergency cipher to be used if he lost his codebook. It was based on a transposition derived from a keyword which he carried in his head. When Preetz's messages were deciphered most of the material was disappointing, consisting mainly of requests from Preetz to change broadcasting signals and for information to be repeated. Foolishly Preetz based himself in Dublin in order to live a flash lifestyle, not realising that this would affect the quality of the broadcasts he made. Hayes was able to prove that the German High Command had contacted Preetz asking him to communicate weather and tactical reports back to them.

Having no means of obtaining accurate meteorological data, Preetz used reports from English newspapers and observations made from looking out his window, and sent these back to Berlin. Having obtained a sophisticated reading of Preetz's enciphering system, it was decided that Hayes would personally interrogate Preetz in order to extract more information out of him. In order not to endanger himself or his family, G2 had given Hayes the alias 'Captain Grey', a humorous reference to his reserved demeanour.

---

4   In cryptanalysis, frequency analysis is the study of the frequency of letters or groups of letters in a cipher text. The method is used as an aid to breaking classical ciphers. Frequency analysis is based on the fact that, in any given stretch of written language, certain letters and combinations of letters occur with varying frequencies. Moreover, there is a characteristic distribution of letters that is roughly the same for almost all samples of that language.

It was a moniker he would use in any interactions with German agents he was interrogating.

Dr Hayes was a master tactician, figuring that the best approach was not to appear aggressive with captured German agents, and that by bringing agents on side with him he could extract the maximum amount of information possible. After several initial conversations with Preetz, Hayes deduced that he was of 'junior clerk mentality and not altogether too bright'. When Preetz's messages were fully deciphered it was noted that he had made references to an accomplice named 'Bates', but there was nothing further to ascertain if this person existed.

When the interrogation was concluded Preetz was convicted of entering Ireland illegally, and having in his possession an illegal wireless transmitter. The authorities believed that Preetz had communicated to Berlin the effect of Luftwaffe raids in England and made considerable efforts to investigate this. Following his conviction Preetz was taken to Mountjoy Prison in Dublin. When he entered the prison yard for the first time one of the first people he met was none other than his Abwehr colleague Walter Simon. Preetz rushed up to Simon exclaiming joyfully, 'Walter, are you here too?' In his rough intonation Simon barked 'Idiot' at Preetz before continuing on his way.

Thanks to Richard Hayes's innovations in the field of codebreaking, Bryan and G2 were having considerable success in their work against Abwehr agents. Hayes was effectively a one-man army, and proved himself to be an invaluable resource in the battle with Nazi Germany. However matters were to become further complicated with the arrival of further agents to Ireland. The continuing problem of Hermann Görtz being at liberty also plagued G2. It was believed that he was being harboured by elements in Irish society in political and social spheres that were in some ways sympathetic to his cause. Unbeknownst to G2 other German operations for Ireland were already underway and more agents were preparing to land on Irish soil.

——

By late June, with France defeated, Churchill was extremely anxious that Ireland could be used to land German troops by sea or air. The Northern Irish Prime Minister, Lord Craigavon, had suggested an All-Ireland defence policy in the event of a German invasion, something that was rejected by the Taoiseach, who was eager to preserve Irish neutrality at all costs.

Sensing an opportunity to take advantage, Abwehr Chief Admiral Canaris decided to send saboteurs to England via Ireland, beginning their missions in Norway and northern France; the clandestine mission was given the codename 'Operation Lobster'. The agents would use surface craft and depart from their start-off points without the use of prearranged contacts. World-famous yachtsman Christian Nissen, better known as 'Hein Mück' from his days in the Royal Ocean Yacht Club in London, was selected to transport the spies. A thin, fair-headed, tall man, Nissen had served in the German Navy in World War I, and had his ship torpedoed by the British off the coast of Cork. He had been interned in Templemore, Co. Tipperary and Oldcastle, Co. Meath as a result.

Nissen was approached by the Abwehr for the mission in June 1940, and received training at the Sabotage School in Brandenburg. There he was instructed to find a vessel suitable for carrying three agents. Nissen travelled to France to source an appropriate vessel, eventually finding one in Brest. He commandeered a 36-foot fishing vessel which, on closer inspection, had no motor. Undeterred by this, Nissen chose to use the vessel, hoping that wind power alone would suffice for the mission. He was instructed to transport two South African Germans and an Indian national to Ireland. The Abwehr were confident that Nissen's reputation as a noted yachtsman would provide sufficient cover for him to complete his mission.

The South African agents were Dieter Gärtner and Herbert Tributh. Both men were unusual choices for spies, given that they were both students with little knowledge of English and no experience in espionage. Nissen described them as young and idealistic and perhaps unsuitable for such a mission. The Indian man accompanying them was Henry Obéd. He was to act as their interpreter and alone out of all three could boast of experience working for the Abwehr. Obéd had an open and sometimes volatile dislike of all things English, and prior to the war he had lived in Antwerp in Belgium, where he had owned a pet shop and dealt in Indian spices.

None of the three agents had any sailing experience, so in order to make the crossing safely Nissen asked the Abwehr for an assistant. He was supplied with a Breton fisherman who, though old, proved an able companion. With all the crew on board the party set sail for Fastnet Rock, 13 km off the Cork coast. Nissen had twice sailed in an ocean race from Cowes on the Isle of Wight to the rock, and so was familiar with the area.

The party left Brest harbour at midnight on 3 July. The vessel was 45 miles west of Fastnet Rock when the Breton seaman spotted two British cruisers. Tributh, Gärtner and Obéd were all asleep in their bunks, having been suffering from seasickness since they left Brest. Fearing that they would be boarded, Nissen became apprehensive. However, at the last moment the cruisers turned away. Clearly their cover had worked. Later that day a British flying boat flew low overhead, observing the vessel by doing multiple low circles. The Breton fisherman had raised the French tricolour on board prior to their departure from Brest, and the ruse worked. The flying boat continued on its flight path, eventually leaving the area. A Portuguese steamer also passed close by, but the agents and their vessel failed to raise its suspicions.

Shortly after sunset Nissen docked in Baltimore Bay, and the agents bade him farewell. He would have to wait almost a day for the wind to pick up so that he could sail away from Ireland. En route to France he encountered a British patrol boat and calmly sat and peeled a potato on board as the British boat eventually sailed on. When he reached France Nissen contacted the Abwehr office in Brest to inform them that his mission had been success. Nissen then travelled north-west to Brittany, where he stayed and from where he would later attempt to take on more Abwehr missions to transport German agents to Ireland.

As Nissen sailed away, Tributh, Gärtner and Obéd climbed into a dinghy and rowed ashore. Before they left the landing site they buried their wireless transmitter and tried unsuccessfully to hide the dinghy they had rowed ashore in. Hiking in the rain across a beach to a nearby road, the men were nothing but conspicuous in the West Cork countryside. While

Tributh and Gärtner carried suitcases, Obéd in particular is alleged to have stood out due to his insistence on wearing a silk Indian suit and a straw hat. However, the veracity of this account is disputed, and photographs taken shortly after the men's arrest show him wearing a double-breasted suit and white hat. Complete in their unusual attire the men trekked to Skibbereen, arriving late in the evening.

In Skibbereen they hoped to get a bus to Dublin, but due to the late hour of their arrival they had missed the last one. They got a lift on a creamery truck from Skibbereen to Drimoleague, where they boarded a bus to Cork City hoping to catch a train to Dublin once they arrived there. Obéd's appearance and demeanor attracted considerable attention, and a local Garda became suspicious of the trio. The Garda rang ahead to Union Quay Garda Station in Cork to alert them to the arrival of the three strange men.

It wasn't long after the men arrived at the station that Gardaí driving in a patrol car noticed them and stopped to question them. The trio maintained that they were students on a sight-seeing trip. When Gardaí opened their suitcases they became immediately suspicious and promptly arrested the men. One of the officers placed a phone call to alert military intelligence and G2 were immediately dispatched to Cork to investigate. In Dublin, Hempel panicked when he heard the news, and claimed that the agents were probably provocateurs sent by the British to provoke a dispute in German–Irish relations.

When G2 examined the agents' suitcases they were shocked at what they found. The trio were carrying eight incendiary bombs eight ounces in weight, four tins of gun cotton and six detonators, along with six fuses which were 2½ feet long stored in the belts of Obéd and Gärtner for safe keeping. The men were also carrying two reels of insulating tape, two sets of cutting pliers and £839 in cash, as well as a book that G2 speculated could have been used for enciphering messages. Obéd had an alarm clock, which detectives speculated was going to be used as a timing device for their explosives.

Despite the youth and naïvety of Tributh and Gärtner, they refused to answer any questions when interrogated by both the Gardaí and G2.

Obéd proved to be more talkative, especially since he was isolated from the rest of the group on racial grounds while incarcerated. In the midst of his interrogation he admitted that he intended to link up with German invasion troops in England. Obéd, Tributh and Gärtner were all convicted under the Emergency Powers Act and the Emergency Powers Order on 25 July 1940.

Each of them was sentenced to three years' imprisonment for landing in Ireland illegally. They were also given a seven-year sentence under the Explosives Act, which was to run concurrently with the three-year prison term. Tributh and Gärtner pleaded guilty, but Obéd maintained his innocence, and attempted to appeal his sentence through the Court of Criminal Appeal. All three men were transported to Athlone to serve their sentences for the remainder of the war.

Meanwhile Görtz, who was still at large, was furious that the three agents had been sent to Ireland. He felt they were undermining him and his mission. Scathingly he wrote to his superiors:

I was assured by the High Command before my flight that no other officer nor any other person would be landed in Ireland unless requested by me. This agreement was to remain in force as long as I was entrusted with my mission. Actually nobody was sent by the High Command but unfortunately a subordinate department did so. I did not know why it had happened. As soon as I had contact with the High Command, I complained bitterly about it. The answer I received was that nobody knew anything about these arrangements. From the very beginning the help these Germans could render was not comparable to the harm that they could do, my comrades did not know why they were sent to Ireland – the responsibility for this lay with others. But now they had to pay the penalty for it – as 'war criminals', 'suspects' or whatever they were called by our enemies.

The capture of Tributh, Gärtner and Obéd had further complicated Görtz's mission in Ireland and made it almost impossible to carry out his duties efficiently. He was without money and a safe roof over his head, and

G2 were closing in on him at every turn. With Görtz at his wits' end and with the IRA–German link severely compromised, the Abwehr would have to think quickly in order to restore any hope that Görtz's mission would succeed. In the interim they had been busy with an unexpected Irish visitor who they felt might help provide a solution.

――――

The former IRA Chief of Staff Seán Russell had made his way back from the USA to Germany and was eager to resume his role as the head of the organisation. Russell had been living in the country outside Berlin, where he was being protected by an Austrian non-commissioned officer who acted as his full-time bodyguard. The Abwehr planned to instruct Russell in the use of materials for the purposes of sabotage, and he was taken to an Abwehr laboratory that specialised in the use of sabotage techniques in Tegel in north Berlin.

Russell was trained in the use of Abwehr explosive materials, particularly the use of chemicals to produce explosives. The Abwehr planned that, given the approval of the Kriegsmarine, they would transport Russell back to Ireland via U-boat and equip him with two operators who were trained in wireless communication. Having gained the approval of the Navy, Russell was to be transported to Ireland once a U-boat became available. When he landed at a suitable location in Ireland he was to bury the sabotage equipment, transmitter and other materials in an appropriate location before returning to collect them with his IRA men once he had them mobilised.

Despite the Abwehr's best intentions and careful planning it was to take more time before Russell could embark on his mission, as there was some apprehension about sending him. During this period IRA man Frank Ryan, who had been on the left-leaning side of the IRA, had made his way to Germany. Ryan had volunteered to fight with the international brigades in the Spanish Civil War, and had recently escaped from captivity in Burgos Prison. He was transported to Berlin, and met up with Seán Russell on 4 August 1940.

On his arrival in Berlin, Ryan was introduced to SS Colonel Dr Edmund Veesenmayer. Veesenmayer, as part of his SS and German Foreign Ministry brief, was involved in the planning of all Abwehr operations to Ireland until 1943. The day after arriving, Ryan was asked by Russell to accompany him to Ireland as part of 'Operation Dove', the codename given to Russell's mission. Both Russell and Frank Ryan departed aboard U-65 from Wilhelmshaven in lower Saxony on 8 August. Russell became ill during the journey, and complained of stomach pains. U-65 was not equipped with a doctor, and he died on 14 August, 100 miles short of Galway. He was buried at sea and the mission was aborted.

Following the return of the submarine to Germany an inquiry by the Abwehr was set up to investigate Russell's death. This inquiry included the interrogation of U-65's crew and Frank Ryan. The conclusion drawn was that Russell had suffered a burst gastric ulcer and, without medical attention, he had died. Rumours soon began to circulate that Russell was poisoned, as he had become too much of a threat to the Abwehr. However Russell's brother maintained that it was more likely that his death was due to the ulcer, as he had suffered with the problem for many years prior.

Ryan was dropped as a possible agent in further covert Abwehr and German Foreign Ministry plans and operations. He was approached in late 1943 for his opinion on the feasibility of a secret transmitter propaganda operation in Ireland for broadcast to the United States, but the plan never reached fruition. Ryan died in June 1944 at a hospital in Dresden. His funeral in Dresden was attended by Helmut Clissmann's wife Elizabeth and Francis Stuart. Clissmann eventually forwarded details of Ryan's fate to Leopold Kerney in Madrid, who forwarded them to his family in Dublin. According to Stuart and Clissmann, the cause of Ryan's death was pleurisy and pneumonia. Ryan's body was eventually repatriated to Dublin and buried in the republican plot in Glasnevin Cemetery.

Meanwhile, back in Ireland, Hermann Görtz remained unaware of the operation relating to Russell, and was growing increasingly paranoid and distressed at his situation. With things going from bad to worse, Görtz began more and more to place his faith in some of the many women with whom he was romantically involved. Some of these women were fervent nationalists, whose prowess at safeguarding Görtz when he was at large was remarkable, given that IRA Chief of Staff Stephen Hayes was unable to guarantee his safety.

Most of the women involved with Görtz were hardline supporters of the IRA who had taken the Anti-Treaty side in the Civil War and who had not joined de Valera in his foray into constitutional politics with the formation of Fianna Fáil in 1926. In many ways they regarded de Valera as a traitor for having taken the oath of allegiance to the British Crown upon his ascension to power in 1932, and some openly despised him for this. The republican pedigree of Görtz's many female associates was without question.

One of the foremost leaders in the Irish War of Independence had been Cathal Brugha. Brugha served as Minister for Defence from 1919 to 1922, Ceann Comhairle of Dáil Éireann in January 1919, President of Dáil Éireann from January 1919 to April 1919 and Chief of Staff of the IRA from 1917 to 1919, and served as a TD from 1918 to 1923. Brugha was also active in the 1916 Rising, the War of Independence and the Civil War, being involved in fighting in the Four Courts during the Civil War. In the midst of this battle he approached Free State troops brandishing a revolver, and sustained a bullet wound to the leg which 'severed a major artery causing him to bleed to death'. He died on 7 July 1922, 11 days before his 48th birthday.

Brugha's wife Caitlín served as a Sinn Féin TD from 1923 to 1927. She established a drapery business, Kingston's Ltd, in 1924, and following her exit from politics devoted much time to the venture. She also harboured Görtz, and aided him financially. Given her open animosity towards England, it was felt by the Irish and British Authorities that her sympathies very much lay with Nazi Germany in the fight against British Imperialism.

Two of the most important female contacts for Görtz while he was at large in Ireland were sisters Mary and Bridie Farrell, who lived at 7 Spencer Villas in Glenageary in South Co. Dublin. The sisters, both republicans, gave Görtz lodgings and financial aid.

Unbeknownst to Görtz and G2 a secret meeting was taking place in Berlin between Lt Gartenfeld, the Heinkel pilot who had flown Görtz to Ireland, and high-level agents in the Abwehr in which was discussed the feasibility of sending more spies to Ireland. Gartenfeld was asked whether dropping another agent by seaplane was the correct method, or whether they should be dropped onto inland lakes in rubber rafts. During the meeting Gartenfeld and the Abwehr conferred on the location of a suitable lake for such an endeavour, but the idea was soon dropped.

By mid-1940, the Abwehr felt that the time was right to send another agent to Ireland on a similar mission to Görtz. He was to arrive by parachute into Co. Wexford carrying an illegal transmitter and a substantial amount of cash. This new agent was carrying with him an ingenious coding system that the Germans thought would be unbreakable. After a few technical problems his mission to Ireland was cancelled in July 1940, but rescheduled in September 1940. The first attempt to drop him in Ireland failed when the Heinkel He111 was forced to return to base in Amsterdam on 5 March 1941. However one week later the planning for his mission began again. With Hermann Görtz still at liberty, G2 and Dr Hayes now faced another ruthless foe.

V

THE SPY WITH THE MICROSCOPE

'This was a very closely guarded "top secret" in German Intelligence. Nobody knew of the Microdots outside of Germany.

GÜNTHER SCHÜTZ, Abwehr agent

On a bitterly cold night on 13 March 1941, a black Heinkel He111 bomber departed Schiphol Airport in the occupied Netherlands. On board a German agent prepared his parachute while the pilot plotted out their route. Flying Officer Lt Gartenfeld was familiar with dropping agents into Ireland, having flown on the mission carrying Hermann Görtz the previous year. The agent accompanying him went by the alias 'Hans Marschner', and carried a fake South African passport with that name.

In reality he was Sgt Günther Schütz, a German agent who had been dispatched to Ireland by the economic section of the Abwehr in Hamburg. The 29-year-old Schütz was a wiry, athletic and extremely able agent who hailed originally from Schweidnitz in Silesia, having been born into a prosperous upper-middle-class family that owned a metal manufacturing business. Like so many German families of his class, the Schützes were drawn to National Socialism, and Hitler's promises of a new Germany filled with opportunity.

As a young man Günther served in the local army reserve unit from 1934 to 1935, and attended a five-week training course with the Mounted Artillery Regiment at Oldenburg in 1938. From 1938 to 1939 he attended the

German Commercial College at Eaton Rise, Ealing, in London, and it was here that he first became connected with the Abwehr. Having a good grasp of economics, Schütz was asked by his masters to keenly observe matters in London while he attended the college. From here he was expected to regularly report back to Berlin on economic matters.

At the outbreak of the war in 1939, Schütz was called to report to his local artillery regiment in Oldenburg to serve in the Wehrmacht. However, given his time in London he was soon acquired by the Abwehr for a special mission more befitting a man of his talent and supposed intellect. The Abwehr were interested in Schütz re-establishing his links with England via a neutral country. The link, which had broken down since the onset of the war, was deemed by the German High Command to be valuable to the ongoing war effort against Britain.

Schütz travelled to Spain, where he made connection with a former German agent named Werner Unland, who had fled England to Ireland with his English wife, and was believed to be living in Dublin. Because of his correspondence with Schütz, Unland was eventually identified by G2 in May 1941 and interned with other Germans in the Curragh Camp. Despite the fact that he wasn't on 'active service' with the Abwehr at the time of his arrest, Unland was to spend five years in detention in Ireland.

Schütz was eventually summoned back to Hamburg, where he was briefed on his next mission by the head of the Economic Section of the Abwehr, Dr Friedrich Karl Praetorius, who impressed upon Schütz the need to carry out 'his patriotic duty'. Schütz was tasked with successfully penetrating Ireland, where he was to radio daily weather reports back to the Luftwaffe, observe British convoy movements and carry out economic espionage at any given opportunity. The most crucial part of Schütz's mission, however, was to report on economic matters in Northern Ireland. The Abwehr were particularly interested to find out what was going on in the Belfast Shipyards, as well as information on employment figures in Harland and Wolff and the shipping yard's military production output.

Schütz was given the use of No. 46 Merrion Square to stay in, an address which had previously belonged to Werner Unland during his time in Dublin. He was also given the address of the German Legation in Ballsbridge, but was given strict instructions to contact them only in the most dire emergency. Schütz's fake passport had been doctored by the Abwehr, having originally belonged to his South African school friend Hans Marschner. Before he left Hamburg, Schütz was also given training in the use of a wireless set, and was equipped with a form of encryption that the Germans believed would baffle the world's greatest cryptographical minds.

Schütz was equipped with an English pocket version of the novel *Just a Girl* by Charles Garvice, the title of which was to be used as the keyword. The Abwehr retained a copy of their own for ease of communication. The encryption method was standard for book-based codes. If Schütz were to send a message on 13 March, that being the 13th day of the third month, he would turn to page 133 and subtract a prearranged number before turning to a stipulated page and use letters from the first line of that page as his code.

Despite the security of his book code, however, the most ingenious part of Schütz's encryption method was based around a series of 'microdots'. Schütz was instructed not to transmit messages in long sentences, but to instead communicate in short bursts based on numerical sequences. To avoid overcomplicating matters he was not tasked with carrying his instructions and the numerical code for transmitting his weather reports in his head. He was instead equipped with a microscope and a cutting from an English newspaper on a botanical theme. His instructions were hidden in the punctuation marks in the cutting.

Microdots were a brilliant method of deception, which worked by reducing sensitive information to such an extent that it would appear no larger than a punctuation mark in a piece of writing. A normal dot is then carefully removed from a piece of writing and replaced with the microdot containing the instructions or other information. While nothing would seem out of the ordinary to the naked eye, the secret message could be easily read by an agent with a microscope. In a further security measure, the dots could only be read when held obliquely to the light, making them glimmer brightly. The Germans were so confident of the security of the microdots that they didn't bother encrypting the messages contained within.

Schütz's mission had no completion date, and therefore he was at his own liberty to choose when to return to Germany. To keep him going while he was in Ireland he was supplied with £1,000 sterling and $3,200. He was to give £300 of this to Unland once he made contact with him, and Schütz hoped to exchange the dollars at the German Legation once he reached Dublin. Shortly before his departure Schütz asked to meet with Oscar Pfaus to obtain a list of any contacts in Irish society that would aid him. The request was flatly rejected by the Abwehr, who wanted Schütz to avoid any contact with the IRA; however they did provide him with a list of names of sympathetic non-combatant Irish citizens, and a supply of 'G-Tinten' invisible ink, which was hidden in the shoulder pads of his overcoat.

———

As the Heinkel passed over England, Schütz and Gartenfeld didn't have the benefit of the blanket of cloud that had guaranteed Hermann Görtz's safe passage the previous year. As they entered British airspace, almost without warning the aircraft was bathed in the brilliant light of a British anti-aircraft searchlight. Within seconds they were under severe gunfire, and as Gartenfeld manoeuvred them out of the range of one light they were soon picked up by another.

The situation became grave, and the men feared they would soon come under heavy bombardment. Schütz prepared his parachute, fearing he would have to jump at the nearest opportunity in order to save his life. This time he used one parachute for himself and the transmitter. He was determined not to be separated from his wireless, as Görtz had been. Gartenfeld dropped to a lower altitude, and as he passed over Birmingham and then Liverpool he knew that once he reached the Irish Sea he would be out of harm's way.

Gartenfeld was now flying by instruments, as he had no way of knowing where he was, and while he tried to get his bearings Schütz hurriedly donned his parachute and awaited instruction from the flying officer. As the Heinkel entered Irish airspace Gartenfeld cut the engines at 6,500 ft, the bomb-bay door opened and Gartenfeld shouted, 'Achtung, fertig, los!'

Stand by, ready, jump! Schütz shut his eyes and leaped headlong into the darkness.

As he drifted towards the ground Schütz felt blood running down his face. He ran his hand under his nose and discovered that he had suffered a nosebleed from the adrenaline of the parachute jump. As soon as his feet hit Irish soil he quickly separated himself from his parachute and buried it along with his jump helmet and Luftwaffe uniform. As he dug he looked up to find a local farmer staring at him. Schütz and the gentleman stared at each other for a few minutes, as if each was waiting for the other to act first.

The farmer blinked first, and walked back inside his house. Schütz knew he needed to get out of the area as quickly as possible. He threw on his English overcoat and fumbled in his pocket to find his compass and one of the maps he was carrying, but in the darkness all he could do was trudge along until he found a signpost. Unfortunately for Schütz all such signage had been removed as a precautionary measure since the outbreak of the war. However one sign seemed to have been forgotten; Schütz moved closer to read what it said.

Dawn had just begun to break, giving Schütz a little more light to read the sign, which to his amazement read, 'New Ross 10 Miles'. Immediately he reached for his map to see what part of Kildare New Ross was in – and found he was about 90 miles from Dublin. Panic set in and Schütz knew that he would have to act immediately if he were to rectify such a disastrous navigational error. He started to wonder whether they had crossed over south Wales as opposed to Liverpool, as he had previously thought. Bitterly disappointed, Schütz set about walking to safety, carrying with him a cumbersome suitcase containing the wireless set he had been tasked to communicate with. As he strolled down the country road he was struck by the quietness that surrounded him. The suitcase eventually took its toll and he decided to climb behind a hedge, where he rested for an hour.

After starting off again, a mile or so down the road he met a woman on a bicycle. Schütz shouted 'Hello' to the woman, who was startled to encounter the strange sight of the German officer on the deserted Irish country road. The woman said 'Hello' back while looking furtively at

Schütz. Unluckily for him she was the wife of a local Garda. The two went about their way, and a short time later Schütz bumped into a young man with an ass and cart whom he promptly asked for a lift to Dublin. The reply was a stern 'No' from the young man, who assured Schütz that he was travelling in the other direction.

Schütz had landed far from his jump zone, which was in Newbridge, and was actually near the village of Taghmon, between New Ross and Wexford town. He would have a three-day march ahead of him if he were to reach the safety of Werner Unland's apartment on Merrion Square. As he trudged along the road the lady he had met on the bicycle hurried to the Garda station in the village of Carrickbyrne, where she reported the sighting of a strange man on the road between New Ross and Wexford heading south-east towards Wexford town. In the interim Schütz had decided to make his way to Wexford town to get a bus to Dublin. Before arriving he decided he would have one last nap in a nearby ditch – a mistake that would prove fatal to his mission.

After Schütz awoke from his second slumber he put on his jacket, picked up his suitcase and took off down the road. He walked for an hour or two before stopping to have a draught of the brandy in his hipflask and to snack on a frankfurter while he plotted out his next move. As Schütz ate he noticed two bicycles in the distance. The riders seemed to be travelling in the same direction as he was, although they had their backs turned towards him.

Sensing something was out of place, Schütz stepped behind a hedge to what he thought was relative safety. There he would wait until the men disappeared over the rise of the hill ahead. A flash of curiosity struck him, however, and Schütz lingered a little longer to see if he could identify who the men were. His sense of foreboding was well placed, as the two gentlemen were Gardaí who had been dispatched from the local barracks to find Schütz after the lady on the bicycle had reported him. As Schütz prepared to disappear behind the hedge one of the policemen suddenly turned around. It was too late – he had been spotted!

Schütz noticed one Garda whispering to the other before they beckoned to him to come forward. As the parties approached each other one of the Gardaí said, 'Hello, nice morning.' To which Schütz sheepishly replied,

'Very nice morning indeed.' The Garda asked Schütz if he was a stranger, and Schütz concocted a story about getting a puncture to the wheel of his car and how he needed to get to New Ross as soon as possible. The ruse wasn't working with the Gardaí, though, as they grew more and more suspicious of the suitcase Schütz was carrying. 'That's a fine suitcase you have there,' one of them said, as Schütz gripped the handle tightly. 'Are you in the haberdashery business?' asked the other Garda. 'Yes,' replied Schütz. When one of the Gardaí asked if he could look inside his suitcase Schütz knew the game was up. He was alone and unarmed on a country road with two foreign policemen, and while he had a parachute knife he wasn't prepared to use it on the two policemen. Without protest Schütz handed over his suitcase and the two Gardaí opened it and stared in amazement at the contents. While one Garda examined the transmitter, money, microscope and assortment of frankfurters, the other removed the handcuffs from his belt and placed them on an ashen-faced Schütz, who was slowly coming to the realisation that his mission was over in less than 24 hours of landing on Irish soil.

Unfortunately for Schütz, his lack of knowledge of rural Ireland had proved his downfall. The farmer he had spotted when he landed was a member of the IRA, and might have given him shelter if he had approached him instead of the lady on the bicycle. His mistake was a costly one. Fearing they didn't have time to reach the local barracks, the Gardaí took Schütz to a local pub, Rochfords (known today as O'Sullivans), in the village of Taghmon, where the officer bought the confused German sandwiches and a few pints of Guinness.

While Schütz ate his sandwiches, one of the Gardaí slipped out to ring for reinforcements and a crowd of bewildered townsfolk began to gather to get a look at the German spy. A squad car soon arrived outside, and as it ground to a halt Schütz sheepishly asked one of the Gardaí, 'What will happen to me? 'Don't worry, we'll hang you, that's all,' replied the Garda with a chuckle. His humour was lost on Schütz, who grew suddenly pale. Gardaí drove Schütz to the site where he had buried his parachute and he promptly handed it over, along with his overalls and steel jump helmet. They then put him back in the car and drove him to the Bridewell Jail in Dublin; from there he was transferred to Arbour Hill prison, where G2 were waiting to interrogate him. Before he left the Bridewell, Schütz managed to dispose of his invisible ink in a toilet.

Before leaving Wexford Gardaí made an inventory of Schütz's possessions and then contacted G2. One item of particular interest was a picture of a gentleman who was later identified as Werner Unland. When Dan Bryan heard of Schütz's arrest he was furious that he had not been informed immediately, and that Schütz had been allowed to spend money intended for espionage on pints of Guinness in the pub in Taghmon. He asked to see Schütz's possessions and immediately recognised Unland when he saw the photograph. Unland had been placed under surveillance, and Bryan guessed there must be a link between the men. His hunch was confirmed when he noticed a piece of paper in Schütz's possession with a lipstick mark on it similar to messages monitored by G2 that had been sent by Unland.

———

When Schütz arrived in prison he freely admitted to his captors that he was a German agent, but he didn't tell them his real name, preferring to stick to his cover story that he was Hans Marschner, a native of South Africa. Such was the level of his deception that the Schütz family were answering post addressed to the Marschners at home in Germany. Sensing that their guest was being less than truthful, Dan Bryan suggested that Schütz be subjected to a more thorough interrogation by Dr Hayes and Commandant Éamon de Buitléar. Hayes, using his cover name 'Captain Grey', calmly walked into Schütz's cell and began addressing the spy in German.

Hayes felt that Schütz was a more intelligent man than Preetz, and that he would find being incarcerated quite difficult – an ideal situation for soliciting more information from him. Hayes asked Schütz about his microscope, commenting that it was a Hensoldt/Wetzlar-branded model. Sensing a trap, Schütz replied that it was for stamp collecting, which he assured Hayes was a keen interest of his. Hayes laughed softly at Schütz, saying, 'G'way, you didn't bring a microscope all the way from Germany to examine stamps.'

Realising his ruse wasn't working, Schütz insisted the microscope was for amateur botany. Hayes laughed again, and smiled at Schütz, all the while reading the German's mannerisms and personality. Both Hayes and de Buitléar continued to visit Schütz every evening at teatime, and engaged him in conversation in his native tongue. The prison governor, Commandant Lennon, would visit early in the day and play chess with Schütz, luring him into a false security. Hayes and de Buitléar would then continue the ruse and causally slip questions into conversation with Schütz, asking him about his mission and the IRA. Their determination would soon pay off, as Schütz slowly but surely opened up to them.

He admitted he had no knowledge of the IRA or indeed Walter Simon and Wilhelm Preetz, and the true reason behind his carrying a microscope became clear. Hayes became fascinated by some newspaper clippings that Schütz was carrying. At first, to the untrained eye, they appeared to be totally innocent. They included hotel advertisements and testimonial letters for medicine, and when Dr Hayes pressed him further Schütz gave him clues which helped him break the code he was using. Hayes asked Schütz why he was carrying a German newspaper article with him. Schütz replied, 'For no special reason.'

Hayes took the articles and examined them. In a eureka moment Hayes looked at one of the articles using the microscope, and to his amazement he noticed that one of the dots on a letter 'i' contained 30 small microdots containing messages. Schütz blurted out that he had the newspaper cuttings with him as he was interested in purchasing some of the medicines advertised in one of the articles. It was too late! Hayes was able to read the set of instructions Schütz had been given by the Abwehr as he looked through the microscope, and was astonished that the Germans hadn't bothered to encipher the instructions. He noted that the microdots could only be read by a microscope that could magnify up to 400 times the size of an image, and put it to Schütz that it was the reason for him having the state-of-the-art Hensoldt/Wetzlar microscope in his possession.

Hayes took down notes of the various names, addresses and phone numbers of people that Schütz was to contact when he landed in Ireland. Schütz was shocked that his method of concealing information had been broken. The microdots were a closely guarded 'top secret' in Germany, and he was utterly dismayed that they had been discovered with relative ease by the softly spoken intelligence officer he would only learn years later was Dr Hayes. As Hayes finished with his notes he turned to Schütz and smiled gently before excusing himself. After Hayes left the room he promptly contacted Dan Bryan to tell him of his discovery.

––––

In the end, Hayes succeeded in breaking the cipher without too much difficulty:

> This cipher was also a simple transposition of the same type as the Preetz cipher. The keywords were obtained from the bottom of a periodical. The cage was twenty spaces wide. In fact all German transpositions throughout the war were in cages twenty spaces wide. This illustrates the difficulty Germans seem to have in avoiding 'method' where method is a disadvantage. If they had adopted variable widths in their cages it would have required staff four times as large to produce the same results in the countries which were trying to break their ciphers.

Hayes also solved Schütz's emergency cipher with relative ease, and surmised that the Germans were ill-equipped to adequately encipher their messages correctly.

> Marschner's (Schütz) emergency cipher was based on a 15 letter keyword. If any of the German agents, such as Preetz and Marschner … sent out with these simple transpositions had read Herbert Yardley's book 'The American Black Chamber'[5] they would have realised that an efficient system for breaking their ciphers was in use in 1916. It is difficult to understand how this book escaped the notice of the German cipher experts. Apart from this book, of course, the ciphers would

5   *The American Black Chamber* is a 1931 book by Herbert O. Yardley. The book describes the inner workings of the interwar American governmental cryptography organisation called the Black Chamber. The cryptography historian David Kahn called it 'the most famous book on cryptology ever published'.

have been broken by any competent cryptographer in a few hours. The amazing thing is that the Germans made no attempt to conceal the 'ch' diagraph by substituting another symbol for it or placing some agreed nulls in a position to split it. The lesson to be drawn from this is that there should be continuity between the cipher departments from one war throughout the peace to the next war. The colossal blunder the Germans made can only be explained on the assumption that the cryptographical staff in 1939 had no continuity with the staff of 1914–18.

Hayes translated over 30 pages of Schütz's instructions as well as his contact list; in less than two weeks he had rendered his whole mission obsolete. Schütz believed it was Commandant de Buitléar who had discovered his secrets, such was the unassuming nature of Dr Hayes, who maintained friendly relations with Schütz all the time he was in prison. It was a relationship that was to prove extremely useful to Hayes, G2 and the Allied Powers. Hayes was the first person in the world to discover the secrets of the German microdot system. It was a discovery that was to win him the admiration of MI5, the cryptographers in Bletchley Park and the Office of Strategic Services in the United States, all of whom spoke glowingly of the achievements of the mild-mannered librarian.

As well as breaking Schütz's code, Hayes obtained a sophisticated analysis of how it worked, enabling him to elicit more information from Schütz in aid of the wider war effort. He quizzed Schütz about organisational structures in the Abwehr, and after gentle persuasion Schütz eventually complied. He provided for Hayes and G2 a thorough picture of the Abwehr's operations and his dealings with them during his time in Hamburg. He also told Hayes abut Werner Unland, how he was operating clandestinely in Dublin and about personnel he came into contact with during his espionage training. Despite maintaining the ruse that he was simply delivering a transmitter to an agent in England who was to report on bomb damage from Luftwaffe attacks there, Schütz had given enough information to incriminate both himself and Unland.

While he was being questioned he asked that some letters be delivered

Colonel Dan Bryan, Director of Irish Military Intelligence G2, 1941–1952 (*Courtesy of the Military Archives of Ireland/Defence Forces*).

James 'Jim' O'Donovan, IRA Head of Munitions and Chemicals. He set up the IRA–Nazi Link.

Ernst Weber-Drohl, circus strongman and Abwehr spy *(Courtesy of the National Library of Ireland).*

Eduard Hempel, German Minister to Ireland between 1937 and 1945 in the build-up to and during the Emergency *(Photo courtesy of Dr David O'Donoghue,* Hitler's Irish Voices: The Story of German Radio's Wartime Irish Service*).*

Site of the former German Legation in Ballsbridge where Eduard Hempel operated an illegal wireless transmitting set.

Captain John Patrick O'Sullivan, an Irish Army Signals Officer who monitored the German Legation from listening stations in Collins Barracks and his home in Chapelizod.

Guy Liddell, MI5's Director of Counter-Espionage during World War II (© *Bettmann/ Getty Images*).

Dr Richard Hayes, Director of the National Library of Ireland during World War II. He was also Ireland's most prolific and brilliant codebreaker, as well as a formidable interrogator of captured German spies.

The Hayes family on a trip to Greystones. Pictured (left to right) Richard, Faery, Mervyn, Jimmy, Clare and Bertie. Joan is behind the camera.

A Heinkel He111 plane was used by the Abwehr to drop Hermann Görtz and Günther Schütz into Ireland.

Dr Hermann Görtz in Luftwaffe uniform *(Courtesy of the National Archives UK)*.

Abwehr headquarters, 76–78 Tirpitzufer Berlin *(© imageBROKER/Alamy Stock Photo)*.

G2 headquarters during the Emergency, North Circular Road, as they stand today.

Laragh Castle, Co. Wicklow *(© National Inventory of Architectural Heritage)*.

7 Spencer Villas, Glenageary. Görtz's safe house and home of the Farrell sisters.

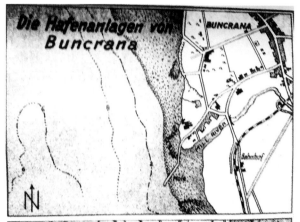

Operation Green invasion
map for Buncrana and
Rathmullan, Co. Donegal
*(Courtesy of the Military
Archives of Ireland/Defence
Forces).*

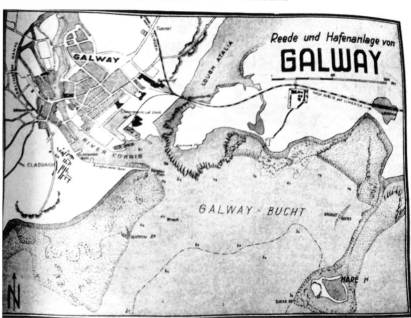

Operation Green invasion map for Galway city *(Courtesy of the Military Archives of
Ireland/Defence Forces).*

Hans Marschner, aka Sgt Günther Schütz, Abwehr agent *(Courtesy of the Military Archives of Ireland/Defence Forces).*

Hans Marschner, fake South African passport used by Günther Schutz *(Courtesy of the Military Archives of Ireland/Defence Forces).*

GARDA SIOCHANA

£500 REWARD

The above sum will be paid to any person giving information resulting in the arrest of HANS MARSCHNER, German internee who escaped from custody at Mountjoy Prison on the night of 15th February, 1942

30 yrs. of age, 5ft. 9ins., complexion pale, hair dark brown, eyes brown, scar between eyes and on left cheek. Speaks English well.

Information may be given to any Garda Station.

Proportionate rewards will be paid for information concerning this man which will assist the Garda in locating him.

A wanted poster from An Garda Síochana for Hans Marschner, aka Sgt Günther Schütz, following his escape from Mountjoy Prison in 1942 *(Courtesy of the Military Archives of Ireland/Defence Forces).*

Burnt fragments of the Görtz cipher, reconstructed on glass plates by Dr Richard Hayes *(Courtesy of the National Library of Ireland).*

Hayes's codebreaking notes on the Görtz cipher *(Courtesy of the National Library of Ireland).*

Hermann Görtz's handwritten cipher notes for coding messages *(Courtesy of the National Library of Ireland)*.

Hermann Görtz's handwritten cipher notes for coding messages *(Courtesy of the National Library of Ireland)*.

'Konstanz', 245 Templeogue Road, home of Stephen Carroll Held and safehouse used by Hermann Görtz.

GÁRDA SÍOCHÁNA

£500 REWARD

The above sum will be paid to any person giving information resulting in the arrest of **JOHN FRANCIS O'REILLY**, internee, who escaped from custody at Arbour Hill Detention Prison, Dublin, on the night of 5th-6th July, 1944

Landed by Parachute in Clare, 16th December, 1943, and had been in custody since that date.

DESCRIPTION:—Born Kilkee, Co. Clare, 7th August, 1916; height 5' 11¼"; weight 152 lbs.; fair hair; blue eyes; fresh complexion; slim build; wore dark brown suit with red stripes; black shoes; rubber soles and heels, believed size 10; bare head; sports shirt. May be wearing a light grey showerproof overcoat.

Information may be given to any Gárda Station.

Proportionate rewards will be paid for information concerning this man which will assist the Gárda in locating him.

A wanted poster from An Garda Síochana for SD agent John Francis O'Reilly, following his escape from Arbour Hill Prison *(Courtesy of the Military Archives of Ireland/Defence Forces)*.

Herman Görtz's mugshot following his arrest in 1943 at 1 Blackheath Park, Clontarf *(Courtesy of the Military Archives of Ireland/Defence Forces)*.

Students on the roof of TCD on VE Day, Dublin. The Union Jack was later burned by a group of students led by Charles J. Haughey *(Courtesy of the National Library of Ireland)*.

The funeral of Hermann Görtz, Deansgrange Cemetery, 1947 (© *Topfoto*).

Görtz's headstone, carved himself during his imprisonment.

Grave of Herman Görtz,
German Military Cemetery,
Glencree, Co. Wicklow.

Dr Richard Hayes with books at his desk in the
National Library of Ireland.

Dr Richard Hayes in later life.

St. Bricin's Military Hospital, where Görtz's trousers were searched by Richard Hayes *(Courtesy of the National Library of Ireland)*

Dr Richard Hayes receiving an Honorary Doctorate for his published work.

to his 17-year-old girlfriend in Bremen, Lissolette 'Lilo' Henze, to let her know that he was safe and well. Despite the objections of some of the authorities the request was approved by Frederick Boland at the Department of Foreign Affairs and G2's Col Liam Archer, who both noted that other internees were allowed mail privileges, and there was no logical reason why Schütz should be treated any differently.

Hayes continued to visit Schütz, who eventually gave him an insight into the use of the microdot system within the German military. Schütz explained that the idea was conceived by a group of German scientists attached to the Abwehr, and such was the cutting-edge nature of the microdots that he was the first German agent to leave Germany using them. He explained that he had been given such an honour due to the esteem in which he was held by the Abwehr. The Germans felt that the system was far superior to the use of 'G-Tinten' invisible ink for the purposes of transporting material, in that it could handle greater volumes of information. Hayes eventually deduced Schütz's real identity, dispelling his story that he was Hans Marschner.

He gave Schütz a copy of Ernest Hemingway's *A Farewell to Arms* and asked if he would jot down a few notes on the text for him. Hayes later compared these to handwriting samples intercepted when Schütz had contacted Werner Unland from Spain using his own identity. The examples matched perfectly, but they were signed 'G. Schütz'. Later G2 Director Liam Archer entered the cell carrying a large collection of files to give Schütz the impression that a large amount of information was known about him. Archer had previously been interrogating a man named Günther, and muttered to himself while leafing through the files 'Now, let's see … Günther, what shall we talk about today?' In disbelief, Schütz blurted out, 'How did you find that out?'

Schütz was detained in Arbour Hill prison for a further month and was eventually transferred to Sligo Prison. At the time of Schütz's arrest the Irish government had planned to intern all German agents in Sligo until the end of the war. However he was the only agent held here. He shared the prison with two other inmates, who were serving sentences for murder. When he arrived at the prison Schütz was immediately put into solitary confinement for eight weeks. He felt intimidated by the warders, who would regularly ask him questions to try and get more information out of him. On the outside Hermann Görtz could have arranged for the IRA to break Schütz out of prison, but there was no way for the two agents to communicate with each other, so such a plan never materialised.

During his time in prison Schütz contacted Hempel by letter, but the minister chose not to have any dealings with him, maintaining a distance from and wariness towards Schütz at all times. Schütz was at wits' end in Sligo when, after the eight weeks had elapsed, two detectives from Dublin Castle arrived and transported him back to Dublin, where he was to be interned in Mountjoy Prison. While Schütz was in Sligo the Irish government had decided to convert the prison hospital into an internment camp for captured Germans and members of the IRA. As Gardaí led Schütz to his cell his mind immediately turned to one thing: escape!

———

Dan Bryan knew that with Schütz detained G2 could turn their attentions to Görtz and Unland. Schütz had given them more than enough information on Unland in particular to allow them to act. There was no doubt that his confession and the ease with which he gave it directly contributed to the arrest of Werner Unland. This was a welcome development, as until then Unland had proven himself to be something of an enigma. His arrival into Ireland had predated that of Ernst Weber-Drohl; however, he was more of a 'sleeper' agent, who had integrated himself before beginning his espionage activities.

Unland was born in Hamburg on 6 August 1892, and saw service in World War I. He travelled to England in 1929 and registered himself there in June of that year. His passage to Britain was aided by the fact that he had met an English woman named Muriel Dugarde in 1928 whom he had become romantically involved with. The couple married in 1930 and travelled to England to take advantage of the fact that Muriel had family there. Unland secured a job as a textiles agent and hardware trader. On a visit home to Hamburg he was recruited into the ranks of the Abwehr controlled by Dr Karl Praetorious, the same agent who recruited Schütz three years later. Unland was instructed to report to the Abwehr on any matters that would be of a technical, industrial or intelligence interest. He was given a series of coded letters for the purposes of communicating such messages, as well as a monthly payment of £25 for the information.

When Unland returned to England he was given a managerial role in a fictitious company – a front with an actual physical address in London. In July 1939, Unland travelled to Dublin and set up a bank account with the Grafton Street branch of Ulster Bank, and in August 1939 he and Muriel moved to Dublin permanently. The couple took up residence in the Royal Marine Hotel in Dún Laoghaire before moving to the Gresham Hotel on O'Connell Street, where they would stay until April 1940.

The couple drew suspicion to themselves on several occasions, as other guests found them evasive and felt as though they were deliberately trying to avoid contact with other people. Eager to not draw any more attention to themselves, Unland approached an estate agent with a view to finding himself and Muriel a new home. He gave the estate agent the fake address of his company in London, and when the landlord in London received the letter addressed to Unland he realised that Unland had moved to Dublin without informing him, and without having paid several months' rent. He promptly contacted the Metropolitan Police in London, who passed the case onto the Irish authorities. Both G2 and the Gardaí now had his address at the Gresham; Unland was a marked man.

The couple were immediately put under surveillance by the Garda special branch. However Unland had succeeded in obtaining a new address for himself and his wife, and the couple eventually moved to 46 Merrion Square, the same address that Schütz would later be provided with. Unland successfully communicated with Germany from there. He had originally begun his communications at the Gresham, but the privacy of the address in Merrion Square was a far more suitable location for espionage. The bulk of Unland's transmissions were requests for money, which would prove him to be more of a nuisance than an asset to the Abwehr.

Using a coded letter method Unland began sending information to an address in Copenhagen which was actually a letter drop operated by the Abwehr. What Unland didn't know was that his messages were being intercepted by Gardaí and G2, who copied the messages and kept them on file while monitoring Unland's movements. They noticed that the Abwehr were sending money to Unland by means of direct bank deposits, but were confused as to how Unland was able to make cash lodgements into various banks. G2 grew suspicious that he was receiving payment from the German Legation, a view that was shared by Taoiseach Éamon de Valera.

In order to get to the bottom of the mystery G2 put a closer watch on Unland and began to monitor his telephone calls and purchases at local shops, as well as his banking transactions and outgoing mail. They observed that Muriel was buying large quantities of nail polish and guessed that this was used for some sort of secret writing due to the chemicals in the polish. Suspecting that he was being watched, Unland began to send letters to himself to test if he was under surveillance. Despite his precautions he was eventually caught after Dan Bryan recognised the aforementioned lipstick on Schütz's envelopes.

Unland was arrested on 21 April 1941 on Clare Street in Dublin while out on a rare walk with Muriel. Detectives detained Unland and took Muriel back to the couple's apartment and promptly searched it. Gardaí found a myriad of items of interest, including a portable typewriter as well as various bits of correspondence. They also found a book of instructions in the use of codes and ciphers, as well as details of the couple's account with Ulster Bank on Grafton Street. Muriel was taken to a Garda station for questioning and Gardaí were confident she would implicate her husband in espionage activities.

Their confidence was misplaced, however; Muriel had a background in theatre as an actress, and she proved adept at weaving a false account of both her and her husband's movements. She insisted that Werner was a textiles agent and that they were both innocent of any charges that would be brought against them. Her story was unnecessary, though, as Werner readily confessed once detectives began to interrogate him. His answers were vague, but they conflicted with Muriel's, and he was subsequently interned in Arbour Hill prison. The authorities decided against interning Muriel, despite her complicity in her husband's activities. She wrote to Dr Hempel in the German Legation asking him for financial support while her husband was interned, and after seeking approval from the German Foreign Ministry Hempel finally agreed and paid her a monthly allowance of £30. Meanwhile, in Mountjoy Prison, Günther Schütz was plotting his escape.

——

In prison Schütz had acquainted himself with a number of IRA men he thought might help him escape. Two of them were awaiting execution, and when the hangman arrived from England he brought news that a man named Richter had been caught and executed within 24 hours of landing on the English coast. Schütz had known Richter from Abwehr training in Hamburg, and the news sent a paroxysm of fear through him.

Richter's full name was Karel Richard Richter. Codenamed 'ROBOTO', the German spy was captured on 14 May 1941 when he parachuted illegally into the United Kingdom. Richter was convicted of espionage at the Old Bailey, sentenced to death and hanged at Wandsworth Prison on 10 December 1941. Schütz suddenly started to think that the Garda's jest in the pub in Taghmon may have been more serious than he originally thought; he grew frightened and began to plot his escape from Mountjoy.

Schütz's first attempt to escape involved digging a tunnel but he abandoned this attempt when it filled with water. He soon realised he would need the help of others to escape. The only place in the prison that prisoners could mix was the infirmary, and it was here that Schütz became acquainted with the IRA prisoners and an English embezzler who later supplied him with two hacksaw blades. Schütz gained the confidence of a sympathetic republican-minded prison guard, and asked the guard to purchase him a fur coat, dress, wig, shoes, silk stockings, head scarf and make-up.

The prison governor became aware of the purchases and arrived one morning in Schütz's cell to question him about them. Schütz reassured the governor, Seán Kavanagh, that the items were for his girlfriend back in Germany, and after some persuasion the governor believed him and left him to his own devices. Schütz then proceeded to lock himself away daily to file at the bars of the cell window with the hacksaw. He also enlisted the help of Jan van Loon, the Dutchman who was also imprisoned there for approaching the German Legation and offering his services as a would-be spy.

On 15 February 1942 both men broke through the bars of their cells and jumped the 23 feet to the ground. Van Loon ran to the wall and hoisted Schütz to the top, tossing him some parcels the men planned to take with them. Out of his bag Schütz produced a length of curtain rope he had acquired the same way as the ladies' clothing. Straddling the top of the prison wall, he threw the rope to van Loon, who caught it. As van Loon climbed the wall he lost his footing and fell to the ground below. Schütz called down to him to see if he was okay. Van Loon said that he thought he had broken his ribs; Schütz had a split second to decide what to do. He decided to leave van Loon behind, and climbed down the far side of the prison wall alone.

Schütz was now a free man. But time was of the essence. Dressed in his outfit he made his way to the address of one of the interned IRA men he had met in prison: James O'Hanlon, who lived at Innisfallen Parade in Phibsboro. Darkness was setting in, and the prison officers would soon notice he was missing. He knew he had to be swift, and that by dawn G2 would be searching for him.

Schütz's escape caused huge embarrassment to the authorities. Gardaí immediately put up wanted posters for Schütz using his alias 'Hans Marschner' and offering a reward of £500 for his capture. The poster described him as '30 years of age, 5ft 9 inches of pale complexion with dark brown hair, brown eyes with a scar between them and his left cheek'. It was noted on the posters that he spoke English very well. The escape also caused severe diplomatic problems for Eduard Hempel, who Schütz contacted looking for aid. He informed Hempel that he planned to leave Ireland by motorboat as soon as was possible, and complained to him that he was harshly treated while in Mountjoy.

Hempel looked into this, and was surprised to learn that Schütz had been given first-class treatment. His cell had been furnished with a carpet and he had access to a radio, money and a recreation room, as well as the benefit of visitation rights and access to money. Hempel informed Berlin that Schütz had escaped, but in front of the press he denied all knowledge of him, including the fact that he had been in contact with him. Secretly, the German High Command instructed Hempel to contact Schütz and to tell him to continue with his mission and to furnish him with sufficient funds to allow him to do so.

Schütz had made contact with IRA man James O'Hanlon's brother Joe, and through him met an associate of Caitlín Brugha, who became his intermediary for messages to Hempel. Through this contact Schütz wrote to Hempel on 1 April 1942 asking for £300 to be sent to him immediately, and for a seaplane or U-boat from Brest to be sent to pick him up. He informed Hempel that he had completed most of his mission, and wished to return to the continent to his comrades while the war continued. Hempel was extremely doubtful of Schütz's mission being in any way complete, thinking that he more than likely wished to return to Germany to see his mistress. He informed Schütz that British planes were patrolling the south-west coast of Ireland, and that facilitating his escape would be a PR disaster for the legation.

Hempel also informed Berlin of his predicament, and the disastrous effect it could have on the diplomatic mission to Ireland. The German Foreign Office contacted the Abwehr to advise them that aiding Schütz in his attempts to escape was out of the question, and would put a huge strain on the legation's legitimacy. The Abwehr disagreed, arguing that Schütz should be allowed to stay in Ireland for as long as possible. They felt it would be useful to have him on the ground should diplomatic relations between Ireland and Germany break down at any stage in the future. In reality they feared that the legation would be expelled by de Valera, and that Schütz's presence would provide them with a valuable link to what was happening in Ireland and England.

One problem remained, however. Schütz could no longer communicate with Germany. Despite the lack of a transmitter, the Abwehr thought he could use his supply of 'G-Tinten' invisible ink to send information to cover addresses in neutral countries. The Abwehr could not directly communicate with Schütz through the legation and instead urged Hempel to inform Schütz that he would receive £600 in small instalments through the legation, and that they were reviewing his request to leave Ireland. They also promised him a new transmitter and told him they were investigating the possibility of having this dropped to him via parachute once a safe means of doing so became available.

Satisfied at this response, Schütz decided to remain in Ireland, and for the next two months he moved between various addresses in Dublin during the dead of night. He initially stayed in Blackrock with an elderly couple at the arrangement of Caitlín Brugha. Dressed in a wig, he was brought to the house by Mrs Brugha's daughters, Neassa and Nóinín. Schütz soon became infatuated with Nóinín, who despite being a student had built up a considerable collection of IRA contacts. Nóinín had been engaged to a man named Seán O'Brien, who was a teacher in Dingle. O'Brien, also an active member of the IRA, had recently been captured and was serving a sentence in Mountjoy Prison.

In the meantime, Nóinín had established an intelligence network that communicated from Dublin to the IRA northern command in Belfast. The intelligence network operated through the passing of notes and word of mouth through various contacts, and people Nóinín deemed trustworthy. This network continued to operate while Schütz was staying with the couple in Blackrock.

————

The elderly couple who had put Schütz up fended off curious neighbours and friends, telling them that Schütz was a French foreign exchange student who had been trapped in Ireland after the war had broken out. Eventually keeping Schütz in the house proved more trouble than it was worth, and he was moved during the night back to Caitlín Brugha's house in Temple Gardens, Rathmines. Schütz distrusted Brugha and other IRA sympathisers, considering them to be fanatics with no discernible plan for their goals, but despite his reservations he was willing to put up with them in order to maintain his freedom.

Brugha explained to Schütz upon his arrival that the IRA link with Germany had been broken when Görtz was arrested, and she implored him to re-establish it. He was also asked to help secure arms for the IRA.

Brugha was determined that Schütz not suffer the same fate as Görtz, and had Schütz hide in a cellar if she heard any strange noises outside. Schütz was alarmed at some of the IRA activity he observed going on while in the house. He witnessed explosives being transported as well as a unique method of delivering messages to IRA leaders throughout the city. Mrs Brugha would give various messages to her children who would cycle to the houses of IRA leaders with the important communiqués.

Schütz also became acquainted during this time with members of the Belfast IRA, who offered him a deal. They proposed to arrange for a boat to drop him off near Brest in occupied France in return for arms, ammunition and money to be used to rebuild the IRA, which by this stage was under serious pressure for resources and finances. The boat's captain was to be Charles McGuinness, an IRA member who was colourful, to say the least. McGuinness was an adventurer, author and sailor, alleged to have been involved in various acts of patriotism and nomadic adventures. His history is shrouded in myths and mystery, making many of its details questionable to say the least.

McGuinness was born on 6 March 1893 and raised in Lower End in Derry. His mother, Margaret Hern, was of Spanish descent, and his father, Charles McGuinness, was an Irish ship captain. McGuinness started out his military career fighting for the English in Africa. He was enlisted in the Cameroon region, but deserted in 1916 when he heard about the rebellion for independence taking place in Ireland. He then joined the Afrikaners and fought against the British. It was shortly after this that he is rumoured to have been captured by the Germans. He convinced them that he was on their side, and fought with them for a time in their East African Campaign.

McGuinness returned to Derry in 1920, becoming involved in defending the Catholics during the Derry Riots, and was soon made the commander of the 3rd Battalion of the IRA's Northern Unit. After the War of Independence, McGuinness's adventures expanded even further, from Australia to Java and then to Easter Island, Indonesia, as well as Russia, Antarctica and China. During this time he took part in riots and mutinies on many different boats. Before World War I, he was gold mining in Australia, and went on adventures to the Mediterranean, Black Sea, Africa, Mexico, the West Indies, Brazil, China and Japan. His unique lifestyle earned him the nickname 'Nomad'.

Hempel was wary of McGuinness, considering him unreliable and easily bribed. In 1942 it came to his attention that McGuinness had volunteered to pass information about Ireland to Germany, and had been arrested in Cork on such a mission. Hempel informed Berlin of the news, and it transpired that McGuinness had obtained an organisational chart of the Irish Navy, and had planned to bring this to Hempel in the legation before his subsequent arrest. McGuinness knew nothing of the Abwehr, and as such proved to be no further threat to Hempel or any reasonable aid to Schütz. McGuinness was interned for the rest of the war, and eventually drowned in December of 1947, when his schooner bound for the Caribbean ran aground in a fierce gale off Ballymoney Strand in Co. Wexford.

During his stay with Caitlín Brugha, Schütz had been translating documents into German for his host. One in particular was a stinging attack on the 'dictatorship' of Taoiseach Éamon de Valera. Schütz also composed a coded message that he hoped to send to the Abwehr through the legation, informing them of his situation:

> I am safe for the last four weeks with help from the IRA. Country organised. Require 10 transmitter cases to be sent. Important plan for Northern Ireland urgently awaits your help. To stay is very dangerous. Cause Embassy Dublin to deliver 100 pounds to me at Kingston private. Embassy behaves as if to put me off. Wait on U-Boat or flying boat. Arrange with Minister. Have valuable material. Greetings to Lilo, Parents. Günther.

Schütz was confident his message would get to the Abwehr unhindered. However unbeknownst to him Dr Hayes had been monitoring messages from the Northern IRA group to Caitlín Brugha and Schütz through the listening station headed by Capt. John Patrick O'Sullivan at Collins Barracks. Hayes was able to write down a complete log of communications and successfully broke the code that was being used to encipher the messages. Although Schütz successfully communicated his message to the Abwehr, Hayes was able to inform Dan Bryan about the content of the messages.

At this stage Schütz was also growing increasingly suspicious that Hempel and the legation were trying to give him a wide berth. He wrote a letter to his superior officer and the man who had recruited him in Germany, Dr Karl Prateorius, telling him of his desire to return home. He also sent a cipher to the legation which was to be forwarded to the Abwehr, telling them that he planned to return to Germany.

———

Schütz's luck ran out on 30 April 1942. While staying with Caitlín Brugha he had received word from the IRA that he would be brought to Bray, where a ship was waiting to take him back to Germany. Schütz, dressed in his ladies' outfit and with a full face of make-up, waited calmly in the living room expecting two members of the IRA. Instead he was greeted by G2 officers and the Gardaí, who promptly arrested him. Caitlín Brugha had gone into Dublin leaving one of her daughters to look after Schütz, and she had opened the door without first checking who was outside.

Realising that the game was up, Schütz exclaimed, 'I'm the one you're looking for.' In an effort to escape arrest Schütz gave Gardaí a fake address and name, but the officers knew immediately that they had found the elusive Hans Marschner. One of the officers shouted, 'That's Marschner!' before quickly grabbing him. Gardaí conducted a similar raid on Mrs Brugha's business, Kingston Shirts, and later arrested both Caitlín Brugha and her daughter Nóinín. As officers handcuffed him Schütz cursed the IRA, who he felt had taken advantage of the rewards for his capture, and were ultimately in his eyes the architects of his downfall.

Schütz was taken to the Bridewell before being transported to Arbour Hill prison. On arrival at Arbour Hill he was taken in for questioning, where he told authorities that he had escaped as he wanted to return to Germany because of 'prison-phobia', but since returning was now impossible he would rather join his interned friends. A special section of the prison in Mountjoy that had once held female internees was cleared and now devoted to captured German spies until a suitable location could be found for them. Schütz was taken here and interned alongside Preetz, Obéd, Simon and Unland.

The prisoners lived in relative luxury, each with his own private bathroom. The men also had access to a private common room and a garden. Schütz himself was ironically lodged in a cell that had once been occupied by Éamon de Valera during the War of Independence, and during his time there G2 made sure that any outgoing mail from Schütz and other prisoners was heavily scrutinised and censored. On his return to prison Schütz was filled with dread and apprehension. He was no longer the harmless spy who had entertained the Gardaí while drinking pints of Guinness in Wexford. Instead he was now a recently escaped convict who had become embroiled in political intrigue against the Irish state.

His thoughts turned to Karel Richter, and he worried that he would suffer a similar fate. As he sat in his cell and pondered what would happen to him the door of his cell suddenly opened, and he was greeted by Commandant de Buitléar and Dr Hayes. De Buitléar looked Schütz up and down and said ominously, 'Mr Marschner, you were moving in very deep waters,' while Dr Hayes calmly studied the anxious German spy. Schütz tried to defend his actions, but he had incriminated himself, such was the volume of written material found in his possession. In the end de Buitléar and Hayes were able to extract every piece of information they needed from him, apart from who sheltered him before the Brughas.

Schütz feared the worst, thinking he would be put on trial and executed. In reality his lot was not to be as severe. He was placed in solitary confinement for three months before being rehoused with the rest of the prison population. He was shocked to find that the luxuries he had enjoyed before his escape were now removed, as he was locked up in a basic cell. He was eventually returned all of his possessions with the exception of course of the women's clothing he had escaped in. His spying equipment had been confiscated by G2 for future study and use for counter-intelligence. Despite the fact that he was subsequently recaptured, the Abwehr were pleased with his initial escape, and promoted Schütz in absentia to the position of lieutenant.

Eventually he was given better lodgings and access to a radio, library materials and a garden. Despite the concessions Schütz plotted daily to escape, though his schemes were to prove ultimately fruitless. Eventually it was decided to move all captured German agents to a specially constructed camp at Custume Barracks in Athlone, Co. Westmeath. The barracks were taken over by forces of the Irish Free State in 1922 and served as the headquarters of 4th Western Brigade until the brigade was disbanded. During the war sufficient space was made in the camp for the captured spies. The government hoped that relocation to Athlone would remove them from the public eye.

Schütz was transferred to the internment camp, along with van Loon (who had recovered from his broken ribs), Preetz, Unland, Weber-Drohl, Obéd, Tributh, Gärtner and Walter Simon. The Irish government was satisfied with the move, given the inadequacy of Mountjoy and the security threat posed by potential escapes. Schütz had taken advantage of many safe houses during his escape, and it was felt that Athlone was more remote and offered fewer opportunities for escapees to hide. Hempel contacted Berlin advising them of the conditions in which the prisoners in Athlone were housed. He noted that

> Unland had asked that £20 be given to each internee working for the authorities in Germany every two months. They get food and clothing from the Irish, so this would be for laundry expenses, extra food, tobacco, soap etc. Eight are interned at the moment: Unland, Tributh, Gärtner, Anderson (Simon), Preetz, Marschner, the man from India, Obéd and recently also Weber-Drohl who has received Legation support too. Mrs. Unland has received £30 per month and I have sent Unland £25. Please tell me if I should continue this or tell them to combine their reserves brought from home and given by the government – £614 total – for their expenses. As of July 31st, Tributh has £21, Gärtner 18, Simon 186, Marschner 67 and Obéd 322. The prison authorities keep this money but it is at the disposal of the internees, who have designated it as private property for buying personal items. Preetz is hardest up since he has no money at all.

Hempel worked on these financial arrangements secretly for some time, as he was successful in obtaining increases for Mrs Unland outside the prison. The internees refused to share their funds with Obéd and Simon, arguing that they shouldn't have to considering they were not German citizens. It was eventually agreed to put the men on a weekly allowance, but it proved difficult for the Germans to figure out who had responsibility for Simon and Preetz.

Eventually all the men apart from van Loon were given a stipend of £25. From time to time they were checked in on by relevant German government departments. The spies were given spacious cells in Athlone with carpets and a book shelf. They were even afforded the luxury of being allowed to listen to the news on the radio every day at 11 o'clock, although this practice was stopped following Hitler's invasion of Russia in June 1941. Many of the prisoners acquired pets, and Schütz spent much of his time in prison feeding his two cats.

———

With nearly all the German agents apprehended, attentions turned to the one who remained elusive: Dr Hermann Görtz. Fearing that the British would take a dim view of Schütz's escape and the fact that Görtz was still on the run, Minister for Justice Gerald Boland made a statement to the press that Schütz had been picked up, and would be interned until the present period of Emergency was over.

The British and the press may have been placated, but Boland omitted one crucial detail from his statement. When Schütz was rearrested, he was carrying a note that was coded and ready to send. It read, 'I have organised all of Ireland with the help of the IRA. Please send a submarine to pick me up.' Still angered by Schütz's escape, the authorities moved against IRA Chief of Staff Stephen Hayes; however, as it turned out they wouldn't need to. On 8 September 1941 Hayes walked into Rathmines Garda Station with chains on his legs and a revolver in his hand shouting that the IRA were going to shoot him.

On 30 June 1941, Northern-based IRA men had kidnapped Hayes, accusing him of being a spy. By his own account, he was tortured and 'court-martialled' for 'treason' by his comrades, and would have been executed had he not bought himself time composing an enormously long confession. He managed to escape that September, and to make his way to the Garda station in Rathmines. The Northern-based IRA men had taken over the leadership of the IRA and had contacted Görtz about Hayes. Seething with anger over his predicament and blaming Hayes for it, Görtz began to plot that if Hayes were gotten rid of he would be able to take over the IRA. He wrote to the Abwehr, telling them:

> The IRA leaders explained to me that countless treacheries within the leadership of the IRA led again and again to Hayes so they had decided to arrest and try him. He had already made confessions and was now writing them down. They asked whether I had proof against him. I was asked if I wanted him shot. I asked them for a few moments for me to consider. When the young IRA leaders asked what they should do they gave into my hands not nominally but practically the leadership of the IRA. I needed only to order the death of Hayes and I was their leader.

Of course, Görtz's idea was delusional, and it would have only made his predicament more difficult. His time on the run had made him unstable. He had become overwhelmed by paranoia, and sensed treachery at every corner. He thought the IRA had set him up, and was now more determined than ever to escape from Ireland and return to Germany. What he didn't realise was that he was now G2's number one target. With IRA leader Stephen Hayes and the other German agents detained it was surely only a matter of time before G2 tracked down Görtz, and he and Dr Hayes would come face to face. In the meantime however the Abwehr had a few tricks left up their sleeve.

VI

JOSEPH LENIHAN AND THE ARREST OF HERMANN GÖRTZ

'I am a German officer and I demand you treat me as such. I did my work and I did it well.'

HERMANN GÖRTZ, 27 November 1941

With all their agents in prison (with the notable exception of Hermann Görtz), the Abwehr went to new lengths in their efforts to infiltrate Ireland. As German agents were being caught routinely by G2, it was felt that more success might be gained by using Irish natives to spy in Ireland, as opposed to continental Europeans. Such agents would be less conspicuous, and would be able to blend into the population with greater ease. It was this line of thinking that brought Joseph Lenihan into the frame. Lenihan was born in Lickeen near Ennistymon, Co. Clare, at the turn of the 20th century, into what would become a famous Irish political dynasty.

One of five children, his brother Patrick Lenihan, known as P.J., was an Irish Fianna Fáil politician in the early 1960s. He held the distinction of being the only parent to be elected to an Irish parliament where his son was already a member. Two of his children, Brian Lenihan Sr and Mary O'Rourke, served as Irish cabinet ministers. A third, Paddy, served as a county councillor in Roscommon, although in the later stages of his career in the 1980s he left the party to join up with Neil Blaney's Independent Fianna Fáil party. Two of Patrick's grandchildren, Brian Lenihan Jr and Conor Lenihan, served as Minister for Finance and Minister of State respectively in the government of Taoiseach Brian Cowen.

The young Joseph Lenihan was an able student, completing his Leaving Certificate in St Flannan's College in Ennis and earning a scholarship to study Medicine at University College Galway. However, after early forays into the IRA he soon left his college course and took the state examination to join the Department of Customs and Excise, a career path he would follow until 1931. Lenihan travelled to the United States and returned to Ireland in 1933, shortly after Hitler seized power in Germany.

His time in the US fostered in Lenihan an anarchical nature of a sorts that was to get him into trouble on his return to the 'aul sod'. In July 1933 he was convicted of public disorder and received a two-week sentence. Not content to change his ways, he was convicted of forgery in 1935, this time receiving a nine-month sentence. MI5 had been monitoring Lenihan during this period as a suspected subversive, noting that he was involved in gun-running for the IRA and doubled as the producer of forged travel documents, thus the severity of his sentence.

Fed up with Ireland, Lenihan left for England once his sentence was complete in 1940. From here he travelled to the Channel Islands, settling in Jersey on the eve of its invasion by Germany. Between 3 September 1939, when the United Kingdom declared war against Germany, and 9 May 1940, very little changed in the Channel Islands. Conscription did not exist, though a number of people travelled to Britain to join up as volunteers. The horticulture and tourist trades continued as normal, and the British government eased restrictions on travel between the UK and the Channel Islands in March 1940, enabling tourists from the UK to take morale-boosting holidays in traditional island resorts. Lenihan himself had travelled to Jersey in the hopes of obtaining manual work in the agricultural industry on Jersey.

On 28 June 1940 Germany sent a squadron of bombers over the islands and bombed the harbours of Guernsey and Jersey. In St Peter Port, the main town of Guernsey, trucks lined up to load tomatoes for export to England were mistaken by the reconnaissance flights for troop carriers. The subsequent attack on them left many civilians dead. A similar attack occurred in Jersey, where nine people died. In total, 44 islanders were killed in the raids. The BBC broadcast a message that the islands had been declared 'open towns', and later in the day reported the German bombing of the island.

Lenihan had travelled to Jersey lacking a specific destination, content to roam, but with Nazi invasion certainly not being part of his plan he decided to try and escape the island, stealing a motor boat in a rash attempt to reach England. The motor soon flooded and he was washed ashore on the Cherbourg peninsula in Normandy in the German occupied zone, where he was picked up by members of the Gestapo.

Lenihan was taken to a Gestapo headquarters in Cartaret, where he was interrogated for a number of days. News soon began to circulate about the Irish prisoner and, sensing an opportunity, two German officers approached Lenihan, offering to release him if he would work as a spy for Germany. Although far from a committed sympathiser of Nazism, Lenihan agreed. He was taken to Paris and brought to German Intelligence Headquarters at 22 Avenue de Versailles in Paris's 16th Arrondissement. Here, Lenihan was trained in espionage, including the use of wireless transmitting equipment and 'G-Tinten' invisible ink.

On a rare night when Lenihan was let out by himself he was involved in a bar fight in the Normandy Hotel, and served yet another short spell in prison for his efforts. He eventually received further wireless training and was sent to various Abwehr headquarters to be briefed on his mission. He was tasked with parachuting into Ireland, where he would travel to Sligo and set up a weather-reporting station. Once the station was operational Lenihan was to contact Berlin, who would send him meteorological staff to help analyse his reports. For this he was to be paid a salary of 1,000 francs per month. His information was of huge significance to the Kriegsmarine and the Luftwaffe, who both required accurate weather information on England for military operations.

Lenihan was scheduled to be dropped in Ireland on 29 January 1941; however, his mission was to take an unfortunate turn. He took off from France in a Heinkel He111, similar to the crafts that had transported both Hermann Görtz and Günther Schütz to Ireland. But there was one crucial difference between those aeroplanes and Lenihan's. The Heinkel that Lenihan was travelling in had a faulty heater, and when the plane climbed to 30,000 ft it gave out completely. The entire crew apart from the pilot suffered from severe frostbite as a result, and Lenihan lost several toes as well as severely damaging his hands.

He was rushed to hospital in France, where he was nursed back to health and confined to a bed until he was ready to complete his mission. Six months later he was discharged and on 18 July 1941 he was dropped into Ireland, landing in Summerhill, Co. Meath. He was given two wireless transmitters and supplied with £500 and a supply of 'G-Tinten' invisible ink. Lenihan was also armed with a special type of invisible ink that revealed its message when mixed with a red powder, heated to 60°C and viewed under ultraviolet light.

He had with him as well a copy of the *Pan in the Parlour* by Norman Lindsay for use in constructing his coded messages, as well as a typed copy of his instructions. And in case of emergency Lenihan was given two backup novels to be used as book codes: *A Windjammer's Half Deck* by Shalimar and *The Loot of the Lazy*. He was also supplied with a Morse code device that allowed him to transform a standard FM/AM radio into a transmitter.

After his jump and when safely on the ground Lenihan hid his camouflage parachute in a ditch, and hastily made his way to Dublin to contact his family and friends. Within three days G2 became aware of the presence of an illegal parachutist in the Meath area. In a top-secret memo Dan Bryan informed his superiors that

> On Monday 21st, July 1941, a parachute and harness equipment were found at Isaacstown near Summerhill in Co. Meath, under circumstances which reasonably indicated that someone had landed from a plane in this country. The parachute which had been concealed in a watercourse or a ditch was pulled out by cattle drinking.

Sensing that something was amiss, Bryan contacted coastal watch posts to see if any German aircraft had entered Irish airspace in the week leading up to the discovery of the parachute. Bryan was alarmed when the reports came back, noting, 'An examination on the reports on aircraft revealed that a plane had come in over the south coast on the morning of the 18th, flew North to Summerhill where it turned East and Southeast and proceeded to fly out to sea over Co. Waterford.'

Bryan and G2 decided to further monitor the mysterious individual who had entered the country; however, Lenihan's indiscretions would soon incriminate him. On the morning of 24 July the Department of Finance contacted G2 to inform them that the Ulster Bank on O'Connell Street had directed their attention to an unusual lodgement of English currency on 19 July. The manager had not been present at the time, but when the transaction was researched it was found that a man named Joseph Lenihan had made the lodgement, and had given his address as Moran's Hotel on Talbot Street.

It was ascertained that Lenihan had only stayed the previous night in the hotel, and had then travelled to Athlone. The manager had reported the lodgement as he felt that there was something sinister about it. He was also under pressure from his head office in Belfast, who became curious as to the origin of the money. G2 now knew Lenihan's name and his last known whereabouts, and began a widespread manhunt for him. Unaware of the furore he had caused, Lenihan arrived in Athlone at the house of his brother Patrick, who was then managing a textile plant in the town. En route Joseph visited his brother Gerald in Dublin and bought himself an assortment of new clothes with his spy money.

When he arrived at his brother's door he concocted a bizarre story to explain his absence over the previous few years. He claimed implausibly that he had joined the merchant marine and had been torpedoed off Cadiz in Spain en route to Valparaíso in Chile. Gerald initially believed his brother, thinking it at least explained the damage done to Joseph's feet and hands. In Athlone he told Patrick a slightly different story, which was at least somewhat rooted in the truth. He explained to his bewildered brother that he had escaped the Channel Islands with the help of a German non-commissioned officer who had taken pity on him. He had then enlisted in the merchant marine and his ship was then sunk off the Cape Verde islands, and his newfound wealth was back pay from the merchant marine.

Both Gerald and Patrick Lenihan were undoubtedly delighted to see their long-lost brother, but were somewhat wary of him. They contacted their sister Maura to discuss the situation, and she too travelled to Athlone to meet her sibling. Soon word came through to local Gardaí that Lenihan was in Athlone. The family were discreetly informed by a local Garda who rang ahead and Joseph escaped before the Gardaí raided the house to look for him. Lenihan escaped on a bicycle, making his way to Geashill, Co. Offaly. The bike, which he had taken from his sister-in-law, had recently been outfitted with a new basket for shopping, and its commandeering by Joseph caused some upset to his brother's wife.

———

After leaving his family Joseph travelled to Dundalk, where he deposited a suitcase containing a wireless transmitter and his supply of invisible ink in the Lerne Hotel in the town centre. Lenihan then crossed the border into Northern Ireland, where gave himself up to the RUC, sking that he be taken at once to MI5. He was taken to Belfast and put on the next flight to London.

When he arrived in England he was detained under the Arrival from Enemy Territory Act. On 23 July he was taken to a camp for detainees of the intelligence service and was vetted for the Double-Cross system. A significant number of agents passed through the Double-Cross system. Many of these were captured, turned themselves in or simply announced themselves, and were then used by the British to broadcast mainly disinformation to their Nazi handlers back in Germany. Its operations were overseen by the Twenty Committee under the chairmanship of John Cecil Masterman; the name of the committee comes from the number 20 in Roman numerals: 'xx' (i.e. a double-cross).

The Double-Cross system would eventually play a huge role in 'Operation Fortitude', the strategic deception of Germany with regards to the location of the Normandy landings. The system coincided with the use of the Ultra intelligence programme, which derived from Alan Turing's breaking of the Enigma and Lorenz enciphering systems at Bletchley Park. These combined strands would ultimately lead to the winning of the war for the Allies. MI5 chief of counter-espionage Cecil Liddell was somewhat perplexed by Lenihan, and convened a meeting to ascertain if he could be useful for the Double-Cross system or even for espionage in general:

> We had a conference about Joseph Lenihan and we came to the conclusion that the only use we could make of him would be by impersonation. Lenihan was dropped in the Curragh with instructions to send weather reports to Sligo and to proceed to England in order to obtain information about air raid damage. He had given himself up in Northern Ireland because he had a criminal record in the south. He is wanted for unlawful assembly, presumably in connection with an IRA meeting, and he has also done some fraud. The Irish have already discovered his parachute, and his set, which has so far not been taken, is left at a house on the Eire side of the border.

Liddell approved Lenihan for work in the Double-Cross system, giving him the codename 'BASKET', which perhaps was a reference to the earlier theft of his sister-in-law's bicycle. He was given an assignment sending letters to his Abwehr cover address on Plaza de Jesús in Madrid. Lenihan's transmitters were still in the Lerne Hotel in Dundalk; however Liddell and the Irish authorities came up with a unique solution for what to do with them:

> Roger Moore of the Royal Ulster Constabulary has come to an agreement with his contact in the Garda Síochána by which we are to be lent Lenihan's wireless set for eight days. We are to lend the auxiliary one-way set to the Eire government for a similar period. Before the agreement was signed the matter was referred to Éamon de Valera.

Lenihan was given a series of coded phrases by MI5 that he could insert into normal conversations and thus communicated in this fashion. Some of the phrases included: Congratulations on the birth of a son = radio in order. Congratulations on the birth of a daughter = light damage, can be repaired. Congratulations on the birth of a child = radio inoperative. With these codes Lenihan was tasked to report by radio after 10 days.

Despite his recruitment, his entry into Ireland had a negative effect on Irish–British relations in many respects. MI5 were concerned that both the Irish and Northern Irish Observer Corps failed to pick up his aircraft in time and report it to authorities. They were also concerned that his cover story seemed to arouse little or no suspicion among his family or friends, and as a result MI5 decided to put a watch on his correspondence, along with that of all Irishmen on the continent. Copies were sent to G2, who were asked to identify and provide full particulars of any men listed. The wariness of MI5 soon extended to Lenihan's role as an agent, and he was soon relieved of his duties, as it would have been necessary for him to broadcast from Sligo, and since he was wanted by the Irish authorities G2 would have to be included in the mission.

While Liddell felt that Bryan might cooperate with MI5, it was thought that Irish neutrality would ultimately prevent Lenihan from being able to be used. If German agents were to find out he was broadcasting from within Éire it could have caused a diplomatic incident. The Double-Cross system was founded on the principle that the agent be captured soon after arrival and his presence in the country known by as few people as possible. Lenihan's sojourns in Athlone and Dublin certainly precluded him from any further missions; however he was allowed to remain in England after his release from duty with MI5. The RUC had complained to Liddell about Lenihan being used as a possible agent, as they suspected him of communicating important information to people in the south.

Despite these worries Lenihan was well treated while in custody, and seemed to receive special treatment compared to other German agents. In many instances such agents were jailed or even executed. At one stage Liddell considered using Lenihan as an agent on a boat between England and South America. He looked through his file in order to gauge Lenihan's suitability, and eventually decided against it after coming to the conclusion that Lenihan had a laid-back attitude to truth. He noted that he didn't believe his story of how he originally came to be in Ireland, and felt that the only way he could make any future use of Lenihan was to completely wipe out his past and give him a completely new identity.

However they ultimately decided against using him as an agent as they thought it would be almost impossible for him to talk to the Germans without disclosing his identity and explaining how he came into the hands of the British authorities. For the work that Lenihan carried out for MI5 he was given £250 – £50 up front and £200 to be placed in a bank account which he could access after the war on the basis that he 'behaved himself'. He was told to report his movements to MI5 and was warned against going back to Ireland, and furthermore to never again leave England.

These orders notwithstanding, in 1942 Lenihan applied for a permit to holiday in Éire. Liddell contacted Dan Bryan through an intermediary, who replied to Liddell that he had no problem with such a visit, and that the Irish authorities would do their utmost to 'keep him under constant supervision but cannot guarantee 100% supervision due to the man's habit and character'. Lenihan, unhappy with this decision, took matters into his own hands, and was caught in July 1942 trying to join the crew of a fishing boat leaving Fleetwood, Hampshire to fish off the coast of Donegal. From this point on Lenihan returned to civilian life in England, and tragically had little if any contact with his family in Ireland thereafter.

He eventually moved to Manchester, where he got a job in a sorting office with Royal Mail. He seemed to have few friends, and often spent his spare time in the local library reading voraciously. In 1974 the Lenihan family received a phone call to say that he had died. They travelled to Manchester and his body was repatriated to Ireland. He was buried in Esker Cemetery in Lucan, where Professor Robert Dudley Edwards, then Professor of History at UCD, gave the graveside oration. In the years after the war he never tried to profit from his story. He was also held in good esteem by MI5, with Cecil Liddell writing in complimentary terms of Lenihan, likening him to a politician, such was his gift of the gab: 'Though of rough appearance, he was fairly well educated, intelligent and with a phenomenal memory for facts and faces. He gave more fresh and accurate information about the Abwehr in the Netherlands and Paris than any other single agent.'

Much of the information provided by Lenihan and the transmitters that he left behind were invaluable in apprehending other German agents on the loose in Ireland. Such information was paramount in the capture of Hermann Görtz.

————

Görtz had in the interim grown increasingly frustrated with his situation in Ireland. While he now had a functioning transmitter, most of the messages that the Abwehr received seem to be concerned with Görtz escaping to France as soon as possible. In addition to this they were of poor quality, and frequently scrambled. On one occasion Görtz ludicrously suggested that he steal a boat and sail out to sea, where he would unfurl a swastika flag to attract the attention of the Luftwaffe, who could then bring him to safety.

Such a plan was the idea of a man acting more in desperation than with an analytical and tactical mind. In reality the Abwehr had decided to wash their hands of Görtz, having come to the conclusion that he was more trouble than he was worth. On 20 September 1941 he had tried one last time to escape, this time by motor cutter, but the attempt ended in failure. As a result the Abwehr began to develop severe doubts about Görtz's competency, as well as his mental state. Indeed even the IRA had communicated with them to voice their anger with him.

With nobody left to turn to, Görtz attempted to turn to some of the figures that he had befriended in Irish society, many of whom visited him at a safe house he was staying in near Dalkey. Among those who visited him were Fianna Fáil senators who had once been in the ranks of the IRA with Éamon de Valera. It was even speculated that rogue elements in the Irish Army had offered to transport Görtz back to Germany; however this plan too would ultimately founder. In a final attempt to rectify his situation Görtz arranged a meeting with the new IRA leader, Pearse Paul Kelly, to see if he could persuade him to join with rogue elements in the Irish Army in an attempt to complete Plan Kathleen.

Time was running out for Görtz, however. With many of his colleagues in jail and with few options left he returned to the house of the Farrell sisters at 7 Spencer Villas in Glenageary. G2 had been monitoring the house, and on 24 September a search warrant was served on the residence. Gardaí discovered a $100 bill in the living room, and the sisters were arrested and brought in for interrogation. However, neither volunteered anything in the interviews. Detectives decided to keep an eye on the house, and the next day they returned to question the sisters once more. The authorities' diligence paid off when they found an envelope under the front door marked 'Doc – most important and urgent'. The Gardaí also targeted the house of Görtz's lover, Mrs Coffey, and found a novel in Germanic script.

In November Görtz moved to the house of Patrick Claffey at 1 Blackheath Park in Clontarf. It was to be his last residence as a free man. Görtz had been moved into the house by a man named Joseph Andrews, who had some involvement in republicanism; however Andrews was an opportunist, and informed the Gardaí that Görtz was staying at the address. Despite being warned by Pearse Paul Kelly, Görtz decided to stay in the house anyway.

On 17 September Görtz began to notice strange noises, and became convinced that he was about to be captured by MI5. He left the house but returned a few weeks later, and on 27 November Görtz finally met his date with destiny. Gardaí burst into the house, and Hermann Görtz was placed under arrest and held under the Emergency Powers Act. Gardaí were actually raiding the premises next door and decided to investigate as they noticed suspicious people outside the house.

When Gardaí discovered Görtz in the sitting room he was sitting calmly in an armchair smoking a cigarette. Gardaí placed handcuffs on Görtz, who immediately became aggressive and belligerent towards the officers. He demanded he be treated as a German officer. He began shouting that he did his job in Ireland well, and as the officers hauled him out the door of the house he bellowed, 'You are arresting the best friend Ireland has. Your government know why I'm here!'

Pearse Paul Kelly was also arrested; he had come back to the house to find Görtz, as they had planned to travel to Germany together. As Kelly knocked on the front door of the house, expecting Görtz to answer, he was instead greeted by two detectives brandishing revolvers. He, like

Görtz before him, was placed under arrest and held under the Emergency Powers Act.

Before they left Clontarf Gardaí searched Görtz for any incriminating material. They couldn't believe their luck; he had been carrying a diary, a set of keys and a Luftwaffe identity book under the alias 'Heinz Kruse', as well as his Wehrmacht identity card and £25. The diary contained plans for his escape as well as the addresses and contact details of many of his lovers. Gardaí brought Görtz to Arbour Hill prison, where he continued to insist he was Heinz Kruse, although eventually he admitted his true identity.

In reality G2 were well aware of who he was, as they had been tracking his movements since he had landed in Ballivor over a year previously. When Hempel heard of Görtz's arrest he became extremely anxious, and decided that he would avoid contact with him at all costs. His caution would come to no good, and in January 1942 Görtz wrote to Hempel asking him for help. Görtz wrote, 'I am an officer of the Luftwaffe. I ask you urgently to get in contact with me as I feel the honour of the German Wehrmacht is involved. Heil Hitler.'

News of Görtz's arrest soon spread; it was only a matter of time before it reached Germany. The German Foreign Ministry contacted Hempel and aided him in drafting an official response to the unfortunate turn of events. Hempel was to state categorically that Görtz had been sent to Ireland to facilitate attacks on England with the help of the IRA, and that he at no stage posed any threat to Ireland, its people or its neutrality. Hempel met with Joseph Walshe of the Department of External Affairs and informed him that if Görtz had in any way involved himself politically it was of his own volition.

Hempel told Walshe that any political intrigue on Görtz's part was probably due to his disturbed state of mind or through his clear personal anxiety and wish to return home to Germany. Within days of being caught most Irish newspapers carried stories of his arrest. The *Irish Independent* carried a headline that read, 'German parachutist arrested in Dublin', while other papers identified Görtz and linked him to the raid in Templeogue the previous year. Such was the furore caused by Görtz that his arrest was also reported in British papers.

The Abwehr were some of the last to learn of his fate; shortly afterwards they prepared an official statement claiming that 'Captain Görtz had a mission as a German officer against England but was unfortunately delayed in Ireland en route to England.' In truth the German authorities were not too concerned with Görtz's arrest, and put the blame on him for getting involved with rogue elements in the Irish Army, particularly Gen. MacNeill. The sole ambition of the German authorities was now to protect Hempel's mission in Ireland, and Görtz was now superfluous to this.

Privately Hempel was delighted that Görtz was out of the way, and that his own diplomatic mission to Ireland was not under the same stress as when he was released. Of all the German spies that came to Ireland Görtz was at liberty for the longest. Most had been detained within 48 hours of their arrival on Irish soil, but Görtz was free for over a year. There are a number of reasons why this might have been the case. The authorities may have simply repeatedly missed him each time they went to arrest him. Or G2 may have let him remain on the loose in order to arrest IRA members with whom he was acquainted. Or perhaps, most sinisterly, Görtz was allowed to remain at large by de Valera until the Taoiseach was sure what way the tide of the war would turn. Indeed Görtz would have been an extremely useful asset if it had turned in favour of the Germans.

To this day many in IRA circles claim that Görtz's arrest was an accident, and that the authorities were actually looking for Pearse Paul Kelly. Once Görtz was arrested and the press found out about his incarceration it was impossible to release him again. Whatever the reasons for his capture, Görtz was taken to Arbour Hill, where he was interrogated by Gardaí and G2.

When news filtered through that Görtz had been captured, Dan Bryan contacted Richard Hayes and tasked him with interrogating the new prisoner. Mindful of the threat posed by information leakage from Görtz's coded messages, Dr Hayes was eager to meet the new arrival. What followed was a game of cat and mouse between the cunning Nazi spy and the genius Irish librarian.

VII

GLASS PLATES AND SPY TROUSERS: BREAKING THE GÖRTZ CIPHER

'This was the best Cipher in our experience used by the Germans during the war. It was evidently used for very special purposes.'

DR RICHARD J. HAYES

Outside of Arbour Hill Görtz's arrest was causing all sorts of trouble for his colleagues and fellow conspirators. His radio operator Anthony Deery was arrested on 12 March 1942 at 47 Upper Clanbrassil Street after a tip-off from an undercover soldier, and Hempel and the legation were left fielding embarrassing questions from the press in the wake of his arrest. Deery was eventually sentenced to 10 years in prison. He was found in possession of a wireless set belonging to Hermann Görtz, which was seized, as was a series of enciphered messages that had been hidden inside a piccolo. These were brought to Dr Hayes, who studied them in detail and soon broke the code used to encipher them. Although Deery had been able to communicate with Germany, the Abwehr didn't rate his messages very highly, and regarded his reports as over-exaggerated nonsense. In truth they only entertained them on the basis that while they continued they could maintain some link to Görtz.

As Hermann Görtz sat in his cell in Arbour Hill he began to formulate a story to tell the intelligence officers that wouldn't jeopardise any ongoing Abwehr operations. Suddenly the door of his cell opened, and in walked a small, unassuming man who introduced himself as Captain Grey.

Accompanied by Commandant Éamon de Buitléar and posing as a Nazi sympathiser, Dr Hayes questioned Görtz in German about how he had arrived in Ireland. The initial exchange went on for a few hours. Görtz was impressed by his interrogators' fluency in his mother tongue, and slowly but surely he began to open up to them. Hayes sat opposite Görtz and smiled at him gently as the German recounted his journey, telling a story that was a mixture of fact and fiction. He recounted to Hayes that Jim O'Donovan had first learned of his presence in Laragh from a broadcast he had made from Northern Ireland, and that the operator of the set had heard that he had arrived in Co. Tyrone and instructed him to inquire for him at three addresses, one of which was Mrs Stuart's.

In an effort to exonerate his lover, Görtz insisted that Iseult Stuart had not told O'Donovan about him. He further elaborated that the fictional radio operator (a student from Belfast), who was in no way connected with the IRA, had visited him a few days after his arrival and helped him with his radio set, which was too weak to broadcast to Germany. Görtz insisted that if he had been dropped in Northern Ireland the man would have been able to contact Germany for him. Hayes listened intently to Görtz, jotting down various observations in his diary.

He asked if the messages he sent were in code, to which Görtz replied, 'Of course,' adding that he had received the code in Germany and that he and the Belfast student aiding him had met there. Görtz said he thought the Belfast man posed so much of a threat to his mission that his transmitter would have been discovered and his plans ruined. He told Hayes that he advised the Belfast man to discontinue transmissions, and for him to join the British Armed Forces in order to draw attention away from his illegal activities.

He explained that he was to install a wireless transmitter in Northern Ireland to be codenamed 'Gustl'. This would then be used to communicate with a station in Germany called 'Irene' at stated times every week. Hayes asked Görtz how he planned to replace the wireless set that he had lost during his initial parachute jump. Görtz explained that a replacement was to be sent once the German High Command had proof that he landed safely. In order to inform the Abwehr that he had arrived safely, he continued, he had been instructed to send two postcards to addresses in

Spain which would then be forwarded on to Germany. The stamps were to be strategically placed on the postcards, acting as a signal to the Abwehr that he had safely arrived on Irish soil. If this failed he would get in touch with the German Legation through Mrs Stuart, and the High Command would sort out any issues with the Foreign Office.

Hayes noted Görtz's observations before asking him if he had made any transmissions in the south. Görtz replied that he hadn't, and to his amazement Hayes took out a sketch of a transmitter from his notes, saying that it had been seized in a raid of IRA leader Stephen Hayes's house. He asked Görtz if he could explain the origins of the sketch to him. Staring at the drawing in disbelief, Görtz explained that he had drawn the sketch for the IRA when asked for advice about the setup of communications between Éire and Northern Ireland, and that he had known it was illegal to be in possession of a wireless set in Ireland. He told Dr Hayes that he had asked the IRA leader about the legalities of owning a wireless set, but that he had been misinformed.

Görtz also explained that the IRA had selected the Dingle Peninsula as the base for the landing of arms as the IRA had indicated they had good men there, and that a U-boat would not be able to cruise close to the rocky coast so they would need a motorboat to ultimately bring the arms ashore. Dr Hayes listened to Görtz's story, all the while picking holes in the narrative. Instead of confronting him, Hayes thanked Görtz warmly for his time, smiled and excused himself.

Görtz was delighted with himself, thinking his ruse had worked and that he had done enough to avoid getting himself in further trouble. But Hayes had other plans for him. During the raid on Stephen Held's house in Templeogue, many pages of ciphers had been recovered. Hayes decided to bring one in to Görtz for him to solve. Eager to convey the idea that he meant no ill will towards Ireland, Görtz began work on the cipher in his cell. Little did Görtz know that Hayes had already solved the cipher, and was merely testing Görtz's trustworthiness. Görtz began to scribble his own censored version of the cipher onto a page for Hayes: 'HE (O'DONOVAN) FEARS I SHALL BE DISAPPOINTED WITH CHIEF… KNOWS NOTHING ABOUT RATHLIN.'

Dr Hayes was fully aware that Görtz was being duplicitous, that the message had no mention of Rathlin and that Görtz had changed its contents, which dealt with Irish coast and air defences. Despite Görtz's many untruths Hayes was able to gain a good indication of the kind of individual he was dealing with. While he didn't agree with Görtz's politics and thought him to be a rogue, the relationship between the men was pleasant. This was essential, as Hayes wished to maintain this for as long as possible, since he knew he would need to get more information out of Görtz at a later stage.

———

Meanwhile Hempel was severely agitated about what to do about Görtz. He feared Görtz would be tried in an open court, which would have been an embarrassment for the legation. However, Görtz was instead interned in Arbour Hill, and it was here that Hayes began to work on breaking his code. G2 had informed MI5 of Görtz's imprisonment and trial, although the details were kept intentionally hazy. Guy Liddell noted in his diary that 'Dr Görtz has been tried by military tribunal condemned to death and reprieved. We have not heard this officially, but we understand this to be the case as a pretext for pressing the Eire government to forgo its neutrality and turn the Germans out. There is fairly conclusive proof that Görtz was working in close conjunction with the IRA.'

It was clear to Dan Bryan that they would have to yield a positive result from Görtz's arrest in order to appease the British. As G2 and MI5 quarrelled over the issue, the German High Command instructed Hempel to make an official statement about Görtz to the Irish government. Hempel approached the Taoiseach directly though the Department of External Affairs in which de Valera was the minister in situ. Hempel assured the Taoiseach that the German government had never sent anyone to Ireland with political motivations, and that no action had ever been taken against Ireland. He also gave assurances that the German government regretted that more attention had been given to this case than was necessary.

Hempel stressed that Germany's attitude towards neutrality was in no way changed by recent events, i.e. the entry of the United States into the war. He went further, stating that 'the attitude of the German government is exactly as it was stated by the Taoiseach at the outbreak of the war'. Hempel was eager to preserve the status quo, and in many ways his own role in Ireland, at all costs. However, Görtz was growing increasingly frustrated with being in prison, and began to concoct an escape plan. He decided to try and smuggle messages out to his supporters, such as the Farrell sisters and the wife of republican Austin Stack, hoping that a plan could be conceived to help him escape.

Görtz tried to win the favours of military guards in the prison to try and smuggle out his messages. He approached Sgt Power and Cpl Lynch, who were working in the prison, and offered them money to carry his messages. The men refused, and brought the messages to Dr Hayes, who copied them and immediately began working on deciphering them. Despite the fact that he had seen samples of Görtz's cipher the previous year, after the Held raid, Hayes felt that in order to break the cipher he would need to gain some knowledge as to what the keyword was, or get a better idea of the intricacies of the system Görtz was using.

Hayes decided that Görtz should be approached directly about his enciphering system. He and Commandant de Buitléar asked Görtz how his system worked, and Görtz decided to go along with them to a certain degree. He told the two intelligence agents that he would show them how his system worked, but refused to give them the keyword. Görtz asked Hayes if he could see some of the messages that had been seized during the Held raid, and began to decipher them. Hayes keenly observed Görtz, and after the messages had been decoded he privately said to de Buitléar that they should go through Görtz's possessions to see if they could find a clue to what his keyword was. Hayes reasoned to de Buitléar that in most cases agents kept keywords in their heads, but that there was always the chance that Görtz might have slipped up and written something down. It was a chance both men were willing to take, but the question remained as to how they could search Görtz's possessions without his consent.

Hayes decided that he would chat to Görtz to try and get a clue. He was eager to break the code as he had become suspicious that Görtz was smuggling messages successfully out of the jail, though he was unable to prove it immediately. He was concerned about the very real danger that Görtz's messages posed to Ireland's neutrality, as well as the greater war effort. He knew that if any information, no matter how insignificant, was leaked by Görtz out of Ireland, it could have a disastrous effect on the outcome of the war.

The British had been using the German agents they had working under the Double-Cross system to strategically deceive the German High Command about the location of the Normandy landings, which had been in preparation since the Americans entered the war after the attack on Pearl Harbour on 7 December 1941. The Germans were being led to believe that the main attack was to come along the Pas-de-Calais, which was almost within sight of England.

Instead the plan was to land troops in Normandy, designed so that the German High Command would think that the Normandy attack was only a feint, and that the main assault was to come at a later stage. If Görtz was able to communicate this plan in any way with the Abwehr it could upset the very delicate strategic picture. Hayes knew that the fate of the country and potentially the outcome of the war rested on his shoulders. His apprehension was well placed, as Görtz had finally convinced an Irish soldier with republican sympathies to smuggle messages out of his cell. The clock was ticking, and only Dr Hayes stood in Görtz's way.

––––

The soldier who was paid a small amount of cash by Görtz to smuggle out messages was Cpl Joseph Lynch. He brought letters from Görtz to the wife of republican Austin Stack, who had died on hunger strike in 1929. She, much like Caitlín Brugha, harboured a deep hatred for the British, and as a result was willing to aid German spies in Ireland. Lynch's failure to alert military intelligence to his activities created a serious security situation; G2 would later discover Lynch's deception, and questioned him on the matter in 1944.

Lynch suffered a nervous breakdown as a result of the discovery of his betrayal, and admitted fully to his part in smuggling the messages. Dr Hayes had been suspicious of Lynch, but since he had no proof, and due to his status as a civilian seconded to military intelligence, he was unable to do anything about it. Despite the setback Hayes was confident that he had come up with a novel way to figure out Görtz's keyword. He would have to act quickly; time was running out.

Hayes continued visiting Görtz in his cell, where the men chatted in a friendly nature, maintaining their good working relationship. On one visit Hayes noticed that Görtz was carrying a considerable bunch of papers with him in his trousers. Görtz was permitted to have papers in his cell which he used to pass the time by writing. During his incarceration he translated into German several stories by W.B. Yeats and wrote drafts of a play. He also kept a diary of his observations and experiences in prison.

Hayes knew that the papers most likely contained a clue to the keyword, but he would have to figure out some way of seeing them without Görtz finding out. He searched Görtz's cell regularly when he was out on exercise, but he never found anything that was of any use to breaking the code. Such was the importance of the papers that Görtz had been taking them with him to the exercise yard. Although Hayes could have confiscated the papers from Görtz, he didn't want to spoil the relationship he had built with the spy, as he was mindful that such a relationship could be useful at a later stage. Hayes would have to find another way. During one of his many conversations with Görtz an opportunity presented itself that Hayes knew he could take advantage of.

Görtz had complained to Hayes about a pain he was suffering from. It stemmed from trouble with a duodenal ulcer, which he had been treated for by a doctor in Blackrock while on the run. However the pain had returned, and Görtz was suffering considerable discomfort from his complaint. Hayes reassured Görtz that he would get him seen by a doctor, and made arrangements with the prison doctor for him to be examined. Görtz was delighted that such attention was being paid to his health, and gladly obliged. The doctor who examined Görtz told him he would need x-rays, and Hayes planned to follow Görtz to the hospital and go through his clothes to find the papers while this was done.

The next day Görtz was transferred under armed guard to St Bricin's Military Hospital in Arbour Hill. Hayes travelled there in advance and hid in the doctor's private room downstairs so that Görtz wouldn't see him. Görtz was taken upstairs to a waiting room, where he changed into a dressing gown. Hayes crept into the room when Görtz went for the x-ray, planning to copy the documents and replace them while Görtz was being seen by the doctor. But to his dismay Hayes couldn't find them. Then he realised that Görtz must have forgotten to take the papers when he changed into a different suit to come for his x-ray. Hayes rushed to his cell and to his relief found the papers in Görtz's other clothes.

Hayes hurried to the GPO on O'Connell Street, where there was machinery for copying documents. The process was slow and arduous, involving first making a negative from which a print could then be made. Hayes had 15 pages of documents to copy, and time was running out before Görtz would be back from his x-ray. In haste Hayes arranged with the doctor to stall Görtz until Hayes gave him the signal that he could be safely let back into the waiting room. However the process had taken much longer than expected. The telephone rang in the GPO and Hayes answered it.

On the other end was the doctor in the hospital, who advised Hayes that Görtz had been x-rayed in every position known to medical science, and that in some positions he had been x-rayed twice. He told Hayes that Görtz was blue with the cold, and asked that he hurry back before his patient became suspicious as to the delay. Hayes told the doctor to delay Görtz for another 10 minutes and the doctor obliged. Hayes then ran to Görtz's cell to place the papers back in the trousers, then took the copies to his desk in McKee Barracks to see if they could yield any clues to Görtz's keyword.

Amazingly Görtz returned to his cell totally unaware that anything out of the ordinary had happened. Hayes and Commandant de Buitléar studied the papers, and while they couldn't find any clues as to the keyword they did find a complete plan drafted by Görtz about how he intended to escape from Arbour Hill. Hayes was shocked at Görtz's ingenious plan, which would likely have succeeded were it not for his intervention. Arbour Hill prison was a two-storey building, and Görtz was being held in a store room with barred windows on the first floor, as opposed to a conventional cell. Immediately above Görtz was an attic, and the ceiling between them was made of plaster.

Görtz had conceived the idea of breaking through the ceiling and moving a few slates before climbing out the roof and sliding down to the parapet on the end of the roof. This was a distance of about three feet, and the parapet was also roughly three feet high, which could conceal him from any of the outdoor sentries posted around the prison. Görtz then planned to crawl behind the parapet right round the prison and jump into a field at the back, where he hoped to be picked up by an IRA contact.

He would then make his way to Laragh to find Iseult Stuart. He had arranged for a signal to be left to indicate if it was safe for him to enter the house at Laragh. Iseult would walk to a clearing in the wood and drop a red handkerchief to indicate to Görtz that the coast was clear and that he could enter the house safely. If Gardaí were in the house someone would drop a white handkerchief instead, and Görtz would wait in the clearing in the woods until the time was right.

———

Thanks to Hayes's quick thinking the prison authorities were now aware of Görtz's plan, and put in place a series of measures to thwart it. The day after his plan had been discovered by Hayes the commandant of the prison called Görtz to his office. He explained to him that he was embarrassed by the state of the room in which he was imprisoned, and that he would like to repair it. He offered to repaint it, which he said would take about two to three days, and asked Görtz if he would mind going to an ordinary cell adjacent to other prisoners' cells while the repairs were being carried out. Görtz was delighted with the attention that was being paid to him and agreed to move temporarily, thanking the commandant warmly. After Görtz was transferred to the first-floor cells his room was repainted and the upper side of the plaster on the roof was reinforced with sheets of galvanised iron laid across the length of the ceiling. These were fixed to laths with two-inch screws. Görtz was then brought back down to his cell, and nothing out of the ordinary happened for about a week.

One morning the military police came in with Görtz's breakfast only to find him blushing and sitting on his bed with white plaster on the ground beside him. One of the military policemen fetched a brush and pan to sweep up the plaster while Görtz ate his breakfast. Nothing was said of the incident by either Görtz or the policemen. He had clearly broken through the ceiling during the night only to be greeted by the sight of the galvanised iron, and so had abandoned his escape attempt.

The incident left Görtz feeling paranoid and suspicious as to how his escape had been thwarted. Desperate to escape, he made a last-ditch attempt to gain his freedom, heating a poker to burn the wood around the lock of his cell door, but he fainted when the smoke overcame him. Hayes decided to keep an eye on Görtz in case he made another escape attempt, and to see if he could ascertain any more clues to his keyword. In June 1943 luck was on his side.

De Buitléar noticed that Görtz had burnt something in the grate of the fireplace in his cell. Thinking that they might be of use he gathered the remnants of the message and brought them to Hayes to see if he could find out what information the message contained. Hayes took the burnt fragments to the Garda technical bureau in Kilmainham for examination, and while he was examining the fragments someone banged a door shut and a gust of wind blew the fragments away.

Incensed by the carelessness of the staff, Hayes gathered the fragments and brought them to Trinity College. Hayes had a friend on the chemistry faculty whose discretion and expertise he felt he could rely on, and together they decided to chemically treat the particles using a specific method. Hayes, who had an amateur interest in chemistry, suggested they procure a bottle of blue-black Swan fountain pen ink, which they used to determine the iron content in the fragments. The fragments were then placed on glass plates, and Hayes used an eyedropper to apply a potassium ferrocyanide solution onto them, pouring off any surplus solution after fully immersing the fragments. The chemist then added a few drops of hydrochloric acid, and as a result the fragments turned a bright shade of blue.

They were now much easier to read. Hayes rearranged them on the glass plates in the correct order, and began to read the message contained within. While some of the particles were missing, the burnt fragments allowed Hayes to piece together Görtz's keyword. The burnt cipher message contained 126 letters, and after much study and testing of various possibilities using frequency analysis, Hayes deduced that the keyword was CATHLEEN NI HOULIHAN. This allowed Hayes to write out the message in plain English: 'Ask –EGP-X whether prepared to put money at disposal immediately after success the more chances x IRA must not know of it x discreet x. Way up to you xx.'

Hayes also reconstructed Görtz's other keywords, which were: ELLEN WIEBKE, ROLF UTE, GERTRUDE MATHIESSEN, DEPARTMENTS OF STATE and AMATEUR THEATRICALS. Hayes continued working on the messages and once he had deciphered them he came to a conclusion that filled him with dread. Someone outside of the prison knew the code word, and Görtz had been successfully getting messages out to them. The message referred to somebody named Andrews, who could have replied to Görtz through a carefully worded insertion in the *Irish Times*.

Hayes immediately informed Commandant de Buitléar of his discovery and the details of how he had broken the Görtz cipher, insisting they immediately inform Dan Bryan, but de Buitléar, acting as his superior officer, overruled him, saying that Bryan would 'only run hotfoot to the British with it'. De Buitléar clearly held a very different viewpoint than Hayes and Bryan, who felt that it was of paramount importance to inform the British of the breaking of the code, despite the likelihood that there would be scant reward in return for their information. They believed that the security of the Irish state would be better served by keeping the British informed of any developments that G2 made in the field of cryptanalysis. But because Hayes was a civilian he was overruled by de Buitléar, and it would be more than a year before Bryan learned that the code had been broken.

During the course of the war relations between Bryan and de Buitléar were often strained. Not only did the men hold opposing views in relation to sharing information with the British, they disagreed to the extent that Bryan viewed de Buitléar as unsuitable for intelligence work given his nationalistic views.

When Bryan eventually discovered that the code had been broken and he hadn't been informed for over a year he was apoplectic with rage, and he remonstrated with Hayes over this tardiness. Hayes understood Bryan's anger, and explained to him that he hadn't been able to inform him as he

had been overruled by de Buitléar. In any case de Buitléar's apprehension
was correct, as Bryan passed on knowledge of the breaking of the Görtz
code to the British, receiving very little in return for his efforts. At all
times Bryan's focus was on protecting Irish security interests; he was never
concerned with being classed as pro-British. He saw his role as to get on
with his British counterpart as best he could in line with government
policy. By contrast Bryan considered de Buitléar, who had perfected his
German in pre-war Berlin, to be 'anti-British to the point of irrationality',
while de Buitléar held the complete opposite view regarding Bryan.

The disagreement was unfortunate, as both men were loyal officers and
great servants to Ireland during the war who unfortunately had different
ways of looking at things. Indeed such a clash of personalities was common
in intelligence agencies at that time. There were similar disagreements
within MI5 and MI6, as well as within the Abwehr and the OSS, the
precursor to the CIA. Despite his actions de Buitléar was never censured,
even though as an act of disloyalty it merited such a sanction. His reprieve
was likely down to Bryan's admiration for his work as an interpreter and
fluent speaker of German, thus making him a valuable asset to the army.

The breaking of the Görtz cipher was one of the greatest achievements
during the war of both G2 and MI5, as the cipher was the most sophisticated
one used by German agents in Ireland, and was clearly reserved for very
special purposes by the Abwehr. Despite the fact that the code was in
existence since early 1940, Görtz was the only German agent who had been
entrusted to use it for the purposes of espionage.

Indeed such was the esteem in which it was held due to its intricacy
and difficulty to break that it was later described by staff at Bletchley Park
as 'one of the best three or four codes used in the war'. Hayes compiled a
complete breakdown of the code cipher, which he noted for its similarities
to a cipher the IRA had received from Soviet Russia in the 1920s. He
observed that

> [t]he Görtz Cipher was the best in our experience used by the Germans
> during the war. It was evidently used for very special purposes because
> although the Germans knew of it in 1940 no agent except Görtz was

trained in its use and other agents were sent out with third class ciphers when this one was available. The Görtz cipher required no book or equipment. The whole system with the keywords could be memorised. A keyword is written into a twenty-five letter square. This forms a basis for turning the clear text into numbers of two digits. The set of numbers are then transposed on the basis of the original keyword. The transposed vertical columns of figures are then substituted into letters by the original square to give the cipher text.

Hayes's success was to be short-lived, however, as Görtz's messages while in prison were prolific and the damage they may have caused was incalculable. There also remained the issue of someone outside the jail knowing the keyword, thus being able to use the code themselves. Hayes, knowing that he and G2 would have to intercept all of the messages in order to avoid them being used, concocted a ruse where G2 would intercept Görtz's messages to the outside, leading him to believe they had successfully reached Berlin. In reality the messages were only getting as far as Hayes, who would reply to Görtz pretending he was the German High Command. In one message Hayes asked for Görtz to give a complete account of his mission in Ireland to date. Convinced he was talking to Berlin, Görtz replied by compiling an 80-page coded report listing all his activities and contacts since his arrival in Ballivor the previous year. G2 even went as far as employing a handwriting expert to mimic Eduard Hempel's handwriting, such was the level of their deception. In order to win Görtz's confidence and perhaps in many ways to poke fun at him, G2 fictitiously promoted Görtz to the rank of Major in one exchange. Görtz was delighted at his promotion, believing that it was in recognition for his exemplary work as an agent in Ireland. In reality the Irish authorities were building up his confidence in case they needed to rely on him for help at some stage in the future.

In Berlin the OKW requested updates on Görtz's condition in prison. The German authorities wished him to know that his wife and children were well, and that if he so wished he could send a message to his wife or mother through the Red Cross. They eventually forwarded a message to him from his wife requesting that he let her know that he was all right.

Görtz's mother, who had contacted Hempel in the legation in a state of distress asking for any information on her son, also wished to hear from him, and would not accept any assurances about his wellbeing unless it came in the form of a handwritten letter from Görtz himself.

Hempel placated her by informing Frau Görtz that her son had kept his rank despite his capture, that he was being well looked after by the Irish authorities and that he was enjoying the comfort of his own quarters, entertainment and company. Hempel was concerned at the prospect of Görtz using the Red Cross to send letters to Germany, fearing that the letters could be intercepted by the British authorities, who were aware of him from his previous spell in prison there. In the end his fear was unnecessary, as Görtz showed no interest in communicating through the Red Cross. Görtz was concerned about his family, however, as Lübeck was the first German city to be attacked in substantial numbers by the RAF.

The attack on the night of 28 March 1942 created a firestorm that engulfed the historic city centre, with bombs destroying three of the main churches and large parts of the built-up area. It led to the retaliatory 'Baedeker' raids on historic British cities, such as York, Bath and Canterbury. Although a port, and home to several shipyards, including the Lübecker Flender-Werke, Lübeck was mainly a cultural centre, and only lightly defended. The bombing on 28 March 1942 was the first major success for the RAF against a German city, and followed the Area Bombing Directive issued to the RAF on 14 February 1942 which authorised the targeting of civilian areas.

Despite receiving assurances that his family were safe, Görtz worried incessantly about them, and blamed himself for the failure of his mission. He fell into a spiral of depression which would characterise much of the rest of his stay in Ireland. Hempel grew concerned about Görtz's mental health, and made contact with Berlin to see if they would make some sort of acknowledgement of Görtz's efforts in order to raise his spirits. The German High Command responded by awarding Görtz the Order of the Iron Cross 1st and 2nd Class. Tributh and Gärtner also received the awards, which were given in recognition of their conduct in very difficult circumstances. Hempel was instructed to pass on his congratulations from the High Command to Görtz when informing him of his honour. Hempel gave the information to the Irish authorities, who instead of informing Görtz held the information back for two years, till a time when they felt it would be more useful to tell him in order to make him more cooperative in other matters.

Despite the fact that he was behind bars, Görtz was causing huge difficulty in the Irish political scene. Senator Desmond Fitzgerald, father of future Taoiseach Garret Fitzgerald and a veteran of the Rising, addressed the 'Görtz case' during his campaign for re-election:

I hope we did something about the parachutist who came here with an invasion plan. As far as I can tell, this was a case where a foreign government sent a man to establish contact with criminal elements to work at overthrowing the present government. Does neutrality mean we don't do anything about things like this? The fact that a man of foreign country, sent here by a plane of theirs, was left with an invasion plan has been used as a reason for jailing people who belong to an organisation which is responsible for many murders. I want to know more, though. Which steps did we undertake against that foreign government? We have protested against American troops in Northern Ireland but not against the bombing of Belfast.

Hempel was furious when he heard Fitzgerald's speech, voicing his displeasure to the Irish authorities.

Escape of course was always foremost in Görtz's mind, and as well as using his code he tried in various ways to contact his supporters on the outside. He was paranoid that the Irish would hand him over to the British and feared that if this were to come to pass he would face execution. He even went as far as throwing messages out of his cell window to passers-by, encouraging them to get in contact with the Farrell sisters, who he hoped could furnish him with the means for escape. In one message he asked for a glass cutter, wire cutter, hacksaw blade and cash to be left in a Dublin café for him.

The Farrell sisters were to put a message in the obituary section in the *Irish Independent* that would allow Görtz to know that they had received his message. Görtz continued to try this method of sending messages several times, often requesting that receipt of messages be acknowledged through advertisements in prominent newspapers.

And while G2 were able to keep abreast of Görtz's messages, they were still perplexed about the individual referred to as Andrews in some of the messages. They suspected this person was operating as an agent in Ireland using Görtz's code. In 1943 MI5 contacted G2 to confirm their worst fears.

———

In February 1943, cryptographers at Bletchley Park decoded a message for the SD (the Sicherheitsdienst, intelligence branch of the SS) and the Nazi Party in Lisbon. It confirmed receipt of a message from an Irish crew member named Christopher Eastwood, who was travelling on board a ship called the SS *Edenvale*. MI6 reported to their colleagues in MI5 that they had intercepted a message from a Portuguese worker named 'Tomas', who was supposed to take the message to the Abwehr but had instead taken it to MI6. Tomas, it turned out, was a double agent for MI6 who took messages to them before delivering them to the Germans.

Through this connection the mystery of who had been using Görtz's code was solved. The name 'Andrews' referred to an Irishman named Joseph Andrews – the same Joseph Andrews with whom Görtz had become acquainted during his time on the run in Ireland, and who had informed on him while staying in Clontarf, where he was eventually apprehended along with IRA leader Pearse Paul Kelly. Andrews, a tall, fair-haired man with piercing blue eyes (who was described by MI5 as an opportunist), lived at 95 Seafield in Clontarf at the time that Görtz was in Ireland. He first became associated with Görtz and his radio operator, Anthony Deery, in September 1941, when Görtz was finding securing shelter in Dublin difficult. Deery had stayed in the house of a friend of Andrews, who introduced them both and eventually arranged for him to meet Görtz.

Andrews quickly won Görtz's confidence despite the fact that others were suspicious of Andrews's motives. He introduced Görtz to his wife, who MI5 described as 'more unscrupulous and able than her husband'. The security service also noted about Andrews that 'he does not appear to have any visible means of support and has been trying to obtain a job. Both he and Mrs. Andrews have for a number of years lived a rather high life and will probably undertake any activity in order to gain money.'

Andrews's unscrupulous nature was clear. He had been employed by B.J. Fitzpatrick and Co. Wholesale Jewellers at 6 Grafton Street, and prior to this had worked for the Irish Hospitals Trust, but had been fired for dishonesty. He had been in charge of all monies of the foreign department for the purposes of purchasing sweep tickets abroad, and mismanagement of this fund led to his dismissal. Andrews had also worked with a number of women in the hospital trust who had dealings with Görtz, and it was through this connection that he first became aware of Görtz's presence in Ireland. He eventually became a driver for Görtz, and obtained his trust to the extent that Görtz authorised him to use his code in the event that he ever got captured.

Andrews's wife Norah, whose maiden name was O'Sullivan, had become quite taken by Görtz, and the two shared a close relationship to the extent that she also gained access to Görtz's code. Andrews had visited the United States prior to the outbreak of the war, where he had become acquainted with members of Clan na Gael, an Irish republican organisation in the United States in the late 19th and early 20th centuries. The group served as a successor to the Fenian Brotherhood and a sister organisation to the Irish Republican Brotherhood.

During his time in the United States Andrews had met with Joseph McGarrity, an IRA member originally from Carrickmore, Co. Tyrone, who had emigrated to Philadelphia in 1892 at the age of 18. McGarrity was a vehement opponent of de Valera and supporter of the s-Plan and subsequent IRA bombing campaign in England during the war. He had allegedly travelled to Berlin in 1939 prior to the outbreak of the war, and was said to have met with Luftwaffe Commander Hermann Göring in an effort to seek arms and ammunition in support of the IRA. He and Jim O'Donovan crossed paths with each other in Germany briefly.

Such was McGarrity's influence in republicanism that the IRA signed all its statements 'J.J. McGarrity' up until 1969, when the organisation split into the 'Official' and 'Provisional' movements. Thereafter the term continued to be used by the Officials, while the Provisional IRA adopted the moniker 'P. O'Neill'. Shortly after his trip to the States it was believed that Andrews himself had visited Berlin, although this couldn't be proven conclusively by either the Irish or the British authorities. MI5 had reason to believe that the German Legation in Dublin had made enquiries into Andrews's reputation and character, with a view to employing him as early as March 1939. They had done so through both official and unofficial channels.

Andrews had also made several visits to the UK, the last in 1940, when he was granted an exit permit to return to Ireland in May of that year. Ever the opportunist, Andrews had travelled to the UK to sell to the authorities there the names of IRA members in the United States, defrauding the US treasury through the Hospital Sweepstakes. This was not followed up by authorities, however, and he successfully sold the names to the US Consul in Dublin, who imposed heavy fines on those involved. Andrews had been involved in trying to establish an alternative channel with Germany but Görtz had been arrested before the system could be set up properly.

Andrews also held strong anti-Semitic views, and was a card-carrying member of both the People's National Party and Córas na Poblachta, which both espoused extreme anti-Semitic views. His reputation as an opportunist was one that was confirmed by many of those who came into contact with him. In an internal memo, Dan Bryan described him as 'an astute and plausible rogue without any fixed convictions and mainly actuated by a desire to obtain money rapidly without due regard as to the honesty of the methods used to secure his ends'. Indeed such was the subterfuge he was involved in that once he obtained the Görtz code he took it to the American Legation seeking money in return.

MI5 were able to keep a close eye on Andrews, as one of his associates, a man named Thomas Joseph Maginn of Church Avenue, Drumcondra, worked as an informant for the Ministry of Defence. Andrews had been arrested in November 1941 and interned in the Curragh due to his connection to one of Görtz's lovers, Maisie O'Mahony. Andrews readily admitted he was working for the Germans, and that he knew Hermann Görtz. He agreed to give information that would lead to the arrest of

Görtz, although the authorities were unaware that he had knowledge of Görtz's code.

As a result of his information he was to receive immunity from trial. After he was released Andrews approached a member of the German Legation for material on a lecture he was giving on Germany, and using his wife as a courier sent the official coded messages. When this proved to be of no use to him he began using the route through Christopher Eastwood on the ss *Edenvale*.

——

The Lisbon route had its difficulties, owing to the fact that the sea route from Dublin to Lisbon was limited to once a month, and on certain occasions the ship didn't call at Lisbon at all. Therefore the messages were often subject to delay. Also, Eastwood himself, much like Andrews, was not a very reliable character. He eventually lost his job on board the ship when he arrived for work one day late and heavily intoxicated. Only for the fact that his workmates insisted he be given a second chance was he able to resume his duties on board the ship.

His dismissal would have scuppered Andrews's communication link. When Andrews's messages did arrive in Germany the Abwehr had considerable difficulty reading them, as they didn't have the keyword. Andrews's messages were boastful in their nature. He claimed that he was a member of Görtz's personal organisation, which in itself was independent of the IRA. He asked that he be picked up by U-boat and taken to Germany, or that another agent be sent to Ireland, along with a new radio and money to be given to him upon arrival.

He also claimed that Gen. Eoin O'Duffy was 'willing to co-operate in active work, especially in occupied Ireland', and that 'General Hugo Mc Neill was sympathetic to the German cause'. Andrews had also seemingly sent the Germans landing instructions for Dublin. The series of coded messages read, 'From Lambay Island go in the direction of mainland, south of Island and go on to the headland coast about 400 metres south of the asylum buildings between water tower and round tower. Land on beach one hundred metres from tower on the northern tip. Avoid one rock obstruction.'

Meanwhile von Ribbentrop at the German Foreign Ministry dismissed his suggestions as impractical and any help from O'Duffy as mythical in nature and to be discounted, reasoning that if such help existed it would be impossible to transport. Despite the Abwehr's lack of interest, the British security service were faced with a problem. They had successfully intercepted Andrews's messages but were unable to read them and break this particular kind of hand cipher – the same cipher that had baffled staff working on ISOS ciphers at Hut 9 in Bletchley Park.

Alan Turing had broken the Enigma and Lorenz codes in Hut 8 during the course of hostilities, but this particular hand cipher proved to be a conundrum beyond the capabilities of the huge staff working at Bletchley. When Dan Bryan shared information with the British they turned to Richard Hayes for help in unscrambling the messages. The British had discovered the Görtz keyword, but they needed Hayes's help in deciphering the text of the messages. Bryan invited the Liddell brothers to Dublin, where they met with Richard Hayes, who explained the workings of the Görtz cipher to them. Guy Liddell was hugely impressed by Dr Hayes and the fact that he had managed to break the Görtz cipher single-handedly while an entire hut at Bletchley Park had difficulty with the same task. To Liddell, Hayes was a one-man army who he later described as having 'gifts in this direction that amounted almost to genius'.

The British were concerned about the messages, as they didn't want to reveal the secrets of their ISOS intercept system, which was how they initially became aware of the keyword. With Hayes's help Liddell was able to read the plain text of Andrews's messages without compromising the ISOS programme. Bryan allowed the messages to run on, letting the British read them without telling them what they might reveal or what Irish nationalists would be compromised. Indeed suspicions about Gen. Hugo MacNeill and his contacts with Görtz were later confirmed through this channel.

Once MI5 gleaned sufficient information from Andrews's messages he was no longer of use to them or G2. He was subsequently arrested in August 1943 and held until hostilities ceased in May 1945. Christopher Eastwood was also detained. Gardaí raided Andrews's house in Clontarf and copies of his messages were found, along with burnt fragments of paper in the grate of his fireplace. These were brought to Kilmainham Garda Station, where the Garda Technical Bureau mounted them on glass plates and sprayed them with chemicals to reveal their messages.

In August 1943 Görtz was transferred to Athlone to be housed with the rest of the German agents. He was furious at the move, and demanded he be allowed to speak to a solicitor. He was angered also because his possessions had been seized in order for the transfer to be made. He was particularly upset about his books and papers being taken, and he demanded that the authorities treat him like an officer instead of a common criminal. Hempel, on the other hand, was relieved at Görtz's transfer, believing it would allow the furore around him to settle down.

The OKW only learned of Görtz's transfer in late 1943. Before leaving Dublin Görtz was able to pass a secret message to them protesting his transferral on the grounds that it conflicted with 'his internationally guaranteed rights as an officer of a country at war'. Such was Görtz's anger that he threatened to go on hunger strike in order to see the matter rectified. Hempel was angered at such a proposal, and confided in Berlin that if 'Görtz wished to choose this method of dying for his country it did not matter when he expired'.

In any case Hempel felt that Görtz's suggestion of such a drastic course of action was proof of his fragile mental state. He toyed with the idea of visiting Görtz to try and lift his spirits, but in the end he decided against it. Hempel was determined to have no other contact with Görtz for the remainder of the war, and was quietly glad that all the publicity the case had brought ended once Görtz was successfully transferred to Athlone. However, as many had come to learn, the future could never be easily predicted when dealing with Hermann Görtz.

VIII

THE GERMAN SPY FROM CO. CLARE

'And now, to my grief, the state, like a thief, Camouflaged by Emergency Orders, Just pockets the coin, with the most knavish design, To bolster its Budget disorders.'

A poem by captured German spy JOHN FRANCIS O'REILLY,

November 1944

From the moment he entered the internment camp in Athlone, Görtz's mind was fully focused on escape. The Irish authorities had succeeded in keeping his messages under control, and having also dealt with Andrews, many in Ireland considered the Görtz case closed. However, Görtz was to prove more trouble than the authorities realised. In September 1942, the Irish authorities had come to the chilling realisation that somebody new was using Görtz's code.

An Irish customs official in Swanlinbar, Co. Cavan, had stopped a man crossing the Irish border and a routine search of his pockets revealed he was carrying a piece of paper with a strange series of codes on it. The customs officer felt that the gentleman in question was acting suspiciously, but as he had no contraband on him he was unable to detain him. To make matters worse, the customs officer failed to take details of the man's identity and address. The piece of paper containing the series of code groups eventually made its way to G2, who passed it on to Dr Hayes to analyse, and it was Hayes who noted that the message was sent using Görtz's code.

There was one discrepancy, however, in that the codes were arranged into groups of four as opposed to five, which was the system favoured by the Abwehr. When Hayes deciphered the message he came to the conclusion that another agent was active in Ireland, and that they were passing messages on to the Germans. Despite Hayes's best efforts the mystery of the sender and receiver of the message was never solved. Ultimately the failure of the customs official to identify the man who carried the message left Hayes and G2 with very little to go on.

Later the same year a restaurant car attendant on the Great Northern Railway was arrested after he was found carrying three letters to the IRA's northern command, which requested a meeting with the southern command, as well as details on Allied troop movements in Northern Ireland. When questioned by the authorities, the attendant claimed the letters he was carrying originated from Kingston Shirts in Dublin, the business owned by Caitlín Brugha. The authorities believed that the IRA may have been interested in sending such information to the Germans for future operations. And Görtz continued sending messages, which were being intercepted by the authorities. Hayes deciphered the messages, and G2, along with the Gardaí, used the information in the messages to build cases against Görtz's accomplices.

Meanwhile in Athlone Görtz was finding it difficult to integrate into his new surroundings. Although concessions had been made to the prisoners in order to provide them with more comforts, Görtz remained tense during his incarceration. He was allowed to associate with the other German internees, however, and he soon formed a relationship with Unland and Preetz. The three Germans gained the trust of the camp commandant, James Power, who played bridge with them once a week. Power was able to gain insights into the men's characters, as they generally let their guard down while playing cards. He noted that Görtz always seemed tense, and held his cards tightly in his hand. The weekly bridge game became something of a novelty in the camp, and eventually the other internees were allowed to attend as spectators.

Unland had appointed himself as leader of the prisoners, something all the prisoners acknowledged apart from Görtz, who often distanced himself from the others. Jan van Loon was the only prisoner Görtz formed a close relationship with, and until the end of the war he acted as Görtz's closest friend.

After biding his time for a short period Görtz's thoughts turned to escape. Within 18 months of the German's arrival in Athlone Unland began painting an eagle and a swastika on the wall of the recreation room in the camp. This was a diversion to distract from the fact that the other prisoners were digging a tunnel in van Loon's cell. Unland had cleverly positioned his mural so that he could keep an eye on the movements of the prison officers. Preetz also stood guard on the lookout for the prison authorities.

The plan was discovered when the prisoners' cells were suddenly raided early one morning. The raids were routine but the Germans blamed Obéd, who was disliked by all. They believed he had revealed their plans to the authorities, despite the fact that they had no evidence to prove this. Preetz eventually showed his disdain for Obéd by throwing a cup of scalding tea in his face one evening in the prison mess.

———

Görtz and van Loon also plotted escape together. Görtz had continued sending messages and had shown van Loon his enciphering method. Van Loon worked diligently in his cell at night by candlelight to encrypt messages that were to be taken to the Farrell sisters and others outside the jail. Both men were unaware that Görtz's code had been compromised, however.

Görtz was so impressed with van Loon's loyalty that he even tried to enrol him into the Waffen SS; such was Görtz's level of delusion in his belief of the seniority of his position as an officer. Görtz duly informed his superiors in Berlin of the promotion – who of course in reality were actually G2. In an amusing turn of events G2, masquerading as Berlin, confirmed van Loon's enrolment, assuring Görtz that he had been fully welcomed into the organisation.

Görtz himself was to prove a divisive figure within the camp, causing the German internees to organise themselves into pro- and anti-Görtz factions. Schütz, Tributh and Gärtner were distrustful of the other group, which consisted of Görtz, Preetz and van Loon. Obéd, who was being detained separately for racial reasons, aligned himself with Schütz and his faction. Weber-Drohl and Simon distanced themselves from either group. The factions arose for a variety of reasons. In terms of status Görtz, Schütz, Tributh and Gärtner were German soldiers and the others were civilians.

Görtz, Preetz and van Loon were also Nazis, having joined the party before the outbreak of the war. This conflicted with the other detainees, who were not open converts to the ideals of National Socialism. Schütz and Görtz in particular clashed regularly. Schütz, for example, liked to listen to English radio broadcasts, an activity Görtz considered to be treasonous. Görtz assured Schütz he would have him executed for this once the pair returned to Germany, and in a somewhat advanced state of paranoia Görtz began listening in to Schütz's conversations.

In one exchange Schütz tried to persuade a prison doctor to send chocolates and silk stockings to his mistress in Germany. At a meeting of the prisoners Görtz used this information to accuse Schütz of being a spy, exclaiming, 'There is a traitor among us and I think that traitor is Marschner.' A fistfight developed, with Tributh attacking Görtz, and the men had to be separated by prison authorities. Dr Hayes visited the internees and later noted that 'Schütz also clashed regularly with Walter Simon who taunted him by calling him a "dirty Jew boy" and threatened to beat him up.'

Weber-Drohl did not fit in with the other internees in Athlone, and campaigned to be transferred to another jail, informing the prison authorities that he would go on hunger strike until his demands were met. At 65 years of age, Weber-Drohl was the oldest of the internees, and he suffered from medical problems which caused him to be a frequent visitor to the prison hospital. He was eventually discharged from the prison hospital for making lewd sexual remarks to a young nurse working there. The doctor on duty refused to keep Weber-Drohl there any longer and he was promptly returned to the mainstream prison population.

Weber-Drohl, an Austrian, felt that associating with the German internees would scupper any hope he had of an early release. In a letter to the Irish Department of Defence, he argued that he had become 'the target of mean and filthy lies and conspiracy of the Germans in the camp'. In one instance he referred to Preetz as a 'teapot thrower', a reference to a fight that Preetz had with Schütz which had resulted in him smashing a teapot on Schütz's head. Weber-Drohl insisted he would refuse all food until he was transferred away from the other prisoners. Such was his displeasure at his situation that he even went as far as contacting the American Minister in Ireland, David Gray, to protest his situation.

Out of all of the prisoners, Obéd seemed to have the most difficult time in Athlone. The Irish climate affected his health, and he soon began to suffer from chronic bronchitis. He was also severely unpopular with the other inmates, who ostracised him and often taunted him. Walter Simon in particular made life difficult for Obéd, accusing Obéd, for example, of playing 'nigger music' in his cell. Preetz, who was by far the most nefarious character housed in the camp, at one stage attempted to assault Obéd, and was only prevented from doing so by the intervention of the prison authorities. When Capt. Joseph Healy of G2 toured the camp to look into the conditions in which the prisoners were being held he noted that Obéd's claims were accurate.

Görtz had positioned himself within the prison as a senior officer, but on various occasions his paranoia got the better of him, and he engaged in petty squabbles with other detainees. He accused Obéd of being an informer who had alerted the prison authorities of one of many of the prisoners' escape attempts. In reality the authorities had found out through Görtz himself. They had gleaned the information from one of his letters which he believed he had sent outside the prison successfully. Gärtner and Tributh, who were somewhat close to Görtz, had a better time in internment in Athlone than Obéd or the others. But even though their lot was easier, Tributh lost all his hair through stress during the six years he spent in incarceration.

In 1944, Görtz grew increasingly frustrated at his situation, and made one last attempt at escape. Writing to the Farrell sisters, he outlined his plan:

My Friends, I ask you to help me get out of this prison. It has become impossible for me to get out without help from outside. At the first opportunity I had sent from here an important message to Germany to support you with all means in your fight against our common enemy. I have reason to believe that this message has reached Germany however I also have reason to believe that in order to make this help real it needs personal contact and explanation. I still think I am the best man to re-establish this contact – perhaps the only man. I think it is best to try and get out of the city the same night and morning by bicycle. If all works well the escape will not be detected before eight o'clock in the morning. A man could direct me to a place outside a place in the fields or bogs or shed where I can rest for the day. I need a road map and compass. Work quick as the ring gets tighter and tighter around me. The nights get shorter – only the actual climbing must be done in complete darkness – moonless nights – let the men darken their faces and have gloves on.

Much like his attempted escape from Arbour Hill, Görtz intended to make his exit through the roof. He had selected the camp's common room ceiling as the best location from which to escape. He would then make his way down the prison walls and out into the fields or bogs, where he hoped to be picked up. When this plot was foiled Görtz resorted to hunger strike in order to try to gain his freedom.

Such was Görtz's determination in carrying out his protest that he managed to last 21 days without food. He eventually had to be fed through a tube and upon its insertion ended his protest. Now at his wits' end, Görtz began to slip back into a state of depression. In an attempt to lift his mood he wrote voraciously and during this period in Athlone he worked on a number of short stories – and a play about Stephen Hayes.

———

The German authorities now had to look elsewhere for spies to send to Ireland. They were fast running out of luck with the agents who had been sent, and it wasn't long before Nazi Germany looked to the Irish expatriate community for solutions. The Irish community during the war was quite small, but it provided an adequate hunting ground for the Abwehr and the SD to recruit from. Irish citizens resident there who supported the Nazi regime were of huge value in terms of propaganda, moral support and local knowledge for planning operations.

Although Ireland was neutral, it didn't declare complete independence from the United Kingdom until 1949. Therefore it was still technically part of the UK. This brought with it a myriad of legal difficulties for Germany if it were to use Irish citizens living in the Reich as spies. Technically any Irish citizen who aided Hitler could have been tried and executed for treason, as Ireland was still part of the Commonwealth of Nations. Despite these peculiarities of international law, several Irish men aided Nazi Germany from within the Reich. One such gentleman was Sgt John Codd.

John Codd was born in Mountrath in Co. Laois but emigrated to Canada in 1929. In 1931 he moved to England and enlisted in the Royal Welsh Fusiliers. After serving abroad he was recalled to England in 1939 on the outbreak of the war. Codd was a self-educated man who spoke a variety of languages, including French, Spanish and Chinese. He was a veteran of the evacuation at Dunkirk, and was wounded providing cover for the fleeing British Expeditionary Force. Codd himself was unable to escape, and was captured and brought to a German field hospital to recover. Once he was well enough he was brought to the Stalag Luft III camp.

The Stalag was established in March 1942 in the German province of Lower Silesia near the town of Sagan (now Żagań, Poland), 160 km southeast of Berlin. The site was selected because its sandy soil made it difficult for POWs to escape by tunnelling. During his time here he was approached by a German, who offered him improved conditions if he would consider working for Ireland against the British. Codd, for whatever reason, agreed to the offer, and was transferred to Friesack Camp. Friesack had been set up as a camp for Irish prisoners of war with the aim of using them as Abwehr agents for espionage missions to Ireland.

Upon his arrival at the camp, Codd was met by an officer recruiting volunteers for espionage work with the Abwehr. The officer promised money, freedom and an eventual return to Ireland for any volunteers. The offer sounded too good to turn down, and Codd eagerly volunteered for German service. He was joined by several other Irishmen who had also been interned at Friesack. Among this number was Private Frank Stringer, a native of Kells, Co. Meath. Stringer had joined the British Navy and later the Royal Irish Fusiliers, and had been in Jersey when German forces invaded in 1940.

Private James Brady of Strokestown, Co. Roscommon was also a volunteer. Brady had been stationed in Norway with the British Army and had also come into contact with the Germans in the Channel Islands. Another volunteer, Private Patrick O'Brien from Nenagh, Co. Tipperary, had been captured at Dunkirk and taken to Berlin to be trained for espionage; however while there he had been arrested for attempted rape and was later transferred to Friesack Camp. The group was completed by five other volunteers, who hailed from counties Louth, Laois, Tipperary and Wexford. Codd, along with the others, was to be given a fake name and transferred to Berlin, where he would be trained by the Abwehr.

The Germans planned to send Codd along with a colleague on a sabotage mission to London, where he would use a radio transmitter to communicate with Berlin. Until the time was ready for him to be called into service he was given civilian clothing and allowed to explore Berlin at his leisure. Codd enjoyed his time in the German capital, visiting beer halls and dating local ladies, as well as many other extravagances that his newfound freedom allowed him. When the time came for him to be put into active service he was ordered to report for intensive espionage training in Potsdam.

During his training his mission objectives changed several times. He was to be tasked with a sabotage mission in the United States, but this was soon abandoned and he was later ordered to report to Cologne for wireless training. Upon his arrival here he was also given an intensive training course in the use of Morse code.

After a series of unfortunate events that resulted in the arrest of many of the other agents, Codd's mission changed yet again. This time he was to be sent to Northern Ireland and was given a new cover name for the purposes of his mission. He was retrained in cryptology but the course was brief, and as a result the encoding method he had been trained in was relatively basic.

In April 1943, Codd was taken to the SD school in Lehnitz for further training in coded radio transmissions and disc ciphers. His training at the SS Training School at The Hague was to be Codd's last, as the events of 6 June 1944 were to drastically alter the course of the war. The location of the Normandy landings came as a complete surprise to the Axis Powers. Hitler had placed Field Marshall Erwin Rommel in charge of protecting the Atlantic Wall, but misinformation spread by captured German agents in the Double-Cross system saw Germany hold back her forces from Normandy.

With German troops now all being diverted to deal with the onslaught, the idea of sending German spies to Allied countries suddenly became ludicrous. Codd avoided being sent to the front line and quietly bided his time until the end of the war at the SD school in Lehnitz. In March 1945, along with his wife he successfully made it to liberated France, and from there made it back to Dublin. Codd was arrested soon after his arrival and was interrogated by G2, who released him when nothing of use came from his interviews.

After the war Dr Hayes interviewed Codd, and noted that he had been trained in using a substitution cipher based on a 25-letter square which was created by first writing the keyword followed by the rest of the text. The first figure in the substituted text was then switched to the end and the figures substituted back into letters to give the final cipher text. Hayes theorised that it was a primitive version of the cipher which Görtz later travelled to Ireland with. Codd was also trained in a new innovation: the SD disc cipher which would later be used to great effect by other German agents.

Codd eventually bought a house at 59 Montpellier Hill, which was only a stone's throw away from G2 headquarters on Infirmary Road. Here he opted to live a much quieter life, although he found it difficult to obtain work. In 1948, he wrote to the Irish government offering to show the Minister for Defence the skills that he picked up during his time in the SD, and asked whether they would be of any use to the Irish authorities. His request was politely declined. Codd received more favourable treatment from the Irish than he might have gotten from the British. His work with the SD was enough to see him executed as a traitor, but the British were never able to trace his location, and he lived out the rest of his days quietly.

————

Apart from Codd, one other prisoner was selected for training in espionage by the Germans. James O'Neill of Co. Wexford had been captured on board a freighter, and had the misfortune to find himself incarcerated in Friesack. Eager to get back to Ireland, he accepted a role with the Abwehr and agreed to train in espionage for a special mission. Given the codename 'Eisenbart', he trained in Hamburg in radio with a view to being sent to Northern Ireland, where he was expected to report on the movements of British and American convoys as well as the shipbuilding industry in Belfast.

The Germans took him to the Spanish border and he was told to make his own way to Ireland. O'Neill was also given cover addresses for the purposes of his mission. He hoped to contact Leopold Kerney, the Irish Minister in Spain, and organise his transport back to Ireland through him. By the time O'Neill had been sent on his mission he had been given a very basic cipher. This was perhaps an indication of the pressure the Germans were under, as well as the fact that they perhaps didn't rate O'Neill very highly.

O'Neill made it to Portugal, where he surrendered to the British. He was eventually interrogated in London by MI5, who released him after coming to the conclusion that he was unsuitable for intelligence work. They felt he was not trustworthy enough for the Double-Cross system, and he was set free rather than being interned. MI5 released him on the basis that he had surrendered immediately rather than attempt to carry out his mission for the Abwehr. His cipher, which used a poem to operate its system, eventually made its way to Richard Hayes, who solved it with little difficulty.

Hayes observed that the cipher was by far the most simple that had been given to any German agent during the war. He noted that it operated by using a sliding rule, and that the poem was used to give a series of letter positions for fixing relative positions of the rule before enciphering each letter. Hayes dismissed the cipher as amateurish in nature, stating, 'It is of a type described in all standard works of cryptography and calls for no further comment.'

By December 1943, G2 were fairly convinced that Germany had lost interest in Ireland. All known agents were now in custody, and since Joseph Lenihan had parachuted into Summerhill there had been no further attempts to land in Ireland by German agents. The Irish authorities believed that Germany hadn't the resources to send agents to Britain or Ireland since the German invasion of Russia. The Führer was now fighting a war on two fronts, and in their estimation his main focus was in the east. While this was certainly true in one respect, the idea of using Irishmen as German agents in the same way as Lenihan still remained an option for the Germans. This set the scene for the arrival of John Francis O'Reilly into Ireland.

O'Reilly, a native of Kilkee, Co. Clare, was the son of Bernard O'Reilly, a sergeant in the Royal Irish Constabulary who had famously arrested Sir Roger Casement on Banna Strand in Co. Kerry during the 1916 rising. John Francis was born in Kerry that same year but moved to Clare with his family once Bernard had retired. After attending school in Kilrush, John Francis attempted to join the Irish customs in 1936, but failed the Irish exam. He decided to move to England to join the priesthood, but only lasted a brief period before moving to London, where he got work as a hotel receptionist. He left London after war was declared in 1939 and moved to the Channel Islands, eventually settling on Jersey, where he worked as a potato picker.

Undeterred by the German invasion of France, O'Reilly stayed on Jersey, and was present when German forces invaded the islands in 1940. Determined to take advantage of any opportunities with the occupying power, O'Reilly took a job at the Luftwaffe airfield on the island and eventually worked his way up the ladder, becoming a translator between the island's Nazi commander and other Irish citizens who had decided to remain on the island after the invasion. O'Reilly eventually gained the confidence of the island commander, and one day approached him, asking him about the possibility of getting permission to travel to Germany for work.

O'Reilly reasoned that he could contact the Irish Legation in Berlin with a view to returning home. The commander agreed on the condition that O'Reilly would recruit other Irish workers to go to Germany with him. O'Reilly agreed, and successfully recruited 72 other Irishmen. The group travelled by train to work in the Hermann Göring plant in Watenstedt. On arrival to Germany O'Reilly volunteered as an interpreter to the German forces, a role that gained him access to and the confidence of the German forces there. O'Reilly's Irish citizenship was to be his greatest asset, and in 1941 he was accepted into the Irish service of German radio, where he worked as a broadcaster. He began broadcasting to Ireland using the alias 'Pat O'Brien', but eventually reverted to his actual name.

O'Reilly's time as a broadcaster was very successful, and during this period he became acquainted with Francis Stuart. Growing tired of working in radio, he made the acquaintance of an American gentleman working for the ss, who informed him of the possibility of obtaining work in Spain contacting sailors who might have news of events in Northern Ireland. The American turned out to be a recruiter for the Abwehr and the sd. The two organisations were in competition with each other, and given a slew of failed security operations, the sd were rapidly gaining ground on the Abwehr.

O'Reilly applied to work for German Intelligence, indicating that he would like to be sent on a mission to Northern Ireland if possible. When his application was accepted O'Reilly stayed with the radio station until he could be accepted for espionage training. After finding a replacement for himself at the radio station he travelled to Bremen, where he began training with the Abwehr in September 1942 for a mission to Northern Ireland. O'Reilly was given the codename 'Agent Rush' and his mission was given the codename 'Isolde'.

O'Reilly was tasked with reporting back to Germany on naval and air intelligence matters from Londonderry, Belfast, Liverpool and Lough Foyle. In order to be given the mission O'Reilly had sexed up information of his contacts within the IRA, and as a result the Abwehr were extremely enthusiastic about their newfound genuine Irish agent. O'Reilly was trained in intelligence in Bremen and became skilled in the use of invisible ink and radio. He undertook an intensive radio course and achieved a degree of competency in Morse code that far outstripped that of any of the other agents sent to Ireland.

O'Reilly also excelled in training he received in clandestine photography and microphotography. With his training complete, the matter of how he would be inserted into Ireland arose. A number of strategies were considered. Initially the Germans considered the idea of transporting him to his home in Co. Clare via U-boat. They also considered transporting him through the Irish consulate in Berlin, a plan that was also eventually scrapped. Eventually O'Reilly's mission was cancelled by Admiral Canaris, who felt that it was a waste of precious resources that would clash with other more important operations.

O'Reilly was then released from duty with the Abwehr, but was soon picked up by the SD, who saw an opportunity to use the Irishman as an agent of their own. While the Abwehr had primarily concerned itself with military intelligence, the SD instead dealt with political intelligence, and they felt that O'Reilly would fit nicely into their plans. After his Abwehr mission was cancelled O'Reilly returned to Berlin, intending to rejoin the radio station that had previously employed him; instead he received a phone call from the SS, who offered him employment. It was an offer that O'Reilly felt was too good to turn down.

He remained in Berlin and began training with the SD, eventually travelling to the south-western suburb of Wannsee, where he received additional training in wireless operation. While his experience with the SD was broadly similar to that in the Abwehr, his mission parameters were to change. O'Reilly was now tasked with collecting political intelligence in England, primarily the infiltration of Scottish national groups. He was also required to join the British Labour Party, with a view to establishing contacts in the British political system.

In addition to these objectives he was also expected to visit Northern Ireland and report on the relationship between British and American troops, as well as naval and air convoys. O'Reilly met with Oscar Pfaus, who briefed him before he set out on his mission. He was equipped with two radios and a supply of invisible ink to be used for ordinary letter correspondence. Before he set off on his mission the SD felt it necessary that he be accompanied by another agent. In conjunction with colleagues in the SS, O'Reilly selected another Irish man named John Kenny to go to Ireland with him.

Kenny was born in Dublin in March 1916 and was raised by his uncle in Kilcummin, Co. Kerry, after his father died while Kenny was still a child. Much like O'Reilly, Kenny left for England to find work in 1937. After working in a series of menial jobs and eager to avoid conscription, he left London for Jersey to work as a seasonal labourer, picking potatoes. Once settled on Jersey, Kenny found work in a hotel as a waiter and driver of a naval engineering officer. It was from here that he was first recruited by O'Reilly.

Kenny answered the door one day to O'Reilly and a Gestapo officer, who promised him that in return for training as an agent he could travel to Germany and wouldn't have to do factory work any longer. O'Reilly also assured Kenny that were he to volunteer he would be back home in Ireland by Christmas. The assurances were enough for Kenny, and he enthusiastically agreed to accompany the two men back for espionage training. Kenny was sent to Berlin, where he was given lodgings in a hotel and a stipend for expenses during his stay.

He was eventually summoned for training at the SD headquarters on Berkaerstrasse, Charlottenburg, in West Berlin. Kenny was trained in the repair and maintenance of wireless transmitter sets, a task that he took to with extreme difficulty. Kenny was not very well educated, and found much of the intelligence training challenging. The fact that Kenny's training was condensed into a very short timeframe further compounded his problems. Despite his clear incompatibility with spycraft, Kenny was given a short course in Morse code, and was dispatched for duty with O'Reilly in December 1943.

O'Reilly was displeased with Kenny's lack of ability, and feared he would jeopardise their mission. Nonetheless, both men were transported to Rennes in the north-west of occupied France to be flown to Ireland and dropped by parachute. O'Reilly pondered his mission as they made their way to Rennes:

> There was a plane leaving the base at about midnight, that night, on bomber reconnaissance and that he had arranged to take the place of the pilot of that plane and had made excuses for doing so … I left the town in his car for the aerodrome and we took precautions by pulling down the car blinds and I sat in the rear well back.

O'Reilly was sceptical of Kenny's motives and suspected he was simply using the mission to get back to Ireland. Despite his reservations he was determined to go ahead with the mission. Kenny and O'Reilly were to be dropped together in Co. Clare on 16 December 1943, but the pilot tasked with carrying out the mission felt that logistically he would be unable to take both men. Instead it was agreed that he would drop O'Reilly first and Kenny the following night.

While O'Reilly made his jump successfully, things became further complicated when thick fog over Co. Clare scuppered chances of Kenny being dropped on the 17th. The pilot of the Heinkel He111 carrying Kenny decided that a successful drop of Kenny was impossible, and opted to return to France instead. The plane was attacked on its way back as it flew over England. The drop was tried again on 19 December, when conditions were more favourable, and this time Kenny landed successfully in Co. Clare.

Lessons learned from Görtz's jump were implemented, and as a result O'Reilly and his suitcase were weighed separately, so that both would reach the ground at the same time. Both agents were also given flares to indicate to the Heinkel crew that they had reached the ground below safely. Despite O'Reilly's safe drop the Heinkel had been spotted. Volunteer John Blake, who was stationed at Loop Head lookout post that night, reported to the air message centre at Limerick that an aircraft of unknown nationality had been sighted about a mile to the north of his post. It was flying from the west in an easterly direction at 500 ft, with both its internal and navigation lights on.

On reaching the coast the aircraft followed the route to Foynes taken by British and American civilian flying boats. The SD thought they were cunning, having planned the drop to coincide with the arrival over Kilkee of a scheduled transatlantic flight from New York. However their plan backfired; O'Reilly's plane had been spotted, and it wasn't long before G2 and the Gardaí were aware of the presence of another illegal parachutist.

_____

O'Reilly was dropped within a mile of his family home, and his family were shocked to say the least when he walked in the front door at two o'clock in the morning. As far as they were concerned he was still in Germany but despite their initial shock they were pleased to see their prodigal son, who hadn't been home in almost three years. Despite the fact that his family didn't notify Gardaí of their son's arrival home the authorities soon found out. O'Reilly's forays into radio had made him somewhat of a local celebrity, and word of mouth in the small town eventually reached the local barracks.

Shortly after 7.30 p.m. Sgt Carroll of Kilkee Garda Station was given confidential information that 'a strange man wearing grey clothes and strong boots and carrying a heavy valise' had made enquiries about the way from Moveen to Kilkee, and that he had arrived on foot in the town earlier that morning. The sergeant was aware of the overflight and suspected that the person in question was John Francis O'Reilly. Gardaí eventually called around to the O'Reilly home, and after discovering that John Francis was out asked his mother to tell him to call into the barracks when he had the chance.

O'Reilly obliged, calling into the Garda station at eleven o'clock that night, where he was questioned and then released. He was rearrested the next morning, and this time was held for further questioning. In the interim Gardaí had discovered evidence to suggest the presence of two parachutes as well as two spades. O'Reilly had also been carrying with him an Abwehr suitcase radio, a Morse key, a transmitter and receiver and a code-wheel for enciphering messages. He was interviewed by Garda Superintendent Dawson, and told the superintendent, without hesitation, that he had 'jumped out of a plane and come down by parachute that morning at Moveen' and, producing his passport, asked if he had broken any law.

The superintendent said that his method of entry into the state was a breach of the Emergency Powers regulations, according to which arrivals and departures from the state could only be made at designated seaports and airports. On the morning following his arrest he made a lengthy statement to Superintendent Dawson, following which he was detained under the Offences Against the State Act. On the morning of 18 December 1943, he was brought to Garda Headquarters, Dublin, where he was interrogated by Superintendent Dawson and two military intelligence officers before being placed in Arbour Hill military detention barracks.

O'Reilly initially tried to mislead G2 as to how his ciphers worked but the systems were later figured out by Dr Hayes. Gardaí searched the family home for the wireless transmitter, which they found in a suitcase hidden in the yard, but the cardboard folder that contained the transmission codes could not be found. Gardaí believed that O'Reilly's father had disposed of the folder. They had more difficulty locating the parachute, however. O'Reilly was brought from Arbour Hill in February 1944 and showed the Gardaí where it was hidden, along with small spades and packing material for the radio set.

———

If O'Reilly's entry into Ireland was eventful, Kenny's can only be described as disastrous. His lack of training in espionage and basic spycraft was to prove to be his downfall. During his jump on 19 December he failed to collapse his parachute on landing, and as a result it caught the wind and dragged him through numerous fields in the Clare countryside, only stopping when Kenny hit a stone wall. He suffered a deep cut to his forehead, and had heavy bruising over his body. After freeing himself of his parachute Kenny made his way to a neighbouring house.

The sight of Kenny bloodied and dazed from the jump frightened the neighbours, who promptly called the Gardaí. Kenny was brought to Kilrush Hospital, and eventually to Ennis Hospital. After he made a significant recovery he was brought to Arbour Hill prison, where he was interned until the end of the war. Dan Bryan, Richard Hayes and others in G2 had hoped that the jailing of Hermann Görtz might have provided some reprieve for them, but O'Reilly's arrival in Ireland brought with it new problems. Writing in 1946, Hayes noted:

During Christmas week 1943, when it seemed that no further ciphers would appear and a period of relaxation might be hoped for, O'Reilly arrived with new types of ciphers in his possession. From January to April these ciphers were studied and the systems analysed. There were no messages in our possession in these ciphers but it took several months to correct all the false statements made by Reilly in relation to the working of his ciphers.

Both Kenny and O'Reilly were given better lodgings than some of the other prisoners in Arbour Hill, and were the only two German agents to remain there during the war and not be taken to Athlone. Kenny's interrogation was to prove to be as fruitless as O'Reilly's, and the authorities quickly came to the conclusion that he hadn't been trusted with any useful information due to his low intellect. Kenny eventually contracted a severe back complaint due to being kept in an unheated cell. He served the rest of his time in Arbour Hill without incident and was released on 11 May 1945. Upon his release he moved to a house in Jones' Road, in the shadow of Croke Park. In 1949, he was charged with arson, but nothing about his fate after that is known.

O'Reilly proved a lot more troublesome to the authorities. His arrival into Ireland had been noted by the US Legation, which proved a source of difficulty for the Irish government. Dr Hayes immediately went to work on a code-wheel cipher device that O'Reilly had brought with him. After a period of time Hayes felt he had garnered sufficient information as to the workings of the code-wheel:

A pair of discs with two jumbled alphabets were used in making this substitution cipher. The relative positions of the discs were designed to be altered before each letter was enciphered in ten positions corresponding to the numbers 0–9. There were two systems in use for providing a long series of numbers to control the alteration of the positions of the discs. The first and simplest was to write down a number followed by the date of the month and number of the month and continued by adding each figure to the figure immediately after it to give an endless series.

Hayes theorised that O'Reilly hadn't intended to use this particular system, and instead his spymasters in the SD had elected for him to use a system of microphotographs to communicate with Germany. The microphotographs contained 400 sets of five-figure groups which could be used from an agreed point. Hayes was able to crack the cipher disc as the letters chosen on it were derived from a predetermined keyword as opposed to a random sequence. Therefore the number of possibilities was greater, and the disc was more susceptible to frequency analysis.

During his analysis of O'Reilly's coding system Hayes made a number of discoveries. The Germans had begun using a method of turning letters into figures on a keyword in such a way that some letters were represented by a single figure and others by a number of two digits. Hayes discovered this new innovation the Germans were using when studying rough work found in O'Reilly's cell; little did he know that he was about to make a groundbreaking discovery that would help turn the tide of the war.

O'Reilly had been asked to prepare specimens of his messages using his disc cipher. While he was initially compliant, he soon abandoned the attempts and refused to do any more specimens. But Hayes had noted the method O'Reilly used by the time O'Reilly destroyed his rough work. Chillingly, by 1944 the Germans had developed an entirely new system of carrying out substitution and transposition ciphers. This new single-and-double-digit substitution system was entirely unknown to the British and the Americans. Hayes shared the information about the system with Dan Bryan, who passed it onto the Americans.

It was later noted by the Allies that a whole series of ciphers could not have been solved without Hayes's discovery. In reality what seemed like a minor detail in O'Reilly's rough work turned out to be of huge significance to the greater war effort. For a period of three months towards the end of 1944 the British were unable to read the ciphers in use by the German High Command. After terrific efforts during which the fullest use was made of calculating machines, all the ciphers were finally broken.

The 'black-out' where the enciphering system was changed coincided with Field Marshall Gerd von Rundstedt's Ardennes counter-offensive to the Normandy landings. The Germans officially referred to the offensive as Unternehmen Wacht am Rhein ('Operation Watch on the Rhine'), while the Allies designated it the Ardennes Counter-Offensive. The phrase 'Battle of the Bulge' was coined by contemporary press to describe the bulge in German front lines on wartime news maps, and as a result it became the most widely used name for the battle. The German offensive was intended to stop Allied use of the Belgian port of Antwerp and to split the Allied lines, allowing the Germans to encircle and destroy four Allied armies and force the Western Allies to negotiate a peace treaty in the Axis Powers' favour.

Dr Hayes's discovery helped play a crucial role in the Allied victory. On 7 January 1945 Hitler withdrew all his forces from the Ardennes, including the ss-Panzer divisions, thus ending all offensive operations. In an address to the British House of Commons following the battle Winston Churchill announced, 'This is undoubtedly the greatest American battle of the war and will, I believe, be regarded as an ever-famous American victory.' Privately it was noted by the security services that the victory would not have been possible without Dr Hayes's work.

———

O'Reilly proved himself to be a well-equipped agent, and perhaps demonstrated how the SD were a more sophisticated group than the Abwehr. Apart from the code-wheel cipher that O'Reilly brought with him, G2 were also anxious to find out how O'Reilly came to be in possession of what looked like a genuine Irish passport. He also was carrying on him an exit permit signed by William Warnock, the Irish Minister in Berlin.

O'Reilly would have had contact with Warnock during his time in Berlin, but G2 felt that Warnock should have been more astute than to give a visa to someone who could potentially cause political fallout. Dr Hayes took the passport to a laboratory in the Garda Forensic Unit in Kilmainham and studied it in detail. Hayes put the document under ultraviolet light and took infrared photographs of it in order to test if it was genuine. He came to the conclusion that the document was authentic, although page 12 of the passport was fake, and had been inserted at a later date. Hayes noted that the visa stamp had been altered to read 1943 instead of 1939, and that William Warnock's job title was out of date, as he had been promoted since the document was originally issued.

The discoveries that Hayes had made in relation to O'Reilly's documents and coding systems were vital to the Allies and the Irish authorities. However O'Reilly was to cause further trouble when he escaped from prison in July 1944. O'Reilly escaped out through a window after allegedly being aided by a sympathetic prison guard. After breaking the window he climbed on top of a nearby unused sentry tower, loosened the barbed wire and made his way over the prison wall.

In the dead of night O'Reilly moved through Arbour Hill, passing undetected by the front door of G2 headquarters on Infirmary Road. He hid until daylight in a potato field near the Phoenix Park, from where he walked to Inchicore to the home of a distant relative. He was given breakfast and, having borrowed five pounds for a train fare, he then left for Kingsbridge (now Heuston) Station bound for his home in Clare. Writing later of the train journey, O'Reilly spoke of his fear of being apprehended:

> During the whole journey I stood chatting in the corridor with a young merchant seaman. He was returning from leave from Portsmouth to his home in Limerick. His description of the German V1 raids on Portsmouth filled many a gap deleted by the heavy hand of the British censor. I thought regretfully of my lost radio transmitter. I arrived at Limerick around 2p.m. As I stepped from the railway station onto the street my heart missed a couple of beats. Walking in front of me I saw two 'Redcaps'. Between them was a young man whose height, build, and hair colour tallied with mine. It occurred to me immediately that this civilian had been taken in mistake for me. I later heard that he was an Irish Army deserter whose guilty conscience had betrayed him at the sight of the military police on the station platform.

In reality O'Reilly had hidden under a seat waiting till the coast was clear. Upon reaching Limerick he borrowed a bicycle and set off for Killkee. The chain broke soon after he left the train station and he was forced to walk the rest of the way.

As dawn broke in Dublin the prison authorities raised the alarm and a major manhunt for O'Reilly began. Given the ease of his escape the authorities suspected that collusion might have been a factor. The Irish government offered a reward of £500 for information leading to the capture of O'Reilly, who was described as being 5'11", weighing 152 lbs and being of slim build with fair hair, blue eyes and a fresh complexion. He was also described as wearing a dark brown suit with red stripes, black shoes and a sports shirt. In a twist to the tale, the reward was claimed by O'Reilly's father Bernard, and John Francis was rearrested within three hours of arriving back in Kilkee.

O'Reilly's father applied for the reward and was granted it. Dan Bryan and Minister for Justice Gerald Boland had debated the merits of paying out the reward to him but ultimately they decided to go ahead with it in an effort not to deter public response to the issuing of any further awards. Upon his arrest O'Reilly claimed that his escape was a protest against the unfair conditions in which he was being held. He was interned once again in Arbour Hill, where he would stay until the end of the war.

In 1944, O'Reilly applied to have his espionage money added to his bank account, but it wasn't given back to him until the end of the war. During his time in Arbour Hill Dr Hayes noted that he felt O'Reilly was 'a cocky young man who believed that the cipher method in which he had been trained in Germany was impenetrable and he fell for a challenge'. Hayes asked O'Reilly to encipher an unbreakable message, but while O'Reilly was out in the exercise yard Hayes collected the burnt notes that O'Reilly had used for the enciphering process from the grate of his cell. He treated these in the Garda Forensic Laboratory in Kilmainham and mounted them on glass slides.

Using this information Hayes broke the code and duly informed Dan Bryan of his findings. Bryan wrote to Cecil Liddell in London, noting, 'messages just read, doctor's notes provided solution'. O'Reilly proved to be a thorn in the side of Hayes, who was unimpressed with the young man's cockiness and 'red herrings'. However by the time the war had ended Hayes had identified most of his codes' secrets and shared these with MI5.

———

O'Reilly was released from custody on Saturday 12 May 1945, receiving the balance of £96 10s 6d of the money he had on his person when arrested. Unlike the German agents in Athlone, who would be interned for another two years, O'Reilly was released within 24 hours of VE Day. Upon gaining his freedom he travelled to Kilkee, where he received a warm welcome from his family. His father presented him with the reward money and O'Reilly found himself relatively wealthy when he combined this with his espionage money.

In October 1945, he bought the Esplanade Hotel in Dublin and later opened a pub on Parkgate Street, a short distance from Irish Military Intelligence Headquarters on Infirmary Road. The pub was named 'O'Reilly's', but it became colloquially known as 'the Parachute Bar', and for many years afterwards O'Reilly himself had the nickname 'the Parachutist'. He serialised his memoirs in a London newspaper, the *Sunday Dispatch*, before eventually moving overseas once more. He was alleged to have lived in Nigeria and Lima in Peru, where he was said to have worked as an electrician.

He was also reputed to have worked as a radio operator for the British in Cairo during the 1967 Six-Day War. O'Reilly married shortly after his release and fathered six children. The marriage broke up and the children were taken into care. The body of his wife was found in Hume Street in 18 April 1956, victim of a botched abortion performed by Mary Anne Cadden, who was convicted and sentenced for her murder.

O'Reilly worked abroad for many years before returning to work in the Shannon industrial estate in the early 1960s. He remarried and fathered another child. During his time back in Clare, O'Reilly taught German classes with Clare VEC, and successfully helped attract German Foreign Direct Investment to the Shannon region using his old contacts in Germany. He moved one last time to England, settling in Westminster. At the age of 54 he was seriously injured in a road accident there and died in Middlesex Hospital on 4 May 1971. He was buried in Glasnevin Cemetery in an unmarked grave.

O'Reilly and Kenny's arrival into Ireland coincided with Hempel's radio set being confiscated by Capt. John Patrick O'Sullivan. Hempel declined the offer of a new set from Berlin, as he feared that the timing might be seen as an act of provocation, and could lead to an Allied invasion of Ireland. The whole episode had caused consternation in the Dáil, and Deputy James Dillon brought the matter up with the Taoiseach. De Valera gave Dillon a quick summary of the facts relating to O'Reilly and Kenny, hoping to placate the deputy. However, Dillon demanded to know why Germany was sending parachutists into Ireland. De Valera explained to Dillon that he could not discuss the matter in any detail, and refused to acknowledge that Hempel had been questioned about the two parachutists.

Angered by de Valera's stonewalling, Dillon angrily replied, 'Good, I'll give you time to think about it', before resuming his seat. The O'Reilly and Kenny landings were significant for a number of reasons. Undoubtedly they helped provide G2 and ultimately MI5 with crucial information with regard to the German enciphering systems, and they also marked the end of German agents beings sent to Ireland. However they were more significant in the fact that they highlighted how the Abwehr had faded in stature and had been superseded by the SD. Perhaps most significantly, it is notable how once in Ireland O'Reilly and Kenny made no effort to get in contact with Berlin, perhaps signalling their motives all along may have been simply to try and get a way out of occupied Europe.

O'Reilly and Kenny's landing in Ireland caused panic within the jails. Görtz and the other prisoners were aware of their arrival as they were able to read news reports in their cells. The prison authorities feared that there would be a prison breakout, and immediately tightened security on the remaining prisoners. In addition to fears of a breakout the authorities also worried that O'Reilly and Kenny would attempt to free the prisoners in Athlone. Such a breakout would have been disastrous, and would have caused huge consternation with the British at such a sensitive time in the war.

The prison governor encouraged informers within the prison to report on any suspicious activity, and the German agents were routinely subjected to cell searches. Two officers arrived in the prison one day and questioned Görtz as to his knowledge of O'Reilly and Kenny. Looking at them incredulously Görtz denied he had any knowledge about the two agents, and berated the officers for thinking he had anything to do with the landing. At this stage the tide in the war had turned. The Normandy landings stretched Hitler's forces to their absolute limit, and after some resistance the Allied forces made their way to Paris.

The Allies entered the city on 19 August 1944, and following intense fighting, the German Garrison under Gen. Dietrich von Choltitz surrendered the French Capital on 25 August 1944 at the Hôtel Meurice, the newly established headquarters of French Gen. Philippe Leclerc. Parisiens celebrated the liberation their city, which had been under Nazi domination since the signing of the second Compiègne Armistice on 22 June 1940. Hitler had instructed Choltitz that Paris 'must not fall into the enemy's hands except lying in complete debris', ordering Choltitz to bomb and blow up all the city's bridges, however, Choltitz disobeyed the order, and personally allowed the Allies to take the city without obstruction.

This prevented the French Resistance from engaging in urban warfare, which would have undoubtedly destroyed large parts of the city. With Paris liberated the long march to Berlin soon began. It was the beginning of the end for the German forces, and Görtz and his fellow agents would soon find themselves in the unenviable situation of being jailed in a neutral country with the Allies looking to recall all German agents worldwide to Berlin to begin a process of denazification. As news filtered through on radio stations throughout Ireland about the Allied successes in the war, the German prisoners knew their lives were about to change forever.

In March 1945, the Irish authorities were struck by good fortune when the German submarine U-260 was scuttled approximately 7 km south of the coast of Cork. The U-boat was deliberately sunk after damage suffered from striking a mine which had been laid by the HMS Apollo, a British Abdiel-class minelayer which had taken part in the Normandy landings before being transferred to the British Pacific Fleet. On 7 June 1944 it was used to transport Supreme Allied Commander Dwight D. Eisenhower, Naval Commander in Chief Bertram Ramsay and Field Marshal Bernard Montgomery to visit the assault areas. Its role as minelayer was to prove vital in yielding more crucial information from the German forces. U-260's crew of five officers and 48 sailors were interned until the end of the war.

As the vessel sank beneath the waves of the Celtic Sea, a sealed box containing some of the most closely guarded German war secrets made its way to the surface. In their haste the German crew had failed to adequately sink the metal box, in which numerous papers had been stored. The box was taken under armed escort to G2 headquarters near Arbour Hill. When Dr Hayes examined the box's contents he could scarcely believe his eyes.

Hayes immediately contacted his superiors to inform them that the box contained the codes and enciphering system of the Kriesgmarine, the German Navy. He began to hurriedly catalogue material and made several observations about the naval code. Hayes noted that the codes were extremely elaborate, and included two substitutions after the original encoding from a code book. He also observed that the substitutions were based on pages of figures and letters which were changed every day. Hayes came to the conclusion that without some good fortune the system was virtually unbreakable, and involved a great deal of work in both encoding and decoding.

In 1940, fragments of decoded messages had been recovered from a crashed German aircraft. Hayes had studied these, and when looking at the naval code ciphers noticed some similarities. He rushed to his notes in an effort to see if a comparison between the two systems could yield any clues. Hayes was able to surmise that the naval code was more sophisticated than the Air Force code, and after studying both systems Hayes came to the conclusion that the naval code system was theoretically close in its make-up to the enciphering system used by Hermann Görtz. The similarity lay in the fact that the process involved substituting letters into numbers and back into letters again. Once Hayes had made his observations G2 contacted MI5 to inform them of their discovery. A cryptographer from Bletchley Park was sent to examine Hayes's findings, which were later noted to be of huge help to the British authorities.

While he worked on the German naval code Hayes also intercepted a British cipher, which was picked up from a transmission to a resistance group inside Germany in March 1945. The cipher was a double transposition, with each transposition being based on the same keyword. Hayes deduced that the keyword was 31 letters in length. Despite gaining an in-depth knowledge of the cipher, Hayes was unable to say whether or not the cipher was in widespread use by the British. After two days Hayes had broken the cipher, and noted its composition for posterity.

Despite these successes the end of the war in 1945 brought with it a myriad of new problems; chief among these was how to deal with the release of the German spies detained in Athlone, as well as the diplomatic fallout from Ireland's dealings with the German Minister and his staff in Dublin. The scene was set for the most dramatic turn of events yet.

IX
HERMANN GÖRTZ'S LAST STAND

'Görtz who is a dangerous person (notwithstanding the ill-informed views to the contrary expressed by some people) will certainly, if given any kind of facilities, resume some of his former contacts.'

COL DAN BRYAN, August 1946

The Ardennes Offensive was Germany's attempt at reversing the tide of the war, but ultimately it was the beginning of the end. In early April 1945, the Western Allies finally pushed forward their forces in Italy and swept across western Germany, capturing Hamburg and Nuremberg, while Soviet and Polish forces stormed Berlin in late April. American and Soviet forces met at the Elbe on 25 April and on 30 April 1945 the Reichstag was captured, signalling the military defeat of Nazi Germany.

This period of the war also signalled several changes in leadership among the Allied and Axis powers. On 12 April, President Roosevelt died, and was succeeded by Harry S. Truman. Benito Mussolini was killed by Italian partisans on 28 April, and two days later Adolf Hitler committed suicide, and was succeeded by Grand Admiral Karl Dönitz as President of the German Reich. Supreme Allied Commander Dwight D. Eisenhower informed the German leadership that the Allied Forces expected 'immediate, simultaneous and unconditional surrender on all fronts'. The war with Germany was soon to be brought to an end.

In his role as leader of Germany, Dönitz sent Col Gen. Alfred Jodl to the headquarters of the Allied Supreme Command in the French city of Reims to attempt to persuade the Allies of an alternative to unconditional surrender. However Eisenhower cut short any discussion by announcing at 9 p.m. on 6 May that, in the absence of a complete capitulation, he would close British and American lines to surrendering German forces at midnight on 8 May, and resume the bombing offensive against remaining German-held positions and towns. Jodl telegraphed this message to Dönitz, who responded, authorising him to sign the instrument of unconditional surrender, but subject to negotiating a 48-hour delay, essentially to enable the surrender order to be communicated to outlying German military units.

Jodl signed the instruments of surrender on 8 May, thus bringing to an end the deadliest conflict in human history. From 1939 to 1945 the war resulted in 50 million to 85 million fatalities, most of whom were civilians in the Soviet Union and China. It included massacres, the genocide of the Holocaust, strategic bombing, starvation, disease and the first use of nuclear weapons in history. Nor had the war left Ireland unblemished. The Luftwaffe had carried out deadly bombing raids in Dublin's North Strand and in Campile, Co. Wexford, while in Northern Ireland, Belfast was one of the most heavily bombed cities in the United Kingdom after London and Coventry.

Despite these atrocities being perpetrated on a neutral nation, Taoiseach Éamon de Valera, on the occasion of the death of Adolf Hitler, paid a controversial visit to the German Legation to express to Minister Hempel sympathy with the German people over the death of the Führer. Hempel was described as being distraught at the news, wringing his hands in anguish. Hempel's family would later claim he held no loyalty towards Hitler and attributed the wringing of his hands to the fact that he suffered from eczema. Sir John Maffey, the British Representative, commented that de Valera's actions were 'unwise but mathematically consistent'.

Douglas Hyde, Ireland's President, also visited Hempel to express condolences, an action which enraged US Minister David Gray as no similar action had taken place on the death of Franklin Delano Roosevelt. This can perhaps be seen more as a reflection of the strained relationship between Gray and de Valera. Indeed de Valera shared a better relationship with Hempel, whose conduct he described at the end of the war as beyond reproach: 'So long as we retained our diplomatic relations with Germany, to fail to have called upon the German representative would have been an act of unpardonable discourtesy to the German nation and to Dr Hempel himself.'

De Valera explained the reasons for his visit by saying he wasn't going to humiliate Hempel in his hour of defeat; however his actions are still questionable given that he would have had some knowledge of the horrors of the Holocaust. Indeed by this stage footage from concentration camps was being played as part of newsreels in cinemas, so such a stance is still perplexing.

BBC broadcaster Richard Dimbleby had accompanied the British 11th Armoured Division (which counted among its number a young James Molyneux, future leader of the Ulster Unionist Party) to the liberation of the Bergen-Belsen concentration camp, and described the scene in a report so graphic that the BBC refused to broadcast it for four days, relenting only when he threatened to resign:

> Here over an acre of ground lay dead and dying people. You could not see which was which … The living lay with their heads against the corpses and around them moved the awful, ghostly procession of emaciated, aimless people, with nothing to do and with no hope of life, unable to move out of your way, unable to look at the terrible sights around them … Babies had been born here, tiny wizened things that could not live … A mother, driven mad, screamed at a British sentry to give her milk for her child, and thrust the tiny mite into his arms, then ran off, crying terribly. He opened the bundle and found the baby had been dead for days.

The footage was viewed all over the UK, and Dimbleby would later describe his visit to Belsen as the worst day of his life.

De Valera's motives for the visit remain shrouded in mystery, and perhaps can only be explained by his desire to maintain strict protocol; or perhaps, more sinisterly, he was appeasing Hempel given the fact that Günther Schütz may have had compromising information of contacts between himself, the legation and government officials. The alleged contacts could have proven to be a major source of embarrassment to the government if they were made public. Despite saving face at home, De Valera's actions angered many in Irish-America as evidenced in a letter to the *New York Times* by one Angela D. Walsh:

> Have you seen the motion pictures of the victims of German concentration camps, de Valera? Have you seen the crematoriums? Have you seen the bodies of little children murdered by Nazi hands? Have you seen the flourishing cabbages – cabbages for German food – flourishing because of the fertiliser, human remains of citizens from almost completely Catholic countries like Poland? These were citizens of a conquered country – and ÉIRE might easily have been a conquered country, neutrality or no neutrality. Have you seen the living dead, de Valera? Skin stretched over bone, and too weak to walk?

The visit to Hempel also did little to improve relations between de Valera and Churchill in the immediate aftermath of the war. Churchill had already been infuriated by de Valera's reluctance to grant access to the treaty ports, and the Taoiseach's refusal coupled with his attitude towards general involvement in World War II prompted the British prime minister to address the issue in a radio broadcast on the BBC on VE Day. In his broadcast Churchill praised British restraint in not invading Ireland during the Battle of the Atlantic:

> The approaches which the southern Irish ports and airfields could so easily have guarded were closed by the hostile aircraft and U-boats. This indeed was a deadly moment in our life, and if it had not been for the loyalty and friendship of Northern Ireland, we should have been forced to come to close quarters with Mr. de Valera, or perish from the earth. However, with a restraint and poise to which, I venture to say, history will find few parallels, His Majesty's Government never laid a violent hand upon them, though at times it would have been quite easy and quite natural, and we left the de Valera Government to frolic with

the German and later with the Japanese representatives to their heart's content.

De Valera's response gained him huge popularity in Ireland, and in many ways solidified his status as a strong leader, prepared to stand up for Ireland:

Mr. Churchill, instead of adding another horrid chapter to the already bloodstained record of the relations between England and this country, has advanced the cause of international morality – an important step, one of the most important indeed that can be taken on the road to the establishment of any sure basis for peace ... Mr. Churchill is proud of Britain's stand alone, after France had fallen and before America entered the war. Could he not find in his heart the generosity to acknowledge that there is a small nation that stood alone not for one year or two, but for several hundred years against aggression; that endured spoliations, famine, massacres, in endless succession; that was clubbed many times into insensibility, but each time on returning to consciousness took up the fight anew; a small nation that could never be got to accept defeat and has never surrendered her soul?

Given the level of cooperation that existed between both countries in terms of military intelligence, such a caustic back and forth can only now in hindsight be seen as an attempt by both leaders to assert their country's authority in the post-war world. In fact Anglo-Irish cooperation during the war wasn't only limited to intelligence.

In 1941, de Valera granted the Allied Powers the use of what became known as the Donegal Corridor, a narrow strip of Irish airspace linking the RAF flying boat base at Castle Archdale in Lough Erne to the international waters of the Atlantic Ocean. Rather than having to fly north towards Londonderry, Catalina and Sunderland flying boats could now fly over Ballyshannon, Co. Donegal in neutral Ireland out into the Atlantic, where they were used primarily in the protection of Allied shipping convoys. The first official flight along the Corridor was on 21 February 1941 by NO. 240 Squadron RAF's flying boats.

Conditions of the concession included that flights should be made at a 'good height', and that aircraft should not fly over the military camp at Finner between Ballyshannon and Bundoran, although these conditions appear to have been ignored by both sides. Such was the strategic importance of the corridor that in 1941 a Catalina flying boat from No. 209 Squadron RAF, also based at Lough Erne, located the German battleship *Bismarck* in 1941, leading to the ship's destruction. Had the corridor not existed it is arguable as to whether or not the *Bismarck* would have been spotted.

———

Despite these huge levels of cooperation between neutral Ireland and the British, the reaction to the end of the war in Europe was met by a largely divided response in Dublin. Much of the cooperation was lost on the general public, and instead there pervaded a distinct sense of nationalism that was further compounded by de Valera's reply to Churchill. On VE Day, future Taoiseach Charles J. Haughey and other UCD students burnt the Union Jack on College Green, outside Trinity College, in response to a perceived disrespect afforded the Irish tricolour among the flags hung by the college in celebration of the Allied victory that ended World War II. It was into this cauldron of mixed public and political opinion that Hermann Görtz and the other German internees found themselves at the cessation of hostilities in May 1945.

Military personnel interned in the Curragh Camp in Co. Kildare were sent back to the continent as early as July and August; however the Irish and the Allies came to an understanding with each other that spies would not be released as quickly. It was largely felt that former German agents could prove themselves to be a nuisance if they were suddenly granted their freedom. The British were particularly concerned about the issue of the spies, so much so that the British representative in Ireland, Sir John Maffey, compiled a list of German agents, including Görtz, who they felt would be 'undesirable to release'.

The British also made it clear that the only way they would agree to any release of internees was if prisoners were subject to deportation orders to Germany. In order to placate the British, the Irish authorities came to an agreement whereby the Germans were allowed to move freely around Athlone during the day under the condition they returned to sleep in the barracks each night. In reality the agreement went much further, and the German spies soon found themselves at liberty to attend social functions and receive guests. Görtz went a step further, writing to Minister for Justice Gerald Boland to request political asylum in Ireland.

On the advice of Dan Bryan and G2 the request was denied. Görtz had every reason to be apprehensive about going back to Germany. Almost immediately the Allied Forces had begun a rapid process of denazification in Germany. The process aimed to rid German and Austrian society of any remnants of the Nazi ideology. It was carried out specifically by removing from positions of power and influence those who had been Nazi Party members, and by disbanding any organisations associated with Nazism. The process had begun shortly after the cessation of hostilities but it was made official policy following the Potsdam Conference, on 30 July 1945.

An Allied Control Council was established in Berlin to execute the Allied resolutions known as the 'Four DS'. Denazification was a major component of this, alongside Demilitarisation, Democratisation and Decentralisation. Plans were also underway to try former Nazis who had been in leadership positions under international law. Görtz felt that his role as a spy in Ireland would ensure that he would be treated badly if he returned home, and from the end of the war his priority was to remain in Ireland for as long as possible.

However by this stage Görtz and the other internees were proving themselves to be a major thorn in the side of the Irish authorities. Both G2 and the Irish Department of External Affairs wished for the prisoners issue to be dealt with as soon as possible, but repatriation was diplomatically a very tricky issue. As well as the interned German spies, the remaining legation staff, including Eduard Hempel, also posed a significant problem for the Irish authorities. In June 1945, American Minister in Ireland David Gray, with whom de Valera had an at times strained relationship, submitted a list of names to the United Nations of diplomats and spies he believed to be hostile to the new global peace arrangements.

The Irish government responded to Gray's action by declaring that it was refusing to deport anyone named on the list who was still resident in Ireland unless the deportation was voluntary. This posed a difficulty for the Irish government, as the Allied Control Commission now held legal jurisdiction over all German citizens abroad who had been involved in the war, including both spies and diplomats. The commission soon exercised its power to recall all such personnel to Berlin to be debriefed and, if the individual case merited it, to face trial. Both the Irish government and the Germans ignored the order.

The Department of External Affairs discussed the issue with the British representative, assuring him that the Germans would not be required to leave unless it was of their own free will. The Minister informed him that 'With regards to the persons who have been detained here because they acted as German agents, it is intended to keep them under detention until such time as, after consultation between the two governments; it is agreed that they are no longer a menace to the security of either country and can, therefore, be restored to liberty.'

Behind closed doors the Irish authorities began a process of reviewing the cases of each of the internees in order to determine which ones posed the greatest problems from both a political and a security point of view. Günther Schütz proved to be the agent who was of most concern. De Valera was sticking to the line that Hempel had behaved correctly during the war and was not involved in espionage in any way. Schütz of course had proof that this wasn't true, and owing to his character it was felt that he was in a position to cause embarrassment to the Irish government if he were released.

In order to thwart this, de Valera had all documents that contained information in relation to discussions with foreign governments destroyed. Having deciphered Schütz's microdot messages, G2 were able to prove that Hempel knew about Schütz's arrival beforehand, and had helped him by supplying him with cash. He also had contact with some of the other German agents active in Ireland, although this wasn't apparent to authorities at the time. When he eventually was released Schütz didn't use this information in any way against Hempel.

———

Dan Bryan reviewed the files on each of the detainees and advised on their characters to the various government departments. Bryan felt that neither Tributh nor Gärtner posed any conceivable threat to national security, and that they were in his estimation foot soldiers rather than serious spies. The same could not be said, however, for Hermann Görtz. Bryan regarded him as someone who was highly likely to cause difficulties in the future if he were released. He cautioned that Görtz would be very likely to resume contacts he had in republican circles, especially through some of the various women he had been involved with. He felt that many of the groups were anti-British to the point of being pro-Nazi.

In the meantime, while de Valera looked into ways in which he might be able to grant political asylum to Hempel, the Department of Justice restricted the entry of Jewish refugees into Ireland. The official line given was that any increase in the Jewish population in Ireland could lead to the rise of anti-Semitism in the country. The government continued to ponder the situation, with the Department of External Affairs noting that in general the internees were not unfavourably disposed to returning to Germany in order to be reunited with their families and friends.

The department noted at one stage during their review into the prisoners' continued detentions that a German ship was docked in Dublin port, and that it could if needed facilitate the Germans' repatriation without having to pass through England. De Valera favoured the idea of repatriating the Germans on the ship as soon as possible, and said that van Loon and Obéd could be repatriated to the Netherlands and India when it became possible. The Department of External Affairs approached the British with a view to securing guarantees of immunity for the prisoners. The British replied that

[t]he control commission would be prepared to accept these men and distribute them to their destinations. The men would be treated in conformity with the policy towards other Germans repatriated from other neutral countries, and so far as the United Kingdom Authorities are aware, there are no charges pending against them which would be likely to lead to capital sentence.

But the fast-moving global political climate, as well as other factors, eventually forced de Valera's hand, and all German spies were released in August 1946 under the Emergency Powers Act. The prisoners were released on the basis that they were to be deported at a later date when such arrangements could be made. Until then they would be allowed to move freely around Ireland. The Department of Justice made the decision to release the prisoners, citing the restricted nature of where they were detained as well as the toll it was taking on their mental health. Minister for Justice Gerald Boland justified his decision by insisting that the prisoners be released, claiming considerable grounds on a humanitarian basis. He also insisted that, following a review of internal security, the Garda Commissioner had informed him that there was no longer any necessity for detaining the men or placing them under any restrictions.

But legal considerations may ultimately have forced his hand. Boland had been informed by the Attorney General and future President of Ireland Cearbhall Ó Dálaigh that Article 14 of the Aliens Order 1935 authorised only 'detention bona fide preparatory to deportation'. Ó Dálaigh also advised the government that any further detention could possibly be challenged by motion of habeas corpus, and could leave the officers of the detention barracks open to action for damages for unlawful imprisonment.

Boland was not prepared to deport the Germans as a definite guarantee of immunity could not be obtained; however, mindful of the fact that the authority with which Ireland could detain the men was at most very doubtful, he ultimately decided to release them. The Department of Defence was tasked with travelling to Athlone to inform the prisoners that they would be released and allowed to remain in Ireland for 'at least the time being'.

The men were requested to register under the Aliens Order and were warned that their stay in Ireland was subject to a number of strictly imposed conditions. The penalty for breaking any of these was immediate deportation. The prisoners were instructed to refrain from discussing or referring in any way to their past activities, the purpose of their entry into Ireland or the reasons for their detention. They were also forbidden from involving themselves in any form of political activity or discussing international politics or the politics of Ireland. In addition to this they were expressly forbidden from engaging in any interviews with members of the press.

Department of Defence personnel travelled to Athlone and Mountjoy to inform the prisoners of these conditions in person. An official also travelled to Tuam, where Wilhelm Preetz had been residing while on parole, to inform him. All of the internees with the exception of Obéd, who was a British citizen, were now subject to the same law as ordinary aliens and as a result had to register with the Gardaí and consistently re-register their addresses so that the authorities could keep up to date with their whereabouts.

Boland retained the right as Minister to deport the men if he felt that it was in the public good. He was also entitled to restrict the men's movements, occupation, employment and frequency of reporting to the Gardaí, as well as possession of any machine or apparatus. In the end Boland didn't have to invoke any of these restrictions, as it was generally regarded that it was in the men's own interest to behave properly and avoid any publicity. Boland also noted that it was unlikely that the state would have to support the men financially upon their release. Schütz, Gärtner, Tributh and van Loon had taken up woodwork while in custody, and it was believed that they were in a position to maintain themselves through these endeavours upon release.

During their time in Athlone the men had made deck chairs, light furniture, wooden toys and table lamps. Such was the four men's enthusiasm for their work that they asked the authorities if they could stay in Athlone until a table they were working on was complete. It was felt that Wilhelm Preetz's in-laws were in a position to offer him a job in their family garage business. Werner Unland's wife had enough money to sustain them until he could re-establish the import business he had worked at in London.

Obéd, who the authorities noted was in the possession of £140, had lived in Antwerp in Belgium in the 1920s, and he planned to return there, as he had a certificate of good character from the Antwerp police issued in June 1946. It was believed he had also applied to the British representative's office for a British passport.

Simon and Weber-Drohl, aged 64 and 67 respectively, had no money. However the authorities believed that Simon, who was a fisherman by trade, could find employment in that industry, and that Weber-Drohl, who was essentially an invalid at this stage, had relatives in America who could be in a position to send him money.

Hermann Görtz informed the authorities that he was in a position to support himself without engaging in business or employment. Despite the fact that Gardaí had seized $20,000 from Görtz on his arrival, it was believed that he most likely had originally brought a much larger sum, and had hidden the balance somewhere to be accessed after leaving confinement.

Immediately upon their release several of the spies moved to Dublin. Tributh, Gärtner and van Loon went into a joinery business together for a brief period, after which Gärtner returned to South Africa, while Tributh moved back to Germany, where he died in 1996.

Henry Obéd was deported to India via London despite his wishes that he be sent to Antwerp to his wife. During his time in India he made several attempts to return to Belgium but his applications were blocked due to his history with explosives. Eventually he was granted an Indian passport after independence and he emigrated to his wife in Belgium in the late 1940s. Obéd was murdered by his wife in 1952 after she discovered that he had been having an affair.

Wilhelm Preetz settled in Tuam to be near his in-laws, but his marriage eventually foundered. He also frequently got into trouble with the law, and in 1947 he was convicted of dangerous driving. Preetz's wife eventually emigrated to the United States, but his own fate remains a mystery.

Walter Simon eventually returned of his own volition to Germany on board a British ship, but his repatriation did little to change his fortunes. After spending many years in a nursing home he died almost destitute in Hamburg in 1961.

Weber-Drohl returned to Bavaria and for the most part seems to have kept in contact with many of the people he met while in Ireland.

Stephen Carroll Held went back into steel manufacturing but eventually sold his factory in 1960 before taking up employment as an accountant.

He maintained for years afterwards that the bad publicity garnered by his arrest and detention had ruined his reputation and that his life financially never recovered. Eventually he and his wife and son left for the United States, never to return.

————

Görtz, however, continued to be a problem for the Irish authorities. He was infuriated by the government's attempts to have him deported, and vigorously tried to fight against them. In the meantime he had taken up a role outside of prison as secretary of the 'Save the German Children Society', a group which had launched a campaign known as 'Operation Shamrock'. The purpose of the campaign was to bring over 400 Catholic German children to Ireland for fostering. The scheme was embraced warmly by the Irish public despite the fact that Jewish children attempting to gain asylum in Ireland were often met by a wall of bureaucracy. Görtz busied himself with his work for the group, earning a meagre salary of £2 per month. In his spare time he read voraciously and devoured any text he felt might aid him in avoiding deportation.

Meanwhile, following the end of the war Dr Richard Hayes had returned in a more full-time capacity to his role as Director of the National Library. And despite being responsible for the day-to-day running of the library, Hayes still involved himself in a more limited role in espionage and remained in contact with both Guy and Cecil Liddell. Görtz's fascination with reading the minutiae of Irish law finally brought him to the library, where he and Dr Hayes would cross paths one final time.

One February morning in 1947, sometime before lunchtime a dishevelled yet familiar figure shuffled into the library's reading room. Hayes recognised the shabbily dressed man as Hermann Görtz, and almost immediately he was overcome with a sense of pity. The last time the two men had met was in the internment camp in Athlone, Görtz then an agent of the Abwehr and Hayes Ireland's master codebreaker. Görtz carried a bundle of books to a desk, and when he took his seat he and Hayes met each other's gaze. Both men nodded tersely at one another and continued with their business. When Görtz returned the next day, Hayes decided to approach him.

In an effort to remedy matters Hayes walked over to Görtz and asked if he would like to join him for a cup of coffee, and they decamped to the quieter surroundings of Anne's Tea Shop on Nassau Street, where they talked for over an hour. Hayes explained to Görtz how he had broken his code, and how it was actually he who had corresponded with him, as opposed to the German High Command. Görtz stared intently at Dr Hayes as the reality that he had been outwitted sank in.

At the end of their conversation Görtz, realising that he had been bested intellectually by Hayes, extended his hand to Hayes and respectfully said, 'I must congratulate you.' Görtz gathered his things and headed home to the house of the Farrell sisters in Glenageary, where he had been staying. Soon afterwards Dr Hayes wrote of the incident to Cecil Liddell of MI5, informing him of the encounter and commenting on another clandestine operation he was undertaking for MI5, unbeknownst to anyone in Ireland:

> H. Görtz who is now free had begun to read all day in the National Library. As was bound to happen sooner or later I walked bang into him yesterday. This morning I took him out for a cup of coffee to soften up the hard points of opposition. Some interesting admissions were made. The operation is proceeding. Details will be released later. Note the following address of an associate of G. Now in Spain who may be a German agent. M.F. de SAN MARTIN, Calle de Belacazzar, 8, Coloniade la Residencia Madrid, Hush; Keep it dark; Please do not refer to this in replying to this address.
>
> Yours ever,
>
> V

Hayes had found Görtz to be somewhat likeable as a person, despite the fact that he disagreed profoundly with his politics. However the encounter probably worsened Görtz's fragile mental state. In September 1946 he threatened to go on hunger strike for a second time in order to avoid being deported to Allied-controlled Germany, complaining that the authorities were treating him as though he were a common criminal. He eventually gave up his protest when he noticed an advertisement in a newspaper looking for crew for an Estonian ship bound for Spain. Görtz wrote to the Irish government asking for permission to join the crew, but to his ongoing frustration the request was denied.

Strangely, during this period of his release he failed to stay in contact with his family. Instead he entertained himself in the company of his fellow internees and Irish friends. The Farrell sisters organised a party in the garden of their home in Spencer Villas in Glenageary for the German prisoners and Görtz attended, joined by van Loon, Tributh and Gärtner. The party was a short-lived moment of happiness for Görtz. While he seemed to be enjoying himself in the company of the others, beneath the surface lay a very troubled and fragile man. Görtz was obsessed with the thought of being handed over to the Russians when he returned to Germany, and the idea that he would be sent to a gulag in Siberia.

For Görtz this would be a fate worse than death. During World War I he had fought on the Eastern Front, and ever since he held an irrational suspicion of Russians, believing them to be akin to barbarians. The wanton destruction of Russian property undertaken by the Wehrmacht during the failed Russian invasion also weighed heavily on his mind, and Görtz was utterly convinced that he would be treated with nothing short of depravity by the Russians should he return home. But Görtz's concerns at returning home ran even deeper.

After World War I Germany had been convulsed politically. From 4 to 15 January 1919 a post-war revolution erupted in Berlin, where various factions clashed over what path the country should follow. This led to the Spartacist uprising, essentially a power struggle between the Social Democrats led by Friedrich Ebert and the Communist Party of Germany led by Karl Liebknecht and Rosa Luxemburg, who had previously formed the Spartacist League. The communists were brutally suppressed by the German Army, and Herman Görtz had been involved in the fighting as a foot soldier. He believed that he would be remembered for his role in quelling the uprising, and would be subjected to severe treatment should he return to Berlin. He knew his only hope of avoiding this fate was to find some legal loophole in Irish law that would allow him to stay.

In the meantime Görtz busied himself by working feverishly to avoid being deported. But time would soon run out for him. By April 1947 the Allies had begun trying war criminals under international law in a series of military tribunals. The trials, held in the German city of Nuremberg, were most notable for the prosecution of prominent members of the political, military, judicial and economic leadership of Nazi Germany, who planned, carried out or otherwise participated in the Holocaust and other war crimes.

In total 24 indictments were handed down to major figures in the Nazi regime, including Martin Bormann, Karl Dönitz, Hermann Göring, Rudolf Hess and Alfred Jodl, as well as the German Foreign Minister who had first helped identify Ireland as a strategic location for espionage, Joachim von Ribbentrop. By the time the trials concluded many of the leaders of Nazi Germany had been executed or sentenced to life imprisonment, and Görtz clearly felt that he belonged in this category. International opinion had shifted, and it was now impossible for de Valera to grant any further asylum to former spies.

A decision was made that diplomats would be allowed to stay, although any former German agents would be deported. The spies were rounded up and returned to custody in Mountjoy Prison. Görtz, Unland and Schütz all fought their deportations on the grounds that they had lived in Ireland for longer than five years, but only Unland was successful. Görtz took his case to the Supreme Court, arguing that under the Aliens Act 1935 he was entitled to three months' notice before deportation. Acting on his behalf were a team of barristers led by future Taoiseach John A. Costello, while the Minister for Justice was represented by Andreas O'Keefe, instructed by the Chief State Solicitor.

During the course of the trial Senior Counsel for Görtz, Mr C. Lavery, informed the court that 'Dr Görtz had not been convicted of any offence and had come before the court as a person who was entitled to the full protection of the court.' The Chief Justice replied by reminding the Senior Counsel that Görtz had committed a crime by landing by parachute and that he came to Ireland as a German soldier to promote the war effort of his country. In reality Görtz had little hope of having his deportation overturned, and the only point upon which the court was called upon to decide was whether or not it could be held that Görtz was 'ordinarily resident' in the country and therefore entitled to his three months' notice of deportation. After a short adjournment the court reconvened and dismissed the appeal, awarding costs to the Minister for Justice. In the end it was decided that the motive for Görtz's sojourn to Ireland was immaterial as to whether not he had resided in Ireland ordinarily for a period of five years or more under the auspices of the Alien Act.

Such was his desperation to stay in Ireland at any cost that Görtz also wrote personally to de Valera during this period. One of the Farrell sisters, Brigid, also wrote to de Valera on Görtz's behalf. In a six-page letter she begged the Taoiseach to personally intervene, citing Görtz's age and rank in the SS as proof that he would be treated harshly if returned to Germany. She further added that

he served his country well as did many Englishmen and Americans in a similar situation and that you should do what is in your power to intervene in the harsh ruling that permits an old soldier and cultured gentleman two full years after the termination of hostilities to face trial ending in his death or at best, long years of imprisonment.

In the end both Görtz and Schütz were given extensions in order to clear up their personal and business affairs. Despite his three-month extension, the news that deportation was inevitable sent Görtz into a deep depression. Schütz, however, had other intentions, announcing publicly that he intended to marry his 25-year-old girlfriend, Una Mackey from Rathmines in Dublin, whom he had met at a dance during his time in Athlone. Miss Mackey lodged a notice of intent to marry to the city registry office in April 1947. Efforts were also made to have the marriage solemnised in a Catholic ceremony. Schütz made an appeal to be granted parole in order to get married, and the Department of Justice agreed to his request, giving the couple a short window in which to have the ceremony conducted and to enjoy a brief honeymoon in Wicklow. Permission was granted on the condition that Schütz surrender himself to the authorities upon his return from the honeymoon. He complied with all the instructions, and after a 'champagne wedding' and a 'motoring holiday' in Wicklow he surrendered himself to Gardaí, and was brought back to Mountjoy Prison to await his deportation. Both he and Görtz were to be transported by plane to Germany, where they would be handed over to the Allies to be debriefed.

Of course in the larger context of the war, in which unspeakable horrors had been carried out in the concentration camps of the Third Reich, Hermann Görtz and Günther Schütz were very minor characters. At most they would have been subject to a prison sentence. However Görtz was convinced that his own role was more important, and that he would face a severe sentence upon his return. His failed attempts at avoiding deportation had troubled him greatly, and severely hurt his pride. He was also greatly angered by news reports that referred to him and Werner Unland as spies. Görtz saw himself as nothing less than a proud German soldier, and he subsequently took a libel action against the *Daily Mail* and journalist John Murdoch for the articles. In reality the action was a last-ditch attempt to defend his honour by a severely paranoid and delusional man. When the action was finally settled, Görtz wasn't able to benefit from the damages.

————

Görtz started to speak openly to others about suicide, bringing it up in conversation with Günther Schütz. In the course of one conversation he explained his fears of deportation, saying, 'I will never go back. It would be the same as surrender and I'll never do that. I shall die like my leaders.' This was perhaps a reference to Hermann Göring, who had committed suicide in October 1946 by ingesting a phial of potassium cyanide in his cell the night before he was due to be hanged. Göring had been found guilty of crimes against peace, crimes against humanity, the waging of wars of aggression and war crimes.

Even the Gardaí he dealt with believed that Görtz would rather commit suicide than be deported to Germany. Fearing for Görtz's wellbeing, the political authorities in Ireland attempted to intervene, and during his parole Görtz met with Dr Hempel at his house in Monkstown. The meeting was arranged by Frederick Boland of the Department of External

Affairs, and in the course of their conversation Hempel tried to reassure Görtz that no harm would come to him when he was deported.

Görtz was unmoved by Hempel's assurances, and outlined the many reasons why he believed he would come to harm if he returned to Germany. He believed that the Allies were determined to exterminate the race of Germans to which he belonged, and that he would be unable to find any work and would therefore be a financial burden on his family. Görtz also stressed to Hempel his apprehension of the communists who had liberated Berlin, and told him his fear of being treated harshly by them.

Hempel was unable to placate Görtz himself, and so suggested that he meet Frederick Boland in person. Görtz agreed, and the three men met at Hempel's house on 15 May. Boland reassured Görtz that he would be not treated harshly in Germany, and that he would be held for at most a period of a few weeks. Boland went further, adding that he had received assurances from the Americans and the British that Görtz would only be subject to close interrogation, and that he would not be arrested upon arrival on German soil.

Boland explained to Görtz that he had received such an assurance from the American Military Governor in Germany, Gen. Lucius D. Clay. The American Representative, David Gray, wrote to Gen. Clay on 12 May 1947 informing him of the discussions he had been having with the Irish authorities in relation to Görtz. Gray was dubious of Görtz's intentions, and believed that he was taking advantage of the goodwill being shown to him by the Irish authorities:

The Minister for Justice told us that Görtz had presented a petition asserting that his life would be endangered if he were returned to Germany. Mr. Boland said that he stated that as a member of the Wehrmacht during the Spartacist Revolution in 1918 he had taken part in the severe repression of the insurrectionists and had been a marked man ever since. On his return home he expected communists to murder him. He therefore asked asylum.

Gray regarded Boland as a man of high character, great courage and iron nerve, combined with a sentimental tenderness towards appeals on compassionate grounds. He believed that in all likelihood Görtz was manipulating Boland, and in reality had nothing to fear if he returned to Germany. Görtz had lived 'unmolested in Germany between 1918 and 1936 and had taken no active part in the Nazi atrocities which had characterised the later stages of the war. While the concentration camps were in full operation Görtz was in prison therefore he was only a minor cog in the large Nazi war machine.'

Gray explained to Clay that he gave no guarantees that Görtz would be immune from prosecution if it were found that he had committed crimes under German law. However he conceded that something should be done to ensure Görtz's wellbeing was taken into consideration: 'I agreed to make strong recommendations to you to provide for Görtz such security as appeared to you to be necessary to prevent him from assassination there in the American Zone and possibly to arrange for the future emigration of himself and his wife, to whom we are informed that he is devoted.'

Gray reasoned with Boland that – as Görtz had arrived illegally in Ireland, was the head of the German secret service in Ireland and had been in hiding for 18 months with the illegal IRA, who had declared war on both the United Kingdom and the United States – they were obligated to deport him. This was compounded for him by the fact that Görtz had constantly reported military information to Germany throughout his time in Ireland. Gray felt that he could in no way accept the deportation of what he considered to be minor German agents and exempt Görtz.

Gray suggested that if Boland wished to avoid any further publicity in relation to the matter he could arrange to have Görtz placed on an American plane, and that he would see that he would not be in a position to cause any harm to himself. He also claimed that such a journey could be arranged without Görtz's knowledge:

In the American zone he would doubtless be safe and provision would be made at your convenience for him to be united with his wife. On the basis of this recommendation the Irish Government has ordered the deportation of Görtz in the aeroplane which you have provided for that purpose and it is the hope of the United Kingdom representative and myself that you will find it possible to afford him the requested protection.

In many ways this arrangement should have been enough to assuage Görtz's fears and reassure him that nothing untoward would happen to him if he returned to Germany. What the Allied and Irish authorities hadn't taken into account was just how fragile Görtz's mental state had become. Boland explained the arrangement that had been reached with the Americans to Görtz, but his reassurances fell on deaf ears.

Görtz, now highly paranoid, refused to believe Boland, and explained in a somewhat agitated state that the Americans could not be trusted and that ultimately he was a marked man. He explained to both Boland and Hempel that the Allies would not keep their word, and that from a standpoint of humanity no grounds existed to deport him. He told the men that he couldn't face another period of incarceration, and the meeting subsequently broke up without any resolution. Boland, concerned about Görtz's welfare, granted him parole, and before Görtz left he agreed to meet Hempel for dinner the following week. It was a rendezvous he would never make.

On 23 May 1947, two letters arrived at the house of the Farrell sisters. One was the aforementioned invitation to dinner from Hempel; the other sent a paroxysm of fear through Görtz. It instructed him to report to the Aliens Registration Office in Dublin Castle that afternoon. He gathered his belongings and put on his overcoat and hat. Before he left the house he went upstairs to his room and fetched one last item – the phial of cyanide that had been given to him by the Abwehr at the start of the war.

It is difficult to assess Görtz's state of mind as he made his way into the city centre. In reality he hadn't much to fear, as many of his Abwehr colleagues who were of similar rank were not subjected to severe treatment at Allied interrogation centres in Bad Nenndorf and Oberursel. It is possible he feared that under interrogation he might implicate members of the IRA or some of the people who had sheltered him, or perhaps he may have wanted to die an officer's death rather than be subjected to criminal trials. The truth about what went through Görtz's mind will never be known. Hempel and Boland had come up with a plan that Görtz could work for the Americans, and as such would not face prison – however, due to a communications mix-up, he never received the news.

Görtz arrived at the Aliens Registration Office a little after 10 o'clock, and as he made his way to the entrance he met Special Branch Detective Sgt Patrick O'Connor. The men exchanged pleasantries and talked about the weather, after which Görtz took a seat in the waiting room. Günther Schütz and his new wife were waiting in an adjoining room, and after a few minutes they heard a terrific commotion from the other room.

O'Connor had returned to the waiting room and informed Görtz that a US bomber plane was waiting at Baldonnel Aerodrome to take him to Germany, and that he was to be detained at the registration office until take-off. Görtz didn't seek to get clarification from Hempel or Boland, but just calmly produced his pipe and began to smoke it. Then, suddenly, he took the cyanide capsule out of his pocket and bit on it. One of the detectives noticed what was happening and shouted, 'That man is taking something!' He ran over to Görtz and grabbed him by the throat. Wrestling with him he shouted, 'What have you taken?', to which Görtz snarled, 'That's none of your business.'

As the two men wrestled, Görtz collapsed. Two detectives loosened his tie and undid the top button of his shirt. One fetched a trolley, and to the horror of the general public the detectives rushed with Görtz's limp and lifeless body downstairs through the passport office before placing it in an ambulance and taking it to Mercer's Hospital in the city centre. The detectives remaining in Dublin Castle burst into the adjoining room and searched Günther Schütz, confiscating his fountain pen. Totally unaware of what had just transpired, Schütz asked the detectives what was happening. The detectives told him they were looking for a poison pen. Schütz, in a state of bewilderment, asked, 'What do you want with a poison pen?' The detectives immediately placed him under arrest and took him back to Mountjoy Prison.

Meanwhile, at Mercer's Hospital the registrar, Dr Marcus Shrage, who happened to be Jewish, began a frantic effort to save Görtz's life. The poison Görtz had swallowed had become stale due to the length of time it had been in his possession; but the dose was still enough to kill him. After 30 minutes the registrar gave up his efforts, and Hermann Görtz, the most senior agent of the German Abwehr to come to Ireland during World War II, was pronounced dead. Görtz's body was taken to a nearby mortuary, where a postmortem was carried out. Two doctors present, Dr Shrage and Dr O'Meara, ruled that his death was due to a heart attack brought on by ingestion of potassium cyanide.

Günther Schütz was allowed into the mortuary under armed guard, where he observed Görtz's body laid out and dressed in his Luftwaffe coat. Detectives noted the cause of death as self-inflicted poisoning and, unaware of the cyanide's origin, immediately began making enquiries in nearby chemist shops. An inquest was held into Görtz's death and, much like his life, it was marred with controversy. De Valera issued a memorandum to all cabinet ministers that any communications between the government and Görtz were not to be disclosed. In it he claimed, 'I am also aware of communications which have been passed between departmental officials and relating directly or indirectly to the late Dr Hermann Görtz. I consider it would be injurious to the public interest that any communication passing between any officials should be publicly disclosed.' This created a situation whereby the Irish government was for all intents and purposes refusing to cooperate with the inquest. Therefore Görtz's death was officially ruled a suicide, and no further enquiry ensued.

Shortly afterwards Günther Schütz was taken under armed guard to Baldonnel Aerodrome, and was placed on a US plane which took him to Frankfurt. He was sent to the US Army internment facility known as 'Camp King' near Oberursel north-west of Frankfurt. During the war it had served as a transit camp of the Luftwaffe and had housed many American and British POWs. Almost all of the Allied airmen shot down during the war spent time in the camp before being transferred to one of the Stalag camps.

After the war ended the Americans used the camp as an intelligence post and an internment camp to put former German agents and military personnel through a process of denazification. Alfred Jodl, Karl Dönitz and Hermann Göring all spent time in the camp. While there Schütz was dressed in black POW's clothes and wooden shoes. He was kept under such close observation that he was even forbidden from shaving. After a period of two weeks this harsh treatment ceased, and Schütz was given his own clothes and driven to Oberursel, where he was detained in a townhouse with other German officers. Their only guard was an American sergeant, who let the prisoners freely associate and take part in leisure activities. Among the prisoners in the house were Dr Schnact, President of the German Bank, Count Lutz Graf Schwerin von Krosigk, the Nazi Minister for Finance, and generals Herr and Feuchtinger, who had been stationed in Milan during the war.

Soon afterwards Schütz was taken away for interrogation by the Americans, who among other things asked him about the extent of Irish neutrality during the war. Schütz was asked whether the Irish authorities had ever violated their neutrality. He informed the Americans that in his view de Valera had stuck rigidly to neutrality, and explained to them that he and his comrades had been interned until the end of the war, and had received no favourable treatment from the Irish authorities. Schütz was also questioned about his time in England and his various contacts within the Abwehr.

By the end of the interrogation the Americans came to the conclusion that Schütz was a minor agent, and he was released. Schütz and his wife eventually moved to Hamburg, where he set up a business selling desk lamps. Shortly afterwards he set up his own import/export business, before quietly moving back to Dublin in the early 1960s. Schütz attempted to profit from his time as a German spy, selling his story to various newspapers in the 1970s, and in his later years he visited the pub in Taghmon where he had been brought for interrogation after his arrest. Schütz lived for many years at Knockanode House near Avoca, where he was involved in the development of a seaside resort at Clogga beach. In 1971 the resort was targeted by a series of mysterious explosions. He bought a hotel in Co. Wicklow which he ran with his wife for many years, and eventually retired to his home in Avoca. Schütz died in his sleep in Shankill, Co. Dublin, in 1991.

———

Hermann Görtz was laid to rest on 26 May 1947 in grave space 12g of the St Nessan's section of Deansgrange Cemetery. His friends had made enquiries as to whether a military funeral could take place but the request was refused by the Irish government. Instead Görtz received a Church of Ireland funeral that was slightly modified to include some Lutheran elements. Reverend K.D.B. Dobbs officiated at the funeral, which was attended by over 800 people.

Among those in attendance were the Farrell sisters and others who had provided refuge for Görtz while he was at large, as well as his radio operator, Anthony Deery, and his fellow spies Jan van Loon and Werner Unland. Jim O'Donovan, Charles McGuinness and Fianna Fáil TD Dan Breen were also present, with Breen acting as one of the pallbearers. Görtz himself was dressed in a Luftwaffe greatcoat, and draped over his coffin was a hand-stitched swastika flag prepared by the Farrell sisters, who proudly displayed his World War I medals on their blouses. As the coffin was brought out of the church several people raised their hands in the Nazi salute and shouted, 'Heil Hitler.'

Hempel had made enquiries to the Irish government as to whether it would be appropriate for him to attend the funeral and was advised against doing so by the Irish authorities, advice Hempel duly heeded. Görtz's grave was initially given a simple marker, but after a petition by his wife in Germany a gravestone with a dagger sheathed in barbed wire was placed over the grave. It had been carved by Görtz himself in prison.

The Farrell sisters also arranged for a plaque to be put on the grave, which read, 'Lt Hermann Görtz', a rank that the unfortunate Görtz never actually held, as he had been falsely promoted to it by G2 during their time communicating with him. With his coffin lowered into the earth Görtz earned the dubious honour of being the last German to be buried with the honours of Nazi Germany, almost two years after the state ceased to exist.

Görtz's mortal remains lay undisturbed until, under the cover of darkness on 26 April 1974, they were removed by a group of German ex-army officers acting on behalf of the German War Graves Commission, and reburied at the German War Cemetery in Glencree, Co. Wicklow. The cemetery contains the remains of 134 Luftwaffe and Kriegsmarine personnel; six of the graves contain the remains of German soldiers held as prisoners by the British during World War I. And, in the far-right corner of the cemetery, under a headstone bearing a dagger sheathed in barbed wire, lie the mortal remains of Major Hermann Görtz; to this day fresh flowers are regularly laid on his grave.

In the aftermath of Görtz's death, Éamon de Valera ordered the burning of any documents relating to Görtz's correspondence with government departments. Such was the diligence given to the task that, when the files were made available to the public 50 years later, virtually nothing remained. When Dan Bryan heard of Görtz's death he was dismayed, and felt that if he had been present that day in Dublin Castle he might have been able to reason with Görtz.

Similarly, Richard Hayes, who was in the United States on a lecture tour as part of his role as Director of the National Library, was saddened at Görtz's death. Despite the fact that he disagreed profoundly with his actions while he was in Ireland, he found him to be one of the more pleasant German agents that he had to deal with during his tenure with G2.

In late 1947 Görtz's wife Eva petitioned the Irish government for the remainder of the money that had been seized in the raid on Stephen Held's house in Templeogue – a sum totalling almost $25,000. 'I am the widow of Dr Hermann Görtz,' the petition began, 'who was interned in Ireland for a period of years during the Second World War, and who died on or about the 27th day of May, 1947, in the city of Dublin, as a result of taking poison when he was about to be deported from Ireland to Germany.' Minister for Justice Gerald Boland informed Frau Görtz that the money had been forfeited to the state, and there the matter came to an end.

Shortly before his death in 1947 Hermann Görtz penned a series of articles for the *Irish Times* where he outlined his entire mission to Ireland.

In many ways it was his attempt to set the record straight on his tumultuous time in Ireland. These articles, as well as the coded report he compiled for Dr Hayes, believing he was doing so for the Nazi High Command, paint a vivid picture of the mission to Ireland of a tragicomic character who, despite the brevity of his time here, became one of Irish history's most notorious figures.

While Görtz had been fighting deportation, Eduard Hempel and other high-ranking German diplomats in Ireland were granted asylum in Ireland. This was mainly down to Hempel's good working relationship with the Taoiseach. In official Ireland Hempel was seen as having behaved in a much fairer way to Ireland than the American and British representatives, and was believed by many civil servants to have better respected Irish neutrality than his Allied counterparts. Hempel returned to Germany in 1949 to be 'denazified', and was subsequently employed in the West German Foreign Service from 1950 until his retirement in 1951.

Hempel died in the West German capital of Bonn in November 1971, and the esteem he was held in by official Ireland prevailed long after his departure from Ireland. This was summed up in a 2011 letter to the *Irish Times* by Michael Drury, an official of the Irish embassy in Bonn, who attended his funeral on behalf of the Irish government:

> Official circles in Ireland recognised that Dr Hempel behaved correctly throughout his mission, given the narrow limits of his position. For example, he respected Ireland's neutrality better than the American minister did. If he were regarded as having been 'Hitler's man', I would not have been instructed, as an official of the Irish Embassy in Bonn, to attend his funeral in 1972.

But even if Hempel had been more respectful of neutrality than other diplomats to Ireland during the war, he also was fully aware of the racist, persecutory and murderous actions carried out by the Nazi regime. The Nuremberg Laws, Kristallnacht and the Final Solution all occurred during his tenure with the German Foreign Ministry, and despite the depravity of many of these actions Dr Hempel voluntarily made the career decision to represent the regime from 1937 to 1945 in Ireland, and received a salary for it. Therefore his legacy is contested.

To some he is regarded as a diplomat who showed Ireland respect as an independent nation, while to others he was simply Hitler's man in Dublin. In any case, he remains a divisive individual in the story of Ireland and its relationship with Germany during World War II. In some ways the favourable treatment towards Hempel characterised official Ireland's attitude towards Nazi Germany. While Jewish refugees were actively deterred from seeking asylum on these shores a plethora of Nazi war criminals and suspected collaborators found sanctuary in Ireland in the years after the war. Otto Skorzeny, Hitler's scar-faced commando who rescued Mussolini from Italian partisans in the Salo Republic, lived in Martinstown House in Co. Kildare for a period, and attended a party in Portmarnock Golf Club in the company of future Taoiseach Charles Haughey and other affluent Dublin socialites where he signed autographs for many of those in attendance.

Indeed Haughey and former Donegal TD Neil Blaney were accused of having procured weapons during the Arms Crisis from Flemish businessman and former member of the Belgian Black Brigade Albert Luykx. An acquaintance of Neil Blaney who frequented his restaurant in Sutton, Luykx was approached by Blaney and asked to help in sourcing arms in Germany with the intention of arming the IRA. Luykx was subsequently tried, together with Blaney and Charles Haughey. He maintained that the operation was sanctioned by the Minister for Defence, Jim Gibbons. All four men were eventually acquitted; however, rumours of Luykx's past were common knowledge. In 1971 it was claimed under Dáil privilege that Luykx was 'a convicted Nazi criminal' who was wanted by the Belgian authorities. A Flemish nationalist, Luykx had escaped from Belgium having been sentenced to death for having denounced people to the SD during the war.

Ireland's leading provider of children's textbooks, Albert Folens, built a considerable publishing empire after being granted asylum in Ireland, although his past was also mired in controversy. Folens is named on the Central Registry of War Criminals and Security Suspects (CROWCASS) list of suspected Nazi collaborators, and was accused in some quarters of having worked as an interrogator for the Gestapo. He had been sentenced by a Belgian court to 10 years' imprisonment and in an interview with a Flemish newspaper he described himself as a 'war criminal in an honourable cause'. Folens maintained his innocence, claiming that he had worked as a translator for the Flemish SD and had no involvement in interrogations, he eventually escaped jail and made his way to Ireland having been smuggled into the country by Trappist monks.

In 2007, a two-part documentary called *Ireland's Nazis* presented by Cathal O'Shannon and produced by Keith Farrell was broadcast on RTÉ. Folens's widow Juliette obtained a temporary High Court Injunction to prevent the use in the programme of a 1985 interview between Folens and journalist Senan Molony in which Folens spoke scathingly about President Roosevelt and other Allied leaders. The Folens family issued a press release denying that Albert Folens was involved with Nazi war crimes or was ever a member of the Gestapo; however they did concede that he was conscripted into the Flemish Legion. Indeed the interview gave no insight into Folens's exact rank during the war, and the nature of his role remains a mystery to this day.

It is unknown exactly how many suspected Nazi war criminals passed through Ireland at various stages. However one thing is clear, in that their level of notoriety didn't act as a warning sign for the Irish authorities and their attempts at concealing their identities may have been enough to thwart the security services. In June 1985, Minister for Justice Michael Noonan was asked a question in the Dáil seeking him to comment on reports that suggested that the notorious Nazi war criminal and chief architect of many of the horrors perpetrated in Auschwitz, the infamous 'Angel of Death' Josef Mengele, may have used Ireland to escape from Europe when he fled for South America soon after World War II ended. Noonan explained that nothing came to light in his department to suggest Mengele had spent time in Ireland. However, he conceded 'That perhaps it is not surprising since what is alleged is that an alien came here under an assumed name – which is not specified – almost 40 years ago and it must be assumed that if there were any records these would refer only to the assumed name.'

Indeed in the years during the war and directly afterwards there existed what was described by some historians as 'a large minority' of pro-German, anti-Semitic sentiment in Ireland, especially in republican circles. This eventually dissipated as the political climate changed around the world. However the legacy of Ireland's heroes who fought Nazism in Dublin and around the rest of Ireland quickly faded into obscurity. Eager to avoid the image of being seen as 'John Bull's best friend', Ireland sought to downplay its role in aiding MI5 and the Allies during the war, and the heroics of Dr Richard Hayes and many other brave Irishmen were soon forgotten. They exist now only in the pages of official memoranda, documents and the anecdotes of those who were fortunate enough to have known such remarkable men.

X

IRELAND'S GREATEST UNSUNG HERO

'Some people share their stories, shouting them from the hill tops. He wasn't that sort of a man. He was a doer and just moved on. Everyone thought he was the Claremorris wonderboy and we were so proud of him.'

FAERY HAYES, discussing her father Richard J. Hayes, September 2017

At the end of the war Dr Richard Hayes returned to a life of mainly academic pursuits, but the lessons he had learned from the war were never far from his mind. He worried daily about how vulnerable Ireland was during the Emergency due to a lack of a sophisticated methods for enciphering Irish Army messages. He felt that huge improvements would have to be made given the new global political climate brought on by the onset of the Cold War.

In 1946 Hayes put his thoughts to paper, outlining his experiences as a cryptographer during the war in a lengthy letter to Éamon de Valera. Hayes informed the Taoiseach that success in dealing with coded messages largely increased with experience and the opportunity to discuss findings with others. He urged the Taoiseach to invest in a permanent cryptography unit within the Army that could be put into action in the future if the need were to arise. Hayes was scathing when comparing the resources he had at his disposal to those available to the British at Bletchley Park:

The British cryptographical staff tried to solve ciphers until there was at least two to three thousand letters of material available. They considered anything less as either impossible or depending on good luck and good luck will not appear unless there are a wide variety of averages to produce it. Here weeks were spent on material of 200 to 400 letters. It requires incurable optimism to carry on with such impossible attempts.

Hayes argued that many codes and ciphers were ultimately solved through diligence and watchfulness, and that could only be achieved through greater numbers of skilled persons working on intercepted messages. He insisted that it was often a case of the other side making a mistake in order to provide a window of opportunity for a cryptographer to carry out their work, and that increased numbers were very important in this regard. Referring to Alan Turing's success at breaking the infamous Enigma code, Hayes explained how one 'horrid' enemy operator had forgot to make the second in a series of double substitutions, and the German coding system was then split open in a matter of hours. This was achieved after much time had been wasted trying to work out the complex substitutions in the preceding months.

Hayes also explained how another error by a German operator led to the solutions for all of the disc-type ciphers used by Germany during the war. He continued that the success of crytographical departments often depends on unending vigilance and, in many cases, a bit of luck: 'An immense amount of mathematical research is necessary but it must also be of the highest standard both of accuracy and imagination but without the lucky break it is not enough. The ciphers of today demand the best brains available in quantity and all the time.'

With a deep sense of foreboding, Hayes concluded by warning the Taoiseach that Ireland 'must not enter the next emergency without a nucleus, however small, of experienced staff. We must start in the next war where we left off in this, not surely from scratch again.' Hayes felt that Ireland had been naïve during the war with its approach to the security of its communications, and that they had been extremely lucky in many respects with their apprehensions of German spies. He felt that a permanent crytographical unit was essential in order to read other countries' communications and to assess the security of their own.

Chillingly, during the war Hayes had broken the cipher which the Irish Army was using to communicate with. He advised the Taoiseach that the cipher was extremely weak, could easily be cracked and that, given contemporary conditions, its security value was very low. He argued that proper enciphering equipment could ensure that greater security could be achieved in the future for the Army's use of coded messages. He even remarked that some of the German spies had come to Ireland with safer encryption methods than were currently available to the Irish Army.

Hayes went further, saying he hoped the Irish Army would never again find itself in a war situation without an adequate version of such an important security tool. Despite Hayes's pleas his words ultimately fell on deaf ears. His work was never preserved within the Army to any serious degree. Instead the Irish government chose to call on Hayes from time to time when they felt they needed his help. In many cases they were simply taking advantage of his good nature and unwillingness to say no.

In 1947, the Irish Department of External Affairs was offered a Swedish cipher machine and government officials contacted Hayes to ask him to test its security capabilities. The manufacturers claimed that the machine's system was unbreakable, but after working with it for a short period Hayes was able to prove them wrong. He explained to government officials that he was able to break the code in a relatively short space of time 'using a tedious but not very difficult method'. Hayes estimated that it could be broken in the space of a few hours with a staff of six cryptographers working to copy and count the various frequencies being used.

———

Even though Hayes's work was crucial to the winning of the war, no one was ever appointed to succeed him in his role as cryptographer for G2. While the Irish government clearly valued his opinions and respected his intellect, they are guilty for whatever reasons for leaving the security of Irish communications as vulnerable to attack as they were during the war. During the Cold War this unfortunately left Ireland exposed to infiltration from other foreign agents. There are no official figures available or indeed any way in which to quantify the number of Russian spies who entered this country during the Cold War, or indeed in the years afterwards. A successor to Hayes would have gone in some small way towards addressing this problem.

Despite the disappointments Hayes faced in relation to his advocacy for a permanent cryptography unit, he achieved great satisfaction through his role as the country's National Librarian. Hayes's varied interests were in no way curtailed during the war years. While working for G2 he carried out a series of scientific experiments on the culture of plants, and in 1943, at the height of his battles with Hermann Görtz, he oversaw the transferral of the Office of Arms from Dublin Castle to the National Library. The Office of Arms was then renamed the Genealogical Office, and took responsibility for the issuing of grants and confirmation of arms as well as the registration of civilian flags.

Hayes also spearheaded a number of important acquisitions for the library during this period, increasing its standing globally. During the war Hayes oversaw the acquisition of the Ormonde Archive from Kilkenny Castle, as well as 60,000 Lawrence photographic negatives covering Ireland in the Victorian and Edwardian eras. An early 13th-century manuscript of the *Description of Ireland* and *Norman Conquest* by Gerald of Wales was also acquired during this period. However it was in the post-war era that Hayes dedicated himself fully to this role, and when his star really shone as a talented director.

Hayes was well liked in literary and artistic circles, and in 1945 he persuaded Nobel laureate George Bernard Shaw to donate his manuscripts to the National Library. When Shaw presented the manuscripts to Hayes they were the only drafts of his literary works that he had chosen to preserve. As time progressed methods for preservation in libraries around the world modernised, and Hayes was always at the forefront of any new innovation he felt could benefit the National Library.

In 1945 Hayes embarked on a project that sought to acquire archival material and manuscripts relating to Ireland that were held abroad. He successfully obtained over 5,000 reels of microfilm for the National Library from archives and other libraries across the world. His work in acquisitions as well as the expansion of collections of estate and family papers had resulted in the library's collection of manuscripts growing rapidly. Ever the pragmatist, Hayes began work on a system for cataloguing the material. It would prove to be his greatest work in the field of academia.

In 1965, Hayes published his 11-volume *Manuscript sources for the history of Irish civilisation*. The publication contained descriptions of Irish archives and manuscripts located in 678 repositories in over 30 countries. It was a major bibliographical work, one which earned Hayes two honorary doctorates in 1967 from Dublin University and the National Library of Ireland. He presented a copy of the work to President Éamon de Valera, and such was the esteem in which it was held that it was still being regularly consulted by students and academics to this day.

During his tenure as director Hayes also campaigned for a new building for the National Library, as he felt strongly that there was a need for increased storage as well as reader facilities. He was aware that the Trinity College library, having been built in the 16th century, received copies of all printed works first published in the United Kingdom. The National Library, which was founded in the 19th century, was not in a position to receive similar texts, and therefore Hayes decided it would be prudent to amalgamate the two institutions, for which he drafted a plan and submitted it to the government. The plan envisaged a cooperative scheme with Trinity College, with the new National Library being built on the Trinity campus. While the two libraries would work closely together under the Hayes plan, they could also both retain their individual identities. Ultimately the government chose not to adopt Hayes's proposals.

———

Over the years Hayes became firm friends with Sir Alfred Chester Beatty, and when Beatty presented his collection of oriental manuscripts to the Irish state he appointed Hayes as his honorary librarian. In order to take up his new role, Hayes retired from his role as Director of the National Library of Ireland in 1967, and was succeeded by his deputy, Patrick Henchy. Hayes devoted the rest of his working life to his role at the Chester Beatty Library. In 1970 he published his last work, the nine-volume *Sources for the history of Irish civilisation: articles in periodicals*.

The work indexed over 150 Irish periodicals that dealt primarily with humanities and sciences.

Hayes's last public appearance was at the opening of an extension to the Chester Beatty Library by President Cearbhall Ó Dálaigh in June 1975. During the opening Hayes gave an interview to the six o'clock news on RTÉ, which was to be the only time that he appeared on television, and to date remains the only known recording of his voice. In the years after the war he had become a member of a committee of cultural experts of the Council of Europe, and during the Cold War he proposed the large-scale microfilming of Europe's printed manuscripts to prevent their destruction in the event of a nuclear attack.

During his later years he served on the board of the Abbey Theatre as well as the Arts Council, the Royal Irish Academy and the Cultural Relations Committee of the Department of Foreign Affairs. However he derived the most satisfaction in life from his family. He was deeply devoted to his children and grandchildren, spending much of his spare time in his later years going to see his son Mervyn play rugby with Palmerstown rugby club. In 1969 his wife Clare died, and this left an aging Richard lost in many ways. Later that year he remarried, to Margaret Mary Deighan, known as Maura to her friends. Maura had been an employee of Hayes's at the National Library, and despite the considerable age gap, his children were happy for him. They saw Maura as someone who gave Richard great friendship and company in his later years.

Despite his numerous notable achievements in the arts and in academia, Richard Hayes was never recognised by the Irish state for his role as a codebreaker during the Second World War. There are a number of reasons for this. First and foremost was his own discreet nature and reserved manner. However, perhaps the most pertinent reasons were Irish neutrality and his work being subject to the Official Secrets Act.

In 1945, Hayes received an invitation to meet with British Prime Minister Winston Churchill, and during the course of the secret meeting he received a medal for his services to cryptography and for the help he had given the Liddell brothers and MI5 during the course of the war. Churchill was said to have been particularly impressed by his work in breaking the Görtz cipher, the German microdot system and the O'Reilly disc cipher system.

An agreement was reached that Hayes would never publicly disclose that the meeting took place, and the awarding of this medal has to date never been officially acknowledged.

Living with the knowledge of the true level of cooperation between the Irish and the British and other Allies during the war was at times difficult for Hayes. He often found it irksome to read articles in newspapers and printed manuscripts that portrayed Ireland as neutral and cowardly during the war. Hayes voiced these concerns in an anonymous letter to the *Irish Times* that was printed on 4 November 1961:

> During the war Irish neutrality was constantly misrepresented in the Allied Press. Security reasons prevented the actual facts and the measures taken to prevent espionage from being published, to counteract this frequently vicious propaganda. It is about time that some of the truth should be released to set the record straight. The Irish government had the situation under complete control throughout the war, and that contrary to the popular belief in the English speaking world this country was not permitted to be used as a centre for espionage. When the full story is told this will be clearer still. – H.G.

Hayes concluded the letter by suggesting that an official history of the period may never be written. Perhaps most interestingly the letter was signed off by the letters H.G.; Hayes chose these letters as a tribute to Hermann Görtz. In the course of the piece Hayes dispelled the notion of Görtz being a man dogged by misfortune. Instead he described him as an extremely lucky individual who would have been in custody a lot earlier had it not been for his good fortune.

Hayes went on in the piece to explain that the Irish security services' control of the security situation was evident in the fact that all of the other German spies who had been sent to Ireland had found themselves in prison within 24 hours of their arrival. Indeed Hayes was right to be proud, as the G2 counter-espionage movement during the war is one of very few examples worldwide where an intelligence organisation achieved 100 per cent of its objectives.

Hayes, like many of those in his secret world, knew that Ireland was never cowardly during the Second World War, and that it did all that it could to help the Allies, bar sending actual troops. This sadly was a truth that Hayes would take with him to the grave. His fondness for tobacco was to come back to haunt him, and he suffered for much of his later years with a bad chest. His health deteriorated further, and after suffering a stroke he was taken to the home of his son Mervyn and his wife Yvonne so that he could be cared for by them.

Hayes was a lifelong atheist, and wished to receive no church service when he passed away. He initially requested that he be cremated; however, he finally came to the decision that he would have a Church of Ireland service. In January 1976, Richard J. Hayes passed away in his sleep. He was buried in Deansgrange Cemetery after a small service attended by close family and friends. As his remains were lowered into the ground his heroics passed with him out of mainstream popular memory.

In 1980, his second wife Maura presented his papers to the National Library of Ireland. The collection contains huge volumes of notebook paper detailing his mathematical workings and calculations, which he painstakingly persevered with during the course of the war. One of the most notable items donated was a child's school copybook belonging to his eldest daughter Joan. When Hayes was helping her with her homework he had a eureka moment with one of the German codes, and scribbled his calculations into the copybook.

Perhaps this exercise book is most telling of the man. Hayes was a forgotten patriot and a man of many talents. He was a loving father, an aesthete, a brilliant academic and librarian, a lover of rugby and, lest we forget, Ireland's most famous Nazi codebreaker. Hayes's contribution to Irish history is huge, yet he is largely forgotten, a tragic cruelty of fate, as he almost single-handedly ensured that Germany decided against invading Ireland during the war, and was instrumental in enabling all German spies to be arrested by the authorities.

Among his greatest achievements was the breaking of the Görtz cipher and the microdot system. His work ethic and diligence in terms of the O'Reilly cipher had a direct effect on the outcome of the Battle of the

Bulge; as such he is spoken of highly in MI5 and OSS accounts of the war. His commitment to his work and his sense of national duty and quiet patriotism helped see to it that Ireland did not suffer the same fate as some of the more active participants in the war. He saw his role as a codebreaker as something to be done to the best of his ability, and when the war ended he simply moved on to the next challenge.

Unfortunately for Hayes he was lost in terms of the historical record, and the narrative that Ireland was cowardly in their neutrality during the war has largely been maintained in mainstream historical discourse. The truth is much different, and the remains of a forgotten war hero lie in the Hayes plot in Deansgrange Cemetery in South Co. Dublin. Sometimes heroes aren't statesmen, they aren't soldiers, they aren't carved into marble statues on city streets. Very often it is those who work quietly in the shadows to whom we owe the greatest debt of gratitude.

——

Hayes's brilliance as a codebreaker was facilitated by the great men who worked with him in G2, especially Col Liam Archer and his successor, the man who recruited Hayes: Col Dan Bryan. Bryan was dynamic in his thinking, and his writings on security policy did much to lay the foundations for Irish security during the war years. Many others failed to recognise the threat that Germany posed, and Bryan often found himself alone in his beliefs.

Undoubtedly his background in the IRA during the War of Independence stood him in great stead, and gave him a thorough awareness of the necessity for secure intelligence and security systems. Bryan was also instrumental in operating the 'Dublin Link' between MI5 and G2. This alliance proved to be highly significant in the defeat of Nazi Germany, and Hayes's work in breaking various codes allowed MI5 to take their policy of strategic deception to new levels. The relationship was to be beneficial to both sides, in that they could call on each other's expertise at various critical junctures during the war.

After the war Dan Bryan transferred to the Military College before eventually retiring from the Irish Army in 1955. During his later years he wrote articles and appeared on RTÉ to discuss the Emergency, although he rarely went into detail on the activities of German spies or the complex security arrangements and relationships that defined most of his career. Bryan passed away in 1985 and was buried in Gowran in his native Kilkenny. He donated his papers dealing with his career to his alma mater, UCD, bringing to an end one of the most secret chapters in Irish history.

Whitehall in London is adorned with statues of Montgomery and Churchill, and Britain's greatest codebreaker Alan Turing has been honoured with a statue in Manchester, yet to most people in Ireland, Hayes, Bryan and other Irishmen who played such a crucial role in World War II sadly remain largely forgotten. This is a wrong that shouldn't be allowed to stand. For when Ireland was at her most vulnerable, and when Britain stood alone in the world against Nazi Germany, our country was spared the horrors of World War II through the patriotism of a few brave men and the quiet heroism of a humble librarian.

BIBLIOGRAPHY

Works Cited

National Library of Ireland
James O' Donovan Papers – MS 21,155, MS. 22,307
Dr Richard Hayes Papers – MS 22, 981 – 22, 984

Private Collections
Dr Richard Hayes Papers (Family Possession)
Captain John Patrick O' Sullivan Papers (Family Possession)

National Archives of Ireland
Department of Foreign Affairs Files:
Parachutists (Joseph Lenihan) – A27
Hermann Görtz – A34
O'Reilly/Kenny – A52 I, A52 II
Bryan – Liddell Correspondence – A60
Francis Stuart – A72
Jewish refugees – D/T S11007B/1
Óbed, Tributh, and Gärtner – S/12013
Charles Mc Guinness – S/12860
Hermann Görtz – S/13301
Hermann Görtz –S/13963

Irish Military Archives
Directorate of Irish Military (G2) Intelligence Files:
Stephen Held – G2/0077
Walter Simon – G2/0207
Francis and Isuelt Stuart – G2/0214
Werner Unland – G2/0261
Unland/Preetz – G2/0265
Séan Russell – G2/3010
Stephen Hayes – G2/3048

Joseph Andrews – G2/3261

Helena Moloney – G2/3364

Jan Van Loon – G2/3748

James O'Donovan – G2/3783

John O'Reilly – G2/3824

Maisie O'Mahony – G2/3997

Sgt Codd – G2/4949

Hermann Görtz – G2/1722

Weber-Drohl – G2/1928

Günther Schütz –G2/X/0703

Óbed, Tributh, Gärtner – G2/X/0345

Joseph Lenihan – G2/X/0805

John Kenny – G2/X/1263

UCD Archives
Memoir of Colonel Daniel Bryan (1900–85) – UCDA P109

Papers of Colonel Daniel Bryan (1900–85) – UCDA P71

British National Archives Kew Gardens
Criminal Files:

Hermann Görtz – CRIM 1/813

Dominions Office Files:

Hermann Görtz – DO 121/86

Reports on German Legation in Dublin – DO 121/87

MI5 Records:

Joseph Gerard Andrews – KV2/3119

Hermann Görtz – KV2/1321

Stephen Carroll Held –KV2/1450

Karel Richter – KV2/31

O'Reilly and Kenny – KV2/119

Joachim Wilhelm Canaris – KV2/167

Newspapers, Magazines and Periodicals

The Banner
An Cosantóir
Donegal Democrat
Evening Herald
Evening Mail
History Ireland
Impartial Reporter
Irish Independent
Irish Press
Irish Times
New York Times
Sunday Chronicle
Sunday Dispatch
Sunday Press
Sunday Tribune
The Bell
The People

Interviews

Captain Daniel Ayotis – Irish Military Archives, Dublin
Yvonne Dixon (Hayes) – Dublin
Keith Farrell – Manchester
Faery Hayes – Dublin
Jim Hayes – Cork
Dr. Mark M. Hull – Fort Leavenworth Kansas
Dr. Chris Smith – Coventry
Marcel Krüger – Dundalk
Gerry Long – National Library of Ireland
Professor Eunan O'Halpin – Trinity College Dublin
Dónall Ó Luanaigh – National Library of Ireland
Professor Gary Mc Guire – University College Dublin
Christine O' Sullivan – Killarney
Sheila O' Sullivan – Killarney

Parliamentary and Official Publications

Dáil Debates

Seanad Debates

House of Commons Debates

Historical Annuals

Greystones Archaeological and Historical Society:

Scannell, James, vol. IV, 2004, 'Major Hermann Goertz and German World War 2 Intelligence Gathering in Ireland'.

Scannell, James, vol. V, 2006, 'John Francis O'Reilly and John Kenny: Irishmen sent by the Germans to spy in Ireland during World War 2'.

Scannell, James, Text of Talk Given to Clontarf Historical Society, June 13th 2017, entitled 'Captain Hermann Görtz – The German WW2 Intelligence Gatherer who came in Uniform'.

Media Sources

RTÉ Documentary On One: *Richard Hayes, Nazi Codebreaker*, 2017

RTÉ Documentary On One: *Codename Paddy O'Brien*, 2007

Ireland's Nazis, RTÉ Television, Tile Films 2007

Caught in a Free State, RTÉ Television, 1983

Published Sources

Bell, J. Bowyer, *The Secret Army – The IRA 1916–1979* (Dublin: Poolbeg Press, 1989).

Biddlecombe, Darragh, *Colonel Dan Bryan and the evolution of Irish Military Intelligence, 1919–1945.* (Unpublished thesis for the Degree of MA, Department of Modern History, Maynooth University, July 1998).

Breuer, William B., *The Secret War with Germany* (Shrewsbury: Airlife Publishing, 1988).

Carroll, Joseph, *Ireland in the War Years, 1939–1945* (Newton Abbott: David & Charles, 1975).

Carter, Carolle J., *The Shamrock and The Swastika: German Espionage in Ireland in World War II* (Palo Alto, CA: Pacific Book Publishers, 1977).

Cass, Michael (ed.), *Intelligence and Military Operations* (London: Frank Cass, 1990).

Churchill, Sir Winston. *The Second World War*. 5 Vols. (Boston: Houghton Miffin, 1950).

Coogan, Tim Pat, *Eamon de Valera, The Man Who Was Ireland* (New York: Harper Perennial, 1995).

Coogan, Tim Pat, *The IRA: A History* (New York: Roberts Rinehart, 1994).

Cox, Colm, 'Militärgeographicshe Angaben über Irland', *An Cosantór*, March 1975, pp. 80–94.

Deacon, Richard, *A History of the British Secret Service* (London: Frederick Muller, 1969).

Duggan, John, *Neutral Ireland and the Third Reich* (Dublin: Lilliput Press, 1989).

Duggan, John, 'The German Threat – Myth or Reality', *An Cosantóir*, September 1989.

Dwyer, T. Ryle, *Irish Neutrality and the USA, 1939–1947* (Dublin: Gill and Macmillan, 1977).

Elborn, Geoffrey, *Francis Stuart: A Life* (Dublin: Raven Arts Press, 1990).

Ferriter, Diarmaid, *Judging Dev* (Dublin: Royal Irish Academy, 2007).

Fisk, Robert, *In Time of War, Ireland, Ulster and the Price of Neutrality 1939–1945* (London: Hutchinson & Co., 1940).

Fleming, Peter, *Operation Sea Lion* (New York: Simon and Schuster, 1957).

Fleming, Peter, *Invasion 1940* (London: Hart-Davis, 1957).

Gellately, Robert, *The Gestapo and German Society* (Oxford: Clarendon Press, 1990).

Girvin, Brian, *The Emergency: Neutral Ireland 1939–1945*, (London: Pan Books, 2007).

Hinsley, F.H., and Simkins, C.A.G., *British Intelligence in the Second World War*, Vol. 4: Security and Counter Intelligence (London: H.M.S.O., 1990).

Hitler, Adolf, *Mein Kampf* (New York: Reynal and Hitchcock, 1939).

Hull, Mark , *Irish Secrets: German Espionage in Ireland 1939–1945* (Dublin; Portland, Oregon: Irish Academic Press, 2003).

Irving, David, *Hitler's War* (London: Hamish Hamilton, 1978).

Johnson, David Alan, *Germany's Spies and Saboteurs* (Osceola, WI: MBI, 1998).

Kahn, David, *Hitler's Spies* (New York: Macmillan, 1978).

Kennedy, Brian, *Dr. Hermann Goertz – A German Spy in South County Dublin*, Pub. (Foxrock: Local History Club, 1989).

Keogh, Dermot, *Twentieth-Century Ireland: Nation and State* (Cork, Cork University Press, 1999).

Keogh, Dermot, *Ireland and Europe 1919–1948* (Dublin: Gill and Macmillan, 1994).

Keogh, Dermot, 'Eamon de Valera and Hitler: An analysis of the international reaction to the visit of the German Minister, May 1945', *Irish Studies in International Affairs,* vol. III, no. 1 (1989).

Kilbride-Jones, H.E., 'Adolf Mahr', *Archaeology Ireland,* vol. VII, no. 3 (Autumn 1993), pp 29–30.

Liddell Hart, B.H., *History of the Second World War* (London: Cassell, 1970).

Liddell Hart, B.H. (ed.), *The Other Side of the Hill: Germany's Generals, Their Rise and Fall, With their own Account of Military Events, 1939–1945* (London: Cassell, 1948).

Littlejohn, David, *Foreign Legions of the Third Reich,* vol. I (San Jose, CA: Bender Publishing, 1981).

Longford, Lord, and O'Neill, T.P., *Eamon de Valera* (London: Arrow books, 1970).

Lucas, James, *Hitler's Enforcers* (London: Arms and Armour Press, 1996).

McGarry, Fearghal, *Irish Politics and the Spanish Civil War* (Cork: Cork University Press, 1999).

McGuinness, Charles J., *Nomad* (London: Methuen & Company, 1934).

Manning, Maurice, *James Dillon, A Biography* (Dublin: Wolfhound Press, 1999).

Masterman, J.C., *The Double-Cross System in the War of 1939–1945* (New Haven and London: Yale University Press, 1972).

Mollet, Ralph, *The German Occupation of Jersey, 1940–1945: Notes on the General Conditions, How the Population Fared* (St Helier: Société Jersiaise, 1954).

Molohan, Cathy, *Germany and Ireland 1945–1955: Two Nations' Friendship* (Dublin: Irish Academic Press, 1999).

Natterstad, J.H., *Francis Stuart* (London: Bucknell University Press, 1969).

Nowlan, Kevin B. And Williams, T. Desmond (eds), *Ireland in the War Years and After, 1939–57* (Dublin: Gill and Macmillan, 1969).

O' Callaghan, Sean, *The Jackboot in Ireland* (London: Allan Wingate Ltd., 1958).

O' Donoghue, David, *The Devil's Deal: the IRA, Nazi Germany and the Double Life of Jim O'Donovan* (Belfast: Beyond the Pale, 2010).

O' Donoghue, David, *Hitler's Irish Voices: The Story of German Radio's Wartime Service* (Belfast: Beyond the Pale, 1998).

O' Halpin, Eunan (ed), *MI5 and Ireland: The Official History* (Dublin; Portland, Oregon: Irish Academic Press, 2003).

O' Halpin, Eunan, 'Army, Politics and Society in Independent Ireland, 1923–1945', in T.G.Frasier and Keith Jeffery (eds), *Men, Women and War* (Dublin: Lilliput Press, 2000).

O' Halpin, Eunan, 'MI5's Irish memories', in Brian Girvin and Geoff Roberts (eds) *Ireland in the Second World War* (London: Frank Cass, 2000).

O' Halpin, Eunan, *Defending Ireland* (Oxford: Oxford University Press, 1999).

O' Halpin, Eunan, 'Aspects of Intelligence', *The Irish Sword*, vol. XIX, Nos. 75 and 76 (1993–4), pp. 57–65.

Ó Luanaigh, Dónall, 'Richard James Hayes (1902–1976)', *Oxford Dictionary of National Biography*, Oxford: University Press, 2004.

Paine, Lauran, *The Abwehr: German Military Intelligence in World War Two* (New York: Stein and Day, 1984).

Peszke, Michael Alfred. *Poland's Navy, 1918–1945* (New York: Hippocrene Books, 1999)

Share, Bernard, *The Emergency: Neutral Ireland, 1939–1945* (Dublin: Gill and Macmillan, 1978).

Singh, Simon, *The Codebook: The Science of Secrecy from Ancient Egypt to Quantum Cryptography* (London: Fourth Estate, 1999).

Stephan, Enno, *Spies in Ireland* (London: Macdonald, 1963).

Stuart, Francis, *Black List – Section H* (London: Penguin Books, 1996).

The Trial of German Major War Criminals, Part I, 20 Nov. 1 Dec. 194 (London: His Majesty's Stationary Office, 1946).

Toomey, Deirdre, 'Stuart, Iseult Lucille Germaine (1894–1954)', *Oxford Dictionary of National Biography* (Oxford: University Press, 2004).

Walsh, Maurice, G2: *In Defence of Ireland, Irish Military Intelligence 1918–45,* (Cork: Collins Press, 2010).

West, Nigel, *The Guy Liddell Diaries,* Vol. I, 1939–1942, (Oxfordshire: Routledge, 2005).

West, Nigel, *The Guy Liddell Diaries,* Vol. II, 1942–1945, (Oxfordshire: Routledge, 2005).

West, Nigel, MI5 (London: Triad Grafton, 1983).

Zeutner, Christian and Bedürftig, Friedrich (eds) Encyclopedia of the Third Reich (New York: Da Capo Press, 1997).